The Mind of NORMAN BETHUNE

The Mind of

Roderick Stewart

NORMAN BETHUNE

Fitzhenry & Whiteside
TORONTO MONTREAL WINNIPEG VANCOUVER

ISBN 0-88902-418-9 Cloth
0-88902-425-1 Paper

Design by Robert Burgess Garbutt

Fitzhenry & Whiteside Limited
150 Lesmill Road
Don Mills, Ontario

Printed in Canada

Contents

Acknowledgements

Having collected these materials from so many persons and institutions in various parts of the world it would be impossible to acknowledge them all on these pages. My failure to do so does not reflect a lack of gratitude for those who aided me.

Foremost among those to whom I am deeply indebted are the relatives of Norman Bethune. In particular, I wish to thank Betty Cornell of London, Ontario, his niece, who supplied me not only with documents and photographs of her uncle but also constant encouragement.

Henning Sorensen, Bethune's interpreter in Spain, and Jean (Ewen) Kovich, his nurse in China, two prime examples of the fact that Bethune attracted only the best people, assisted me with material and information.

In Spain I was able to locate three of the four medical doctors who worked with Bethune. All were helpful, especially Dr. Valentin de la Loma of Madrid who has become a dear friend.

I wish to thank the Government of the People's Republic of China which kindly permitted me a second visit to their country in the spring of 1975. On this occasion I visited every major area where Bethune worked. In my meetings with numerous persons who knew Bethune, I was always able to rely on the able assistance and ready wit of my interpreter Yeh Tung-hai.

Parks Canada authorized my travels to provide for the Bethune Memorial Home. Among those whose expertise and friendship I value are the following: Max Sutherland, Hillary Russell, James Miller, Alvin Austin and Wayne Colwell. Of invaluable assistance were Diane Mew, my editor, and Ramsay Derry, Trade Editor of Fitzhenry & Whiteside.

I am grateful also to the Ontario Arts Council whose generosity has made it possible for me to complete the book.

In assembling the photographs for this book, I have received generous help from many people. In particular, I should like to thank the National Film Board, who allowed me to use photographs of Bethune in China given to them by the government of the People's Republic of China; Dean Harold J. Perkins of the State University of New York at Plattsburgh who has generously allowed me to use their photographs of the panels of the mural, "The T. B.'s Progress;" and Mrs. Yola Sise, widow of Hazen Sise, in conjunction with the Bethune Memorial Foundation, who has kindly granted me permission to publish several photographs taken by Mr. Sise in Spain.

Acknowledgements are also due to the following for permission to reproduce the photographs appearing in this book:

Mrs. Fritz Brandtner: 19, 28
Bethune Family: 1, 2, 3, 4, 5, 6, 7, 12, 35;
Mrs. Charles Comfort: 37;
Paraskeyva Clark: ii, 75, 87, 89;
Jean Ewen: 80;
George Holt: 79;
Geza Karpathi (Charles Korvin): 59, 64, 65;
Joseph Kurung: 12
Michael Lindsay: 103, 108, 114;
National Film Board of Canada: 3, 4, 5, 6, 7, 11, 13, 21, 25, 28, 32, 34, 43, 56, 58, 61, 90, 91, 94, 100, 109, 115, 117, 118, 124, 126, 127, 133, 136;
Parks Canada, Dept. of Northern and Indian Affairs(Government of Canada): 3, 147
Royal Victoria Hospital: 20;
Marian Scott: 31;
Yola Sise: 46, 59;
Henning Sorensen: 51, 68;
Toronto Star: 74, 148;
Trudeau Institute: 10.

My final acknowledgment is to my wife, Norma, who, day after day, typed, retyped, then typed again the hundreds of thousands of words written by Bethune.

Preface

During several years of research I had collected a large number of materials relating to the life of Norman Bethune. Among them were many of his writings.

Shortly after the publication of my biography Bethune (New Press, Toronto, 1973), I was asked by Parks Canada, a division of the Department of Indian and Northern Affairs of the Government of Canada, to act as their historical consultant on the restoration of Bethune's natal home in Gravenhurst, Ontario, which had just been purchased by the Department of External Affairs.

During the next two years I retraced many of those steps that I had earlier taken to collect information for the biography. Once again I visited friends, relatives and associates of Bethune in Canada, the United States, England, Spain, Switzerland and the People's Republic of China. These trips added to my growing collection of materials which included letters, speeches, transcripts of radio broadcasts, poetry, short stories, medical and political articles, drawings and paintings. Eventually I decided that because most of these had never been published, they should be compiled to be presented in book form. This volume is the result of that decision.

The most logical way to present his writings is in the order in which he wrote them. A natural companion are photographs relating to the various stages of his life. These appear throughout the text and provide the historical context for his writings.

The final decade of his life witnessed his greatest achievements. This was also the period in which his writings were the most numerous. Most of these have been preserved and appear in this book. Unfortunately the earlier part of his life is less known and there are fewer of his writings from those years.

The selections that I have made are from the known writings of Bethune. I have excluded certain letters, documents and articles that are inconsequential or too technical. Although the latter quality applies generally to his medical articles, I have included excerpts of these. In some cases where the original material has been lost, I have included contemporary reports. This applies mainly to his speeches in 1937 when he was raising funds for the Spanish Republic which were extensively covered by the newspapers.

In selecting from Bethune's personal correspondence, I have focussed on letters to his friends and colleagues which chiefly relate to his medical and political achievements that have established his historic reputation. While I have quoted from some of these letters in Bethune, most of them are published here for the first time.

At the beginning of each chapter I have sketched an outline of the significant events of his life at that particular time. I have also written a few words of introduction to each of the writings to account for its origin.

Nearly eight years of research and writing about the life of this extraordinary Canadian have not altered my original conviction that he was an unusually complex person. In Bethune I tried to present him from the various perspectives of those who had known him. Now I am attempting to let him speak for himself.

RODERICK STEWART
Toronto 1977

For David

Youth at the Prow and Pleasure at the Helm

ONTARIO

Norman Bethune frequently spoke of his family tradition, and the high standard of achievement of his ancestors doubtlessly influenced him. Reverend John (1751–1815), his great-great grandfather who brought his family from Scotland, built Canada's first Presbyterian church in Montreal. One of his sons, John (1791–1872), became Rector of Montreal and Principal of McGill University. Another, Alexander Neil (1800–1879), was the second Anglican Bishop of Toronto. His son, Charles James Stewart (1838–1932), was an early headmaster of Trinity College School in Port Hope, one of the finest boys' schools in North America.

Another son of the Reverend John was Angus (1783–1851), an aggressive businessman, who rose to prominence in the two great Canadian fur-trading empires, the North West Company and the Hudson's Bay Company.

There were many similarities in both the character and career of his son Norman (1822–1892) and his great-grandson, the subject of this book, Henry Norman (1890–1939). Angus' son Norman, who was educated in Toronto by his uncle, Bishop Bethune, learned surgery in Edinburgh before returning to Toronto to become one of the co-founders of Trinity Medical School in 1850. He was Dean of that institution six years later when the religious authorities ordered him to bar non-Anglican students. Enraged, he refused to accept the ruling and submitted his resignation. When all of his colleagues did the same, the medical school was closed.

Throughout the next fifteen years Norman wandered: in Europe, to act as an observer during the Franco-Austrian War; on the north Atlantic to serve as a ship's surgeon; in Edinburgh to practise surgery and to marry a Scot, Janet Nicolson. In this interlude he acquired considerable skill as a painter and his diaries reveal an aptitude for writing.

In 1871 on the reopening of Trinity Medical School, this time without religious restrictions, he resumed his position on the faculty. He spent the remainder of his life in Toronto teaching and practising medicine.

Norman's only son Malcolm became a Presbyterian minister. Ambitious, somewhat vain, but rigidly determined and frequently outspoken, he sometimes offended the leaders in his congregations with his blunt candour. As a result he never rose in the religious hierarchy.

In varying degrees Norman Bethune inherited many of the traits of his father and grandfather. The most pronounced were evident from childhood: intelligence, ambition, artistic skills, stubbornness and unwillingness to compromise against principles, regardless of the consequences. These would be the source of both his greatest agonies and his most magnificent achievements.

Malcolm Nicolson Bethune (1857-1932) Elizabeth Ann Goodwin (1852-1948)

Norman's mother was an intelligent, strong-willed woman whose fervent evangelism had converted her worldly and errant husband. Malcolm renounced his planned business career and entered Knox College in Toronto to study theology.

This is the earliest known picture of the Bethune family, taken about 1893 or 1894; Norman is on the horse.

The Reverend Malcolm Bethune's first charge was the Presbyterian Church in Gravenhurst, one hundred miles north of Toronto. Norman was born in the manse, where the family remained until 1892.

The children were born at two-year intervals: Janet Louise (1888); Henry Norman (1890) and Malcolm Goodwin (1892). Norman and Janet had a mutual respect which endured until Bethune's death. He was never close to his brother. This photograph (left) was taken in 1900.

There was some inherited wealth which allowed the Bethunes to live beyond the income of a Presbyterian minister. On more than one occasion Elizabeth Ann was able to take her children to visit her relatives in England. Below she is seen with them in 1904.

The restlessness that always characterized Bethune may
have originated in part in the family's constant
peregrinations during his youth. Because his father
moved from charge to charge, Bethune was unable to plant
roots. Before this photograph (right) was taken in Owen
Sound, Ontario, likely in 1905, the Bethunes had lived
in six other Ontario communities. He graduated from
the Owen Sound Collegiate in 1907.

A year's work in a bush camp after graduation was followed
by a teaching position in a one-room school just north of
Toronto. When he became bored after two years at the
University of Toronto he joined Frontier College as
a labourer-instructor in September 1911. At the end
of a full day's work as an axeman in a lumber camp
north of Lake Superior, he spent the evening as a
teacher. His students, almost all of whom were older than
he, were recent immigrants who learned English from
him. When his year was up he went west to work for several
months as a reporter for the Winnipeg *Tribune*. In
September, 1912 he entered medical school at the
University of Toronto.

Just before his third year of medicine was to begin, Bethune volunteered for the army and joined the Royal Canadian Army Medical Corps at the beginning of the First World War. Serving as a stretcher-bearer, he was severely wounded by shrapnel wounds in his left leg at the Second Battle of Ypres, April 29, 1915. Following his convalescence in England he was invalided out and returned to Canada to complete his medical studies.

The remainder of his studies were telescoped into a crash course. With him in the graduating class that received their diplomas in December 1916 was Frederick Banting, one of the co-discoverers of insulin.

In 1917 he joined the Royal Navy, serving as a Lieutenant-Surgeon aboard H.M.S. *Pegasus* and doing active duty in the North Sea. He was demobilized at the beginning of 1919.

He spent part of a year in the nascent Canadian Air Force, apparently as the Senior Medical Officer, carrying out research on the causes of blackout in pilots.

At the end of the war, he began a series of post-graduate studies in several London hospitals beginning (above) at the famous Great Ormond Street Hospital for Sick Children. His training in surgery was extensive, climaxing in the award of a Fellowship of the Royal College of Surgeons in Edinburgh in 1922.

Frances Campbell Penney was an extremely attractive woman from a prominent Edinburgh family. Their courtship lasted three years from their meeting in London. They were married in August 1923. Unfortunately their two personalities clashed soon after the marriage.

The Sirens of Fame, Success and Wealth

DETROIT and SARANAC

Following their marriage in 1923, Bethune and Frances flitted through Europe on a madcap honeymoon for six expensive months. Finally, happily exhausted but almost broke, they went to America where Bethune set up a private practice in Detroit, Michigan, in the late autumn of 1924. Instead of the instant riches that he had expected in the booming automobile capital, he faced mounting debts and an uncertain marriage.

Pressed by creditors, the well-qualified surgeon was at first reduced to teaching a course in prescription writing at the Detroit College of Medicine and Surgery. Then, very slowly, his financial position began to improve. Relying on his charm no less than his surgical skills, he impressed the medical community. Soon he was able to move to a more fashionable residential area, buy a new car and start to indulge his hobby of buying oil paintings.

Success had come, however, not only from his charm, but from long hours and hard work. When Bethune began to tire easily in the summer of 1926, he agreed to a colleague's suggestion that he have a complete physical examination. The results were terrifying. He had contracted tuberculosis in both lungs.

Coincidentally, the finest sanatorium in Canada was Calydor, located in his birthplace, the town of Gravenhurst. He remained there only a month, preferring the famous Trudeau Sanatorium at Saranac Lake, New York.

The favourable medical prognosis on his admission to Trudeau in December 1926, was gradually altered. Before Bethune left Detroit for Calydor, Frances had decided to leave him. In the early months of 1927 he constantly fretted over his disastrous marriage and rapidly accumulating debt. His mounting anxieties and his refusal to accept the prescribed treatment of complete rest aggravated his condition. He soon began to talk of suicide.

Fortunately his stubborn will and persistent curiosity

Founded by Dr. Edward Livingstone Trudeau, an American of Swiss descent, Trudeau Sanatorium was considered one of the finest in North America. Basic treatment was rest, a sound diet and the clean fresh air of the Adirondack mountains.

TRUDEAU SANATORIUM

No. 7513

Name: Dr. Norman Bethune
Address: 711 Selden, Detroit, Michigan

Race: English-Scotch
Nativity: Canada In U.S. 3 yrs.
Occupation: Physician

Saranac Lake Address: _____

Relative or Friend: Father Rev. Malcolm Nicholson Bethune
Address: Grimsby, Ontario

Denomination: Presbyterian
A.M.A.D. Age: 36 yrs

Additional Address, Club, Society, etc., for tracing: _____

Family Physician: Dr. Herbert Rich Address: Detroit Mich Saranac Lake Physician: _____

Tuberculosis Physician: Dr. Herbert Rich Address: Detroit Mich

Admission Date: Dec 16-1926 Classification: R ? M.A.A. Turban ? Side L2

Discharge Date: Dec 1-1927 Classification: Improved Turban III Side L Party

Diagnosis Physical Signs: Inf. L. apex and apex of L. Lower

X-Ray Formula:—Admission: _____

Discharge: _____ Pneumothorax R. Stat L. Party

Sub. Cut. Test:—Dose ____ Constitut. ____ Phys. Signs ____ X-Ray ____

General Condition, Admission: Unfavorable **Favorable** Discharge: Unfavorable **Favorable** Onset Catarrhal

Digestion Admission: Unimpaired **Impaired** Discharge: Unimpaired **Impaired**

Duration of Disease, Admission: 8 mos Discharge: 1 yr 7¾ mos Hospital Days: 350

Weight: Usual 156 On Coming to Mountain 162 Date Dec 16 '26 Standard 168½

Max. in Past History 162 On Admission 161¾ Height 5 ft inches 10½

Min. in P.I. 153 At Discharge 176½ Gain 14¾ Loss ____

Sputum: Tubercle Bacilli Previous to Admission Present When? Sept 15 '26 By Whom Detroit Mich

On Admission: No expectoration During Residence: pos At Discharge: neg

Hemoptysis: Previous to Admission: no

During Residence: none.

Pleurisy with Effusion: no

Fever: Previous to Admission 100 Duration 21 da Average Max.; Adm. 98 Average Max.; Dis. 97½

Pulse: Range on Admission 62 to 88 Range on Discharge 76 to 116

Urine: On Admission Few gran. casts. Res Hyaline At Discharge 100

Complications: Non-tuberculous, On Admission 0 During Residence 0

Complications: Tuberculous, On Admission 0 During Residence 0

Treatment: General – Infirmary – Artificial Pneumo. Exercise at Discharge: Unlimited

Admitted by Dr. Hazel

History Taken By: E.H. Welling Date Dec 24, 1926

History Checked By: _____ Date Dec 27, 1926

The policy of the Sanatorium was to admit only patients in the early stages of tuberculosis. As Bethune's case sheet reveals, his condition upon admission was favourable.

Bethune took great delight in flouting many regulations. With both lungs infected with the disease, he refused to stop smoking cigarettes. Frequently he would evade the nightly nurse patrol and slip through the gate to spend several hours of revelry in the town's speakeasies.

combined to save his life. After many months of studying tuberculosis in medical texts and journals in the hospital library he chanced upon an article describing a little-known and seldom-used treatment called artificial pneumothorax. Excitedly grasping the book, he rushed to the office of the chief physician. Despite the latter's agreement that the treatment might achieve positive results in Bethune's case, he refused to administer it. He feared several inherent risks, including the possibility of puncturing Bethune's lung.

Bethune stormed, cajoled and even threatened until the conservative doctor resignedly acquiesced. A hollow needle was inserted into Bethune's chest through which air was pumped into the chest cavity, forcing the lung to collapse. The theory held that in this condition of rest, a collapsed lung would eventually heal. In Bethune's case it worked and with amazingly miraculous swiftness. Within two months the cavities in one lung had disappeared and were quickly receding in the other. Bethune left Trudeau Sanatorium on the first day of December 1927.

Despite his victory over tuberculosis, he was unable and unwilling to return to his former way of life. During the last weeks at Trudeau he learned that Frances had been granted a divorce which included a court order

Patients were lodged in cottages that dotted the hills that made up the Sanatorium grounds. Here Bethune met an American physician, Dr. John Barnwell (second from Bethune's left) who was his closest friend throughout the remainder of his life.

Tradeau N.Y.

Bethune arranged parties for patients and nurses for which he supplied wine smuggled in from Quebec. This forced bravado was designed to conceal his growing pessimism when he realized that his condition was not improving. He began to discuss suicide, for which he told Barnwell he had devised an excellent method. He would inject himself with morphine before wading into the lake. After a few strokes the drug would take effect and he would achieve a painless death.

obligating him to pay her $25,000. For an already indebted doctor who had lost his practice, it was a staggering sum.

The enforced period of rest had given him time for introspection as he reviewed his past and pondered his future. In one of his black moods he expressed these reflections in a mural that he called "The T.B.'s Progress." Painted on wrapping paper, it ran for nearly sixty feet along the walls of his cottage on the hospital grounds. Several years later, in a magazine article, he described the thoughts that lay behind the mural.

The T.B.'s Progress

Reprinted from "The Fluroscope", Vol. 1, No. 7., Aug. 15, 1932.

Attacked as he is so frequently in early manhood, when the future is beckoning with alluring smiles, the first reaction of the tuberculous to the realization of his disease, is often one of utter despair. Tragedy stares him in the face. Life seems ruined. Crashing down over his ears is the wreck of his future plans and expectations. Doubts and uncertainties fill his days and nights with depressing fears. Many of these fears are unjustifiable, as he will discover later, but the nervousness of many tuberculous patients can only be partly attributable to the disease process, as a large part is caused by worry over financial conditions, the dependence on others' support, the laying aside of long-cherished plans and the uncertainties of a clouded future. The young man who is suddenly told that he has tuberculosis and must stop work and enter a sanatorium, in most cases regards his life as a tragedy with only one possible ending. He begins to realize after a time that this view of his life and his disease is wrong. Hope reenters his heart when he sees his friends returning to the outside world and taking up their normal lives again. In the sanatorium, perhaps for the first time, he has the opportunity to think. Contemplation becomes a substitution for action. The result is a deepening of his intellectual and spiritual life. Realities change their nature—the unimportant becomes the important and the formerly essential becomes the superfluous. It is only the dull and unimaginative who can lie in a bed in a sanatorium for six months or a year and fail to rise a better and finer person. Life should be enriched and not impoverished by this retreat from the world.

I came down with active pulmonary tuberculosis in 1926 when just starting off, in what I had reason to believe, would be a successful medical practice. I fought against the realization of my disease just as many of you have done, but increasing loss of strength, cough and positive sputum, forced me at last to stop work. A large cavity was found by X-rays in one lung with some disease in the other. I was put to bed for a year. On exercise, the cavity began to increase in size. Doubts and fears for the future began to cloud my normal optimism. Then I was given artificial pneumothorax and improved immediately. In a dark moment while taking the early air injections, I drew for the amusement of myself and my cottage mates, the allegorical story of my past life and what I thought the future would be.

The small cottage called "The Lea", in which five of us lived, was one of the oldest in the sanatorium and sat back on the hill behind Dr. Trudeau's first cottage, "The Little Red". The interior was paneled in yellow pine, now darkened by the years. There were four doors and three windows. The continuous coloured drawing, five feet high and sixty feet long, ran around the walls, fitting in the spaces between the roof and the wainscoting, the doors and windows. The title of the drawing was "THE T.B.'S PROGRESS, A DRAMA in one act and nine painful scenes". Below the drawing were bits of poetry (so-called!) describing the scenes. The cottage was torn down last year and the drawings transfered to the Fluroscopic Room of the Tuberculosis Unit, University Hospital, Ann Arbor, Michigan.

The first scene or drawing was a picture of my pre-natal existence. The womb was depicted as a dark cave, with the infant already being attacked by the tubercle bacillus which is represented throughout the drawings as a red pterodactyl—a sort of prehistoric reptile with a long beak and sharp teeth and bat-like wings. Although, for scientific accuracy, the theory of inter-uterine infection is highly improbable, for the sake of artistic design it was too good an idea to neglect! The legend accompanying this was:

> Look, O Stranger, at the danger
> To our hero, embryonic.
> T.B. bats, so red, ferocious,

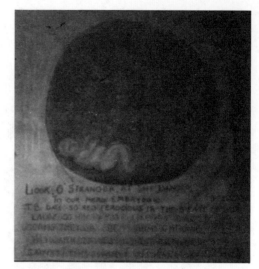

> In the breast of our precocious
> Laddie, do him in just like his
> daddy.
> His dark cave no barrier knows,
> Against this worst of mankind's
> foes.

The second scene shows my entrance into the world, I am being carried in the arms of a beautiful angel with brilliant irridescent wings who is clothed in long, white flowing robes. Facing her, seated on a sort of throne, is a male angel (the Angel of Fate) who unrolls in his hand a scroll on which is inscribed my future. Incidentally, this theory of predestination is probably a relic of my Scotch ancestors. Looking over his shoulder are other angels who, as they read my future, turn away weeping. The legend below this is:

> The angels at his birth,
> Forseeing all his years,
> Restrain not, nor should we,
> The tribute of their tears.

The third scene is my childhood. It is depicted as a dangerous journey through a thick wood where lurk various wild animals. Childhood diseases are shown as cruel terrifying creatures, the ideas of which I took from old medieval illuminated manuscripts. The Measle is a sort of spotted tiger; the Mump, the Whoop, the Dipth, and the Scarlet are various other wild and weird animals, which either lurk behind the trees, or fly in the sky ready to pounce down on the child. This child is shown being attacked by an enormous dragon, called the Dipth and is being defended by a knight in shining armour whose long bright sword kills the dragon. The name of this knight is Sir Schick, referring to the Schick protection against diphtheria. The legend reads:

> From Dragon Dipth, Sir Shick
>   defends,
> From other foes he cannot save.
> The wounds and scars of their attack,
> He'll carry to his grave.

This refers, of course, to the predisposition which we think childhood diseases sometimes give for tuberculosis.

The fourth scene describes my early manhood. I am out of the woods of childhood and have set sail across the Sea of Adolescence. I start off happily on a great ship like a Spanish galleon—"Youth at the Prow and Pleasure at the Helm". Everything seems propitious that my journey will be fine and successful, but half-way across, my ship comes near a rocky coast, and, like Ulysses, the Sirens sing their songs and lure me off my course. I land from the ship as the beauteous creatures (Fame, Wealth, Love and Art) point the way up the rocky cliffs to a splendid castle on the top called the "Castle of Heart's Desire." Just as I am about to enter I am attacked by swarms of T.B. bats who strike me down. The legend below reads:

> On Adolescence troubled seas,
> The sails of argosy are set,
> Alas, he hears the Sirens' song,
> His course is changed, his bark
>   a wreck.

The fifth drawing shows my fall into the Abyss of Despair. I fall head over heels from the high mountain, pursued as I fall by swarms of T.B. bats. As I fall, I look back and see that the Castle of Heart's Desire, which once looked so magnificently substantial from the front, is actually only a Hollywood set. At the bottom of the canyon is flowing a dark red river, representing a hemorrhage. The poetry under this reads:

> Down, down he falls from that
>   high mount,
> Success so near at hand,
> His foes triumphant see him reel
> Down to that bloody strand.

The sixth drawing shows me as I lie in the depths looking upward and seeing, on a high mountain, another castle flying the Red Cross flag. This is Trudeau Sanatorium. Outside the gates is the bronze statue of Trudeau himself. The battlements of the castle are defended by different warriors, the doctors of that place—Dr. Lawrason Brown, Dr. Baldwin, Dr. Heise, Mr. Sampson of the X-ray department, and Miss Amberson, the Superintendent of Nurses. I climb slowly up to this castle where I gain entrance and protection from my enemies. There is a gas filling station (Pheumothorax apparatus) just inside, and music and laughter come through the gates. The little

15

cottage of Dr. John Barnwell, now head of the T.B. Unit, University Hospital, Ann Arbor, is shown under the trees just outside the castle gates. Coming out through the windows are the notes of an old song we played on the gramophone, which will always remind me of the happy times we had together. The poetry under this is:

> On Pisgah's Heights stands Trudeau
> strong,
> Bright sanctuary high,
> Where Heise, Brown and Amberson
> His enemies defy.

Pisgah is the mountain that Trudeau Sanatorium is built against.

The seventh drawing shows my return to the city. Here is where my mistaken pessimism enters. The city is drawn as a rather modernistic impression of skyscrapers seen from above and the people are like little black ants on the street. The air is filled with T.B. bats who attack me again, and I have a relapse of my disease. The poetry underneath this:

> Lured by that Siren, Spurious
> Fame
> Who had no heart nor pity,
> Our hero strives to win a name,
> In the canyons of the City.
>
> Temptations flourish thickly
> there,
> But T.B. bats are thicker,
> They swarm about the foetid air,
> While he grew sick, and sicker.

The eighth drawing shows me starting off to the South-west in pursuit of Health and Happiness, which are shown as two lovely female forms on a bright cloud, with the sun shining above them as they beckon me across the desert. This, of course, is nothing but a mirage. Our hero is very thin and weak and has a small sputum cup strapped to his cadaverous body. With a staff in his hand, he stumbles out across the plain over which are scattered the wrecks of the old-fashioned covered wagon days. The legend under this reads:

> Once more laid flat upon his back,
> Our victim pulls a boner;
> Instead of back to Saranac
> He's off to Arizona.
>
> And so the plains got his remains
> For his disease deceased him;
> He coughed and spat, lost all his fat,
> Kind death at last released him.

This, of course, is rather morbid and entirely imaginative, and from what has occurred since, quite untrue!

The ninth and last drawing shows the Angel of Death holding me in her arms and looking down on me with a kindly and benign expression on her face. She is not a dark angel but just as beautiful and bright as the other angels at my birth. In the foreground is a small churchyard with the five tombstones of the men who lived with me in the cottage. The poetry under this drawing is:

> Sweet Death, thou kindest angel of them all,
> In thy soft arms, at last, O let me fall;
> Bright stars are out, long gone the burning
>   sun
> My little act is over, and the tiresome play
>   is done.

Two of the men who thought they would die in the time we agreed upon (and they helped me suggest the time!) have done so. My own death I put down to occur in 1932. How wrong I was, unless, of course, something happens in the rest of this year. But my natural expectations are to last much longer than that!

My life was saved by artificial pneumothorax and phrenicectomy, and hundreds of you will be like me in this regard. Looking back I can see how my fears and hopeless attitude in regard to the future were wrong. Fear is the great destroyer of happiness, and most fears are unjustifiable. It can be said that man lives by hope alone. Under modern methods of treatment and early diagnosis, nearly every tuberculous patient has a great chance to recover if he is careful and follows the advice of his physician. Never despair, but be cheerful and quiet in your mind; follow the rules and play the game out to the end.

Tuberculosis terrified, depressed, fascinated and finally inspired him. On his way to recovery, he dramatically resolved to commit himself to work in tubercular research and surgery. Coincidentally, Dr. Edward Archibald, one of the North American pioneers in the struggle against tuberculosis, had just begun to develop a tubercular research centre. He was Chief Surgeon of Montreal's Royal Victoria Hospital, fewer than one hundred kilometres from Saranac Lake. Learning of Bethune's qualifications and ambition, he invited him to join his staff.

Straddling Two Worlds

MONTREAL

The first months in Montreal provided a refreshing contrast to the past two unhappy years. He liked his work with Dr. Archibald and he was optimistic about the future. He was preparing himself for the road to conventional success. Even his hopes for a second chance with Frances were revived when she finally agreed to correspond with him from Scotland where she had returned after the divorce. From his residence in the Faculty Club of McGill University he wrote her in the autumn of 1928.

My job here is a combined clinical one in the Royal Victoria Hospital—in the chest clinic and part research work. I told Archibald a couple of months ago I would be forced to leave as I couldn't live on my income. He was keen that I should stay and offered me this fellowship at $1500 a year. I will stay one year I think and then Archibald will be able to place me somewhere. He is the outstanding figure in chest surgery in America and a most charming fellow.

Fortunately I was able to bring to the clinic some new ideas as a result of my Ray Brook research. He has told me he can't hold out any hopes of a hospital appointment here—my appointment is in the university—but I told him I was indifferent to that—all I wanted was a thorough training in chest work—then I can go anywhere. I have been thinking of England next year in a sanitorium.

I have also a tentative offer from Shanghai, China—but not for the immediate present— for next year.

I am in excellent health—have lost a lot of weight this summer and am now down to 164 lbs. I go to bed every afternoon from 2-5. The work is really very light. My pneumothorax is holding well and I have no cough, expectoration or fever. The insurance comes to hand regularly. I feel confident it will hold for another year—and then the future must take care of itself.

I will never return to general practice and am getting prepared to do nothing but chest work— both medical and surgical combined. The way will open out, I'm sure.

An aerial view of the Royal Victoria Hospital, Montreal.

In addition to assisting Dr. Archibald in thoracic surgery Bethune was given a virtually free hand to engage in tubercular research. The nature of his investigations varied but his most significant contribution was the invention of a variety of surgical instruments that were widely used throughout North America. During his eight years in Montreal, he wrote numerous articles describing his various innovations in the laboratory and in surgery. Appearing in learned journals they helped to establish his international reputation.

One of these articles resulted from an operation that he performed on the Hollywood actress, Renée Adorée. Bethune promised to devise a technique to conceal an unavoidable scar that would result from the operation. He later described the process in "A Phrenicectomy Necklace," published in the American Review of Tuberculosis, *Volume 26 (September 1932), pp 319-21.*

A Phrenicectomy Necklace

The practice of surgery has been called an art, and it may be considered so, if that term is not defined too closely. In all its essentials, however, it is a craft, and the surgeon a craftsman, an artisan, a plastic mechanic.

Bound by the rigid and inexorable laws of his medium, the human body, the surgeon is permitted but few of the liberties his fellow craftsmen may take who work with stone, wood or metal. He is a master of makeshift, a ready compromiser, denied, as in no other craft, the relief of substitution. A *tour de force*, although occasionally successful, is more apt to be disastrous. His critics are harsh, unforgiving and of distressingly long memories. He is not allowed the exhibition of playful fancies, wit or humor, which other craftsmen enjoy in their productions. But, for all that, our craftsman often has the soul of a creative artist, although the nature of his plastic medium restricts the free play of his artistic nature. Like most other men, his creative force is confined to one channel and allowed but one escape.

The modern introduction of anaesthesia has liberated the craft from the hurried expediency of the past to the more leisurely procedures of today. Modern surgical craftsmanship with its new leisure and, as an immediate consequence, its new precision, permits and encourages the artistic sensibilities of the

Dr. Edward Archibald was the Canadian pioneer in thoracic surgery. In personality, temperament and political philosophy he was the opposite of Bethune of whom he wrote: "I never really liked him; our outlook on life was too dissimilar."

operator. These artistic desires and their approximate satisfaction are contained, to a large extent, in what is known as "surgical technique." Still, for all the remarkable transition from butchery to bloodlessness, an operation scar still remains a scar, and, regarded artistically, can never be considered else but an aesthetic affront to the human body. Some of these insults may be concealed by clothing, rearrangement of hair or other artifices; those others, beyond concealment, must be borne with whatever resignation their sufferers can command.

The powerful combination of the patient's vanity and the craftsman's artistic urge has produced the cleverly hidden scar of the "face-lifter," the dubious buttonhole incision for the appendix, the transference of the smallpox-inoculation scar from the arm to the thigh (this last representing a well-intended

"The whole backward path of surgery is littered, like the plains of the American desert, with the out-worn and clumsy relics of technical advances . . . . Surgical instruments in use today are a curious collection of the awkward heirlooms of the past, mixed with the new, delicate and efficient tools of contemporary technology."

THE GEORGE P. PILLING & SON CO., PHILADELPHIA

THE GEORGE P. PILLING

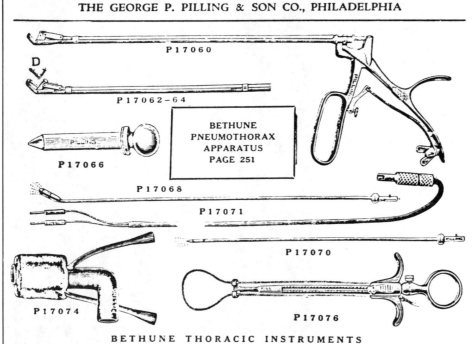

BETHUNE
PNEUMOTHORAX
APPARATUS
PAGE 251

P17060

P17062-64

P17066

P17068

P17071

P17070

P17074

P17076

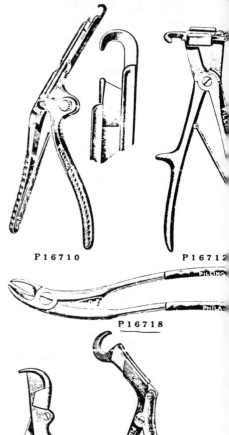

P16710

P16712

P16718

P16722

P16724

BETHUNE THORACIC INSTRUMENTS

The above is a set of instruments for Thoracic Surgery. Designed by Norman Bethune, M.B. (Toronto), F.R.C.S. (Edinburgh), First Assistant, Medico Pulmonary Clinic, Royal Victoria Hospital; Thoracic Surgeon, Department of Pensions and National Health, Dominion of Canada; Consulting Thoracic Surgeon, Mt. Sinai Sanatorium, St. Agatha, P. Q., and Grace Dart Home Hospital, Montreal, P. Q.

P17060—Thoracoscopic Scissors, Bethune, rotatably mounted in handle.

P17062—Interpleural Clip Applying Forceps, Bethune, rotatably mounted in handle (including handle).

P17064—Silver Clips, Bethune (D), for preventing hemorrhage in cutting adhesions. Applied with forceps P17062.

P17066—Intercostal Trocar and Cannula, Bethune, flat-oval.

P17068—Interpleural Transilluminator, Bethune, angled, use through trocar P17066.

P17070—Transilluminator, Bethune, small, curved, for use through Jacobaeus Unverricht Thoracoscope (P17000).

P17071—Connecting Cord, for either of the above transilluminators.

P17074—Air-Tight Empyema Tube, Bethune, with inflatable pneumatic collar for closed drainage. Large or small.

P17076—Lobectomy Tourniquet, Bethune, sliding pull.

P17078—Phrenicectomy Necklace, Bethune, for locating and masking post-operative scar (not illustrated).

FOR ILLUSTRATING CASE RECORDS

P17085—Rubber Stamp, J. W. Cutler, showing the pleural cavity and diaphragm, especially for recording results in artificial pneumothorax and phrenicectomy.

P17090—Chest Charts in "sticker form," Bethune, for heart and lung case records. Printed on gummed paper in pads of 50, perforated for quick detachment like postage stamps. Anterior and posterior views on one sticker.

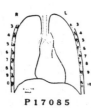

P17085

P17090

THORACOTOM

P16710—Rib Shears, Sauerbruch-Frey, authentic model, for the first upper rib.

P16712—Rib Shears, Sauerbruch, for all ribs other than first, adult or child size.

P16714—Rib Shears, Shoemaker, adult or child size.

P16716—Rib Shears, Doyen.

BONE-CUTT

P16730—Bone-Cutting Forceps, Liston, double action, straight, Swedish rustless steel.

P16732—Same, curved.

P16734—Bone-Cutting Forceps, Liston, straight 5¾, 6¾, 7½, 8¾ and 10¼ inches.

PORTABLE PNEUMOTHORAX APPARATUS

P17092—Pneumothorax Apparatus, Lloyd, one-man, portable; apparatus consists of three-way stopcock with tubing outlets to the chest, the manometer, and a 15 cc. air pump. An air filter and rubber balloon are connected between pump and stopcock, the latter serving as a reservoir for measured dosages and as a buffer. Complete in case with manometer and water reservoir. Reprint of construction and operation on request.

P17092

OTHER PNEUMOTHORAX APPARATUS, SEE NEXT TWO PAGES

The Pilling Company of Philadelphia manufactured instruments designed by Bethune. These below were featured in their 1932 catalogue. He refined some of these and invented others before he left for Spain four years later. Bethune was aware that changes in medical science would render his own inventions obsolete as well. Today only the rib shears have survived.

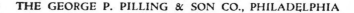

SON CO., PHILADELPHIA

THE GEORGE P. PILLING & SON CO., PHILADELPHIA

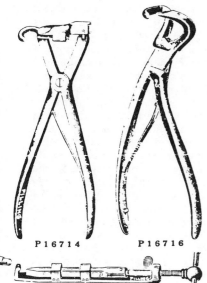

P 16714　　**P 16716**

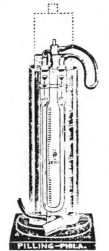

P 16720

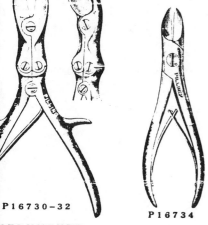

P 16730-32　　　**P 16734**

STRUMENTS

6718—Rib Shears, Bethune, long handles, powerful biting jaws, suitable for all ribs including first rib.

6720—Guillotine for first rib, Lilienthal, screw operated.

6722—Rib Shears, Gluck.

6724—Rib Shears, Stille.

6728—Rib Perforator, Friedrich, for suturing (not illustrated).

FORCEPS

6734R—Same, 7½ inches only, rustless steel

6736—Bone-Cutting Forceps, Liston, curved, 5¾, 6¾, 7½, 8¾ and 10¼ inches (not illustrated).

6738—Bone-Cutting Forceps, Liston, angular, 7, 8¾ and 11 inches, not illustrated.

DR. NORMAN BETHUNE'S PNEUMOTHORAX APPARATUS

P17160—Bethune Pneumothorax Apparatus. The distinguishing features of this apparatus are the transparent, non-fragile material for the two telescopic cylinders that form the displacement chamber, and the method of refilling. The two cylinders are graduated to read directly the number of cc.'s of air inflated. By first raising the inner cylinder above the level of the water in the outer cylinder, and then allowing it to settle, the air confined in the inner cylinder is discharged through the valve. To refill the apparatus it is simply necessary to raise the inner cylinder above the level of the water, a simple and rapid method which eliminates pumping with a bulb or pump. The valve on the base controls inflation, and the arrangement is such that the manometer is always "on." The manometer is protected by means of automatic check valves against the ejection of the water by high positive or high negative pressure.

P17161—Pneumothorax Apparatus combined with Suction Cylinder for Chest Aspiration, Bethune. Similar to pneumothorax apparatus described above, including all the features enumerated, but having mounted on the same base a transparent graduated aspirating chamber. Mounted on a central plate is a commutator valve for controlling the operation of the pneumothorax apparatus, the tubing connections for both pneumothorax and aspiration, a filter and a vacuum gauge for use in aspiration. Negative pressure may be obtained with an electrically driven pump, a foot bellows, or any other available means (not illustrated).

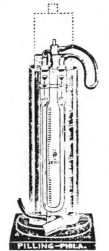

P 17160

CUTLER PNEUMOTHORAX, ASPIRATING AND IRRIGATING MOBILE UNIT

P17175—Pneumothorax Chest Aspirating and Irrigating Mobile Unit, Cutler. Consisting of a complete apparatus for pneumothorax with self-integrating scale for individual inflations, motor-driven suction and pressure pump, with automatic control devices, for recharging the pneumothorax apparatus, for supplying pressure for irrigation and suction for aspiration. All these parts are conveniently arranged in a white enamel cabinet mounted on rubber tire wheels. Ample table space for the required accessories. The pneumothorax apparatus is housed in a separate compartment above the table. Air receptacle is metal. Features are the self-integrating scale for indicating both the amount of air in reservoir and amount of individual inflation, and a specially constructed valve to permit an extremely nice control of rate of inflation.

P 17175

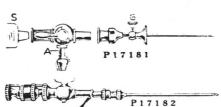

P 17181　　　　　　**P 17180**

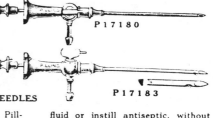

P 17182

PNEUMOTHORAX NEEDLES

P 17183

P17180—Pneumothorax Needle, Pilling-Loving, with two-way stopcock and stilette.

P17181—Pneumothorax Needle Assembly, J. W. Cutler, consisting of needle, two-way stopcock for use with standard Luer syringe. With this assembly it is possible to administer anesthetic, inflate the pleural cavity with air, remove

fluid or instill antiseptic, without exposing the cavity to the outside.

P17182—Pneumothorax Needle, Floyd, with two stopcocks, one controlling inflation, the other intra-thoracic pressure readings.

P17183—Pneumothorax Needle, Saugman, similar to Loving needle P17180, but with opening at the side instead of end.

misdirection), the crease-hidden thyroidectomy incision, artificial teeth, the toupé, the glass eye, the artificial nose and many otorhinolaryngological and orthopaedic operations. Therefore, little apology is offered in presenting another suggestion for the satisfaction of both the patient's and the surgeon's harmless aesthetic vanities.

Since the vertical phrenicectomy incision has been abandoned the scar of the transverse approach has become less noticeable. Yet, even in the same hands, the transverse scar will show slight variations of position from patient to patient: here, a little too far out; here, a trifle too low; here, a half-inch too high;

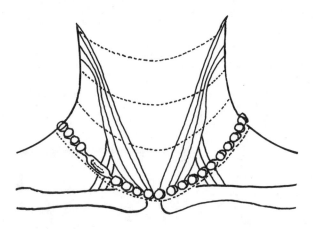

Fig. 1. *Diagrammatic Sketch of Phrenicectomy Necklace in Position*

The lower end of the bar rests on the edge of the clavicular head of the sternomastoid muscle. The scalene muscle (not shown) should be felt below.

and in others, a trifle too long. Now the ideal scar should run neither transversely nor vertically, but obliquely downward and inward to the sterno-clavicular joint, and lie in a normal crease of the neck. It should be three-quarters to one inch in length, although an additional half-inch is sometimes allowable.

To disguise the scar of this incision, the common practice is to place it in a crease of the neck; but with the head turned sharply to the side, as in the operating position, creases are apt to be obliterated. In many young subjects no creases can be seen. Correct anatomical placement and the future ease with which the scar may be hidden may both be obtained by using an ordinary bead necklace. This, of course, must be rolled away to draw on the skin a line in which it lay. Not infrequently, when the beads are

replaced, this line drawn freehand, is found to be just a trifle out of position. This may be avoided in the following way:

> Take an ordinary bead necklace of the "choker" type (a 10¢ one from Woolworth's is excellent) and, after removal of a few beads from the string, introduce a thin, slotted, flexible, silver bar, 1½ inches long and ¼ inch wide. A short link of silver chain, 5 inches long, is placed at one end of the string of beads so that the clasp may be adjusted to give a total length of necklace from 12 to 16 inches. This range will accommodate all but the thinnest or thickest necks. The flexible silver bar can be easily bent to fit the neck as snugly as the original beads. This bar has a slot 1 inch long and ⅛ inch wide. The necklace, after being sterilized by boiling and after the skin has been prepared, is placed in position with the patient sitting upright, head to the front. The beads should lie easily and naturally on the neck and the lower ends cross the sternoclavicular articulations. The adjustable clasp is fastened and the bar is then placed in the correct position by palpating the anterior scalene muscle which is felt below. With a small applicator (a toothpick is useful) dipped in mercurochrome, one then can draw a line on the skin through the slot in the bar, without disturbing the beads. The necklace is then removed and the patient placed in the operating position. The incision is made through the red line. After the operation the patient is informed that a necklace of such and such a length (say 14 inches) will hide the scar from view.[1]

Strange to say, this seems to fill the female breast with the most profound gratitude.

[1]This necklace was made by Pilling and Son Co., Philadelphia, Pennsylvania.

Many members of the medical profession viewed this as cheap showmanship. Even he later admitted that the article ". . . was taken as it was meant to be, as an amusing little trinket."

Undoubtedly his unorthodox frivolity antagonized some of his colleagues and obscured his consistent and very real commitment to the eradication of tuberculosis. In one of his first papers, "A Plea for Early Compression in Pulmonary Tuberculosis" he revealed not only the extent of his concern but his perceptive analysis of the nature of the problem of tuberculosis.

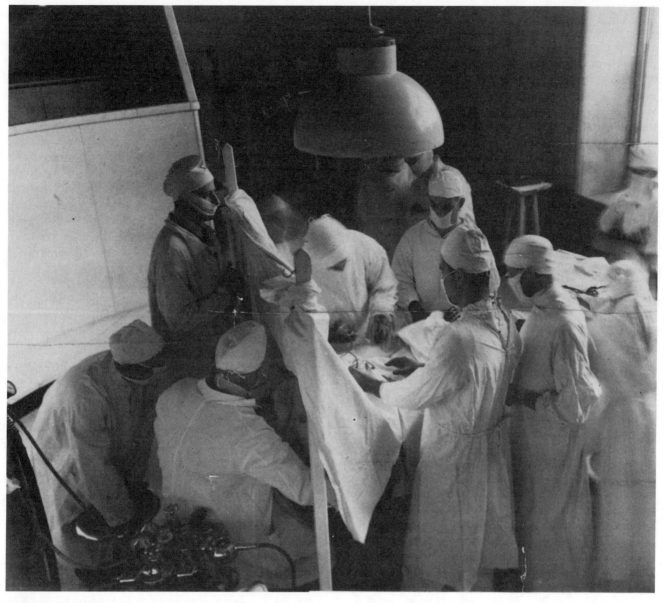

Bethune (facing the camera) is assisting Archibald (to Bethune's right). Admired for his speed and dexterity, Bethune was often accused by his conservative colleagues of taking risks at his patients' expense.

A Plea for Early Compression in Pulmonary Tuberculosis

The Canadian Medical Association Journal, July 1932.

The treatment of pulmonary tuberculosis involves two problems. The first is that of the infected individual, regarded as a whole, acting and reacting in his social and physical environment, and the second, the reaction of that individual's body, and more particularly his lungs, to the presence of the tubercle bacillus. The tubercle bacillus may be considered, as it truly is, just another factor in the environment of man, impinging on him, causing certain changes in his body and modifying its behaviour. The first problem then becomes chiefly an economic and social one, and the second, a physiological and immunological one. In the final analysis they are mutually reactive and inseparable.

25

Trudeau well said, "There is a rich man's tuberculosis and a poor man's tuberculosis. The rich man recovers and the poor man dies." This succinctly expresses the close embrace of economics and pathology. Any scheme to cure this disease which does not consider man as a whole, as the resultant of environmental strain and stress, is bound to fail. Tuberculosis is not merely a disease of the lungs; it is a profound change of the entire body which occurs when man, regarded as an organism acting under the dictation of, and the product of, his environment, fails to circumnavigate or subjugate certain injurious forces acting on his body and mind. Let him persist in continuing in such an environment and he will die. Change these factors, both external and internal, readjust the scene, if not the stage, and he, in the majority of instances, will recover. The sanatorium with its bed rest, fresh air, and good food, is such an external environmental change. The second requirement is to alter the local environment of the tubercle bacilli, and this change is most quickly and effectively obtained by collapse therapy. In the case of a man acutely infected with the tubercle bacillus, activity in his daily struggle to adapt himself to his social and economic environment is almost invariably followed by a coincidental activity of the disease. Rest in the first direction is followed by arrest in the other.

Tuberculosis is commonly regarded as a chronic disease. This only means that the tuberculous takes an unconscionably long time in dying. Did the lung, alas, not "suffer in silence," but did it protest more vigorously, tuberculosis, like syphilis, would be treated in the first acute stage with a high hope of cure, and we would not await the development of the second or third stages, when a satisfactory result is difficult and sometimes impossible. These early lesions are not infrequently missed by a physical examination and a stethoscope. They will be discovered through a careful history and an x-ray film.

Early pulmonary tuberculosis is of all so-called chronic diseases the easiest to cure. The remedy is *rest*. Dr. John Flinn, has well called this the "specific treatment." Pulmonary tuberculosis shows an inherent tendency, a willingness for recovery, which when considered beside chronic heart, kidney or liver diseases, which show little or no tendency to cure, makes it unique among the diseases of long duration afflicting man. Given half a chance, pulmonary tuberculosis will meet the physician half-way towards recovery. Our sanatoriums are filled to-day with the incurable sequelae, the deplorable after-results, the uncollapsible cavities, the avoidable complications of what was once, for many patients, an entirely curable disease in the early stage. The incurable tuberculous who will fill our sanatoriums for the next five years are now walking the streets, working at desks or machines with early curable tuberculosis, and coming into doctors' offices with loss of appetite, loss of weight, tiredness, and are getting bottles of medicine for their stomach complaints or tonics for their fatigue. They eventually will come to the sanatorium with moderately or far advanced disease with cavitation. We, as a people, can get rid of tuberculosis, when once we make up our minds it is worth while to spend enough money to do so. Better education of doctors, public education to the point of phthisiophobia, enforced periodic physical and x-ray examinations, early diagnosis, early bed-rest, early compression, isolation and protection of the young are our remedies.

We, as physicians, can do but little to change the external environmental forces which predispose to re-infection. Poverty, poor food, unsanitary surroundings, contact with infectious foci, overwork, and mental strain are mostly beyond our control. Those essential and radical readjustments are problems for the sociologists and economists. We produce in a sanatorium, for a few short months, a new and harmonious environment and attempt to counteract years of disharmony and maladjustment. All the more reason, since the time is so short, to take advantage of these months by actively altering the local environment of the bacillus in the diseased lung by collapse therapy. Rest, either physiological or so-called mechanical, will not by itself cure the disease; it merely induces local conditions favourable for the re-establishing of the body's defensive mechanism, those mysterious and incalculable elements, the sum total of which are called resistance. Once resistance has been built up it must be carefully protected. This preservation of resistance is the chief problem of rehabilitation and its watchword is "The Fatigue Conscience." It is thus seen that there are three acts to the drama; the first, the predisposing environment and the onset of the acute re-infection; the second, the temporary change of this injurious environment in the sanatorium, with an active attempt to enforce lung relaxation; and the third, the readjustment to the external environment after the sanatorium. The first and last are the important ones and the most difficult problems in the treatment of this disease.

Until that happy day breaks when the immunologist and serologist solve the problem of how to prevent invasion and, once invaded, to

This is the photograph Bethune had taken for professional purposes in 1934.

hasten absorption and induce fibrosis in a lung invaded by the tubercle bacillus faster and more surely than any other procedure is the outstanding fact we know about the treatment of this disease. The treatment of pulmonary tuberculosis to-day is the treatment of neglected cavities. The remedy is earlier diagnosis and earlier compression.

More and more, rightly or wrongly, and I believe, wrongly, we are regarding pulmonary tuberculosis as a disease of a lung instead of the entire body. It is truly a form of scientific despair which will seem absurd when immunology and serology come into their own. Yet, that narrow and empirical viewpoint of the mechanical mind, with its eyes fixed on practically nothing but the local pulmonary lesion, has contributed more to the successful treatment of this disease than a hundred years of forced feeding, fresh air, vaccine and chemicotherapy, change of work, or intermittent rest with exercise.

Who can regard the millions of money lost in earning capacity each year, the high cost of sanatorium upkeep, the poor results of short-time hospitalization, the drain on the patient's, his family's, or his country's purse, the years wasted in curing, and the lives lost, without thinking that sanatoria and short bed-rest are not worth while? The day of the sanatorium as a sort of boarding-house is past. The modern sanatorium is a hospital for active treatment. No sanatorium to-day can call itself modern which does not have at least 50 per cent of its patients under some form of collapse therapy, a distribution of say 30 per cent pneumothoraces, 15 per cent phrenicectomies, and 5 per cent thoracoplasties or extra-pleural wax fillings, etc. Compression saves time, saves money, and saves life. The patient with early tuberculosis who, through economic pressure, can afford to spend less than two to three years in a sanatorium must have mechanical pressure. Lack of time and money kills more cases of pulmonary tuberculosis than lack of resistance to that disease. The poor man dies because he cannot afford to live. Here the economist and the sociologist meet the compressionist on common ground.

He soon became impatient to be on his own. When professional and personal differences began to destroy his once harmonious relationship with Dr. Archibald, Bethune looked for a new position. At the beginning of 1933, Sacré Coeur Hospital, a recently opened Catholic institution in Cartierville just north of Montreal, offered

destroy in vivo the tubercle bacillus, the phthisiotherapist is forced to adopt the mechanistic viewpoint in the treatment of this disease. This is no new idea. It was suggested by William Carson, of Liverpool, in 1821, who said in part—"It has long been my opinion that if this disease (phthisis) is to be cured, and it is an event of which I am by no means disposed to despair, it must be accomplished by mechanical means, or in other words by a surgical operation." He urged artificial pneumothorax and other collapse procedures. While this mechanical viewpoint is a confession of failure to treat this disease directly, while some of the procedures advocated are clumsy, crude, and often dangerous, yet lung relaxation and lung compression must be accepted to-day for want of something better. That partial or complete respiratory immobilization will

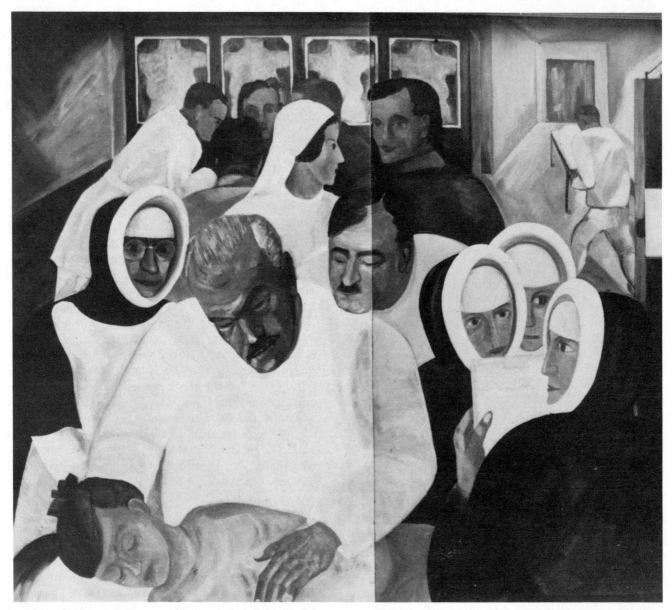

To celebrate Bethune's first operation at Sacré Coeur, his friend, Fritz Brandtner, a well-known Montreal artist, did this painting. Bethune described the occasion in a letter to his old friend John Barnwell: "Ten miles from Montreal—French Canadian and Catholic, twelve hundred dollars a year, one day a week, so the strain is less strained. I cauterized some adhesions there yesterday, and the chorus of oh's and ah's from the nuns rose like a chant at the high altar. My title is 'Chef dans le Service de Chirurgie Pulmonaire et de Bronchoscopie.' I'm going to have a nice big white cap made with Chef marked in front. Really, I'm delighted."

him the headship of the Department of Thoracic Surgery, a position he took up immediately.

During this period he assumed a more prominent role at international medical conferences through his cogent and often passionate arguments in favour of new approaches to tubercular problems. In 1935 he was elected to the Executive Council of the American Association of Thoracic Surgeons.

Ironically he was held in much higher esteem by his colleagues in the United States and other parts of Canada, than by those in Quebec. Every doctor in Montreal knew of Norman Bethune; no one was more controversial in the medical community. One popular view was that he was too willing to criticize, too anxious to attack time-tested procedures. He was impatient and unable to accept gradual progress. His schemes were grandiose, im-

practical, even crack-brained. He was impolite, arrogant and showy. In short, he was an embarrassment to his profession.

A minority opinion held that he was, indeed, a flamboyant gadfly but with a brilliant, imaginative mind that flashed from cause to effect, providing unusually accurate insights that escaped the average doctor. His dislike of regulations, his ability to speak his mind freely, even his oft-questioned operating speed, were all the product of an unusually keen sense of commitment to the patient.

There was little question even among his enemies that he was an extremely skilful operator. He briefly described his feelings after an important operation in 1935.

Nov. 6, 1935
6 P.M.

My child is well.
It was a very beautiful operation.
I felt very happy doing it.
The entire right lung was removed—the first time this has been done—in a child of 10—in Canada and the 45th operation of its kind ever been done in the world. Isn't that nice?

Yes, I will sleep deep tonight—last night was a "nuit blanche"—not whether I could do it but whether I should. I decided I must at 4 A.M., slept till I felt refreshed and "tight" and went at it like a canvas—my picture full in my mind.

It was not easy to assess him. He loved life. He saw it as a great adventure full of riches but one that was clothed in mystery. Riches were not money but the limitless variety of human experience and he longed to get more than his share. He desperately wanted to shatter the mystery, to explore, to create, to achieve. Beneath this ardent longing that usually appeared to onlookers as callous impertinence, there was an unlikely blend of self-doubt and over-confidence. These were always in a warring state.

Not satisfied with his medical achievements, he turned to art and after a few lessons impatiently struck out on his own. His paintings were bold, intense and powerful, a clear reflection of himself. Yet, as in so many other areas of his life, he failed to devote the time necessary to develop

as an artist. Instead, he turned to literature and began to write.

Most of the short stories that he wrote have been lost. The following, "Encounter," is the only extant one from this period and is one of the earliest indications in his writings of his growing interest in Communism.

Encounter

I don't think he had any doubts about me at first. He really thought I was, what, at first glance, I appeared to be—so unguarded, so confident was his approach. Everything about him said, "Why, hello, I know you." Of course, it was rather late, the night was dark, but even so, there was little excuse for his mistake. Well, anyway, this is what happened.

I left my cousin's about one, after a furious, interminable argument about communism. Just to look at these complacent capitalists makes me extraordinary actionary, much less to talk to them. As usual we got nowhere. It was like an argument between two men, one blind. one deaf, about music—say an orchestra and we had slugged at each other all evening with clumsy club-like words. Of course, we had had a lot to drink and that hadn't made it any better, in fact worse, because, as time went on, we appeared, each to ourselves, as the sole-remaining, heroic and desperate defender of our separate citadels of Truth and it became more important than anything in the world, that the God, who was articulate in us, should defeat the Antichrist in the other. I left, licking my wounds, feeling very angry and frustrated. The cool air was a benediction on my head. Quiet and withdrawn, the deserted street stretched up the hill into the night.

He must have watched me coming, for his advance from across the street had a sort of prepared gaiety. At least I didn't take him unawares. He came towards me very friendly-like, very much in a friend-prepared-to-meet manner. Now, I don't know why I did it. Perhaps it was just a continuation of my mood, the last dregs of my anger. I wanted to shake him also out of his too easily accepted assumptions. I certainly didn't do it because I disliked him. In fact, truthfully, I did it because I really loved him. When he was about ten feet from me, I suddenly crouched down on all fours, glared at him and said in a fierce, truculent way, "Wow."

He stopped, I would have stopped too, I expect. In an uncertain, yet with a rising nervous tone, he repeated my salutation. His very nervousness was an incitement to attack, and I advanced towards him slowly, the snow very cold, like little, broken-up diamonds beneath my bare hands. Well, that certainly took him aback. He half-turned and retreated to the opposite side of the street and stood there regarding me, trying to readjust himself, his mental conflict so plain to read, I could have burst out laughing. I can quite understand his mixed emotions, can't you? After all, it was rather late, the street was deserted except for he and I, he had mistaken me for an acquaintance, and I must have looked very curious with my head down, glaring at him. Why had not I simply said, "Sorry, you've made a mistake?"

So he half-backed, half-turned to the opposite side and stood looking at me in bewilderment. Probably nothing more would have happened, if I hadn't taken up the offensive and, without a sound, in an ominous and intimidating silence, advanced towards him on my knees and hands. He stood his ground bravely for a short time, but my attitude was so menacing, that finally his courage broke. He turned and ran—actually fled—between a purple cottage and a white stucco garage and from there he shouted at me. Yes, shouted. I suppose he thought he was safe. I let him think so, got up erect on my legs, returned to my own side and started down the street, not very fast and watching for him out of the corner of my eye.

He must have cut around behind the houses, for he suddenly reappeared a little ahead of me, talking to himself, and probably to me, in a low jittery fashion. I couldn't make out all the words, but "what the hell" and "I'll be damned" were quite clear at least. Well, we went through the same performance again, the advance, the challenge, the doubt, the retreat, the reappearance. Each time his uncertainty mounted and his perplexity increased.

After half a dozen reenactments of this ridiculous performance I got rather tired of it and instead of walking on as before, after one of his disappearances, I hid behind a telegraph pole. It was a big pole, bigger than I was, in the shadow of a house, and from my hiding place I could watch him unseen. He reappeared and stood gazing eagerly up, then down the empty street. No one. Fearing a trap, he walked slowly over to my side, very excited yet very much on guard, Where could I be? When he was about six feet from my hiding place, I pounced out, advanced a step and threw myself at him, shouting loud enough to rattle the windows—"Grrrrrrrrrrrr."

With a cry of mingled terror and supplication he fled precipitously straight up the street. I watched him go with the bitter ironic smile of the misunderstood. "Fool," I flung at him, then turned myself and walked away. After fifty feet I turned again to see what he would do, and what he did persuaded me that I had finally, yes, even against his will, convinced him, for he came back to the pole behind which I had hid, walked slowly around it, smelt carefully every inch within reach of his nose, then ceremoniously pissed against the place, where I had leant.

Yes, I think now his doubts were dissipated. That young, credulous Airedale pup was finally convinced he had met at last that fabulous creature, the Man-Dog of canine mythology. To him had been granted the terrifying yet ineffable bliss of a visitation from the past, a glimpse of the reincarnated One, the Living Legend, the long-awaited, the desperately desired, the ever-to-hoped-for One, who could explain, and only He, the hithertofore unexplainable feelings of sympathy and adoration in his heart for that mysterious superdog, Man, so like himself in life, love and pursuit of shadows, in his fine courage, his slavish cringing, his unconquerable gaiety, that some mutual Origin, some common Ancestor must be postulated to explain their kinship. He had seen Him, the old dog's tales were true, there was a Santa Claus, and never again would he regard with easy familiarity a man as just a man, but in every encounter, any day or night, he might meet the One again. Perhaps tomorrow. Life can be very exciting, can't it, when there is hope?

But I am the one who is afraid to meet him again.

March 31/36

He also wrote poetry. After his divorce from Frances, he met other women, many of whom were strongly attracted to him, although most of these affairs were brief and unsuccessful. He was too demanding, too difficult to comprehend. One who was able to cope with his involved personality was a beautiful and sensitive artist. To her he dedicated these poems.

STRIKE, if strike you must
But warm us first, t'was better so to die
Beneath your fierce flames than perish in the shade,
Cold and alone.

Perhaps, a miracle as happened once, should come
    again
That golden glare were made to stand
And never sink and never leave the land
Desolate and dark,
But stay, suspended overhead,
High, serene and clear
Perpetuate.

Remembrance

I can't pretend
I think of you every hour, why
Such dull days, I'm not aware of you at all,
Any more than the beating of my heart. Thru,
A young tree in the wind.

A white flower in the grass,
A quick bird in flight,
A breath of sun-named air,
And the whole world is emptied of delight
Like a cup turned upside down
And I am hollowed and sick for my love,
But I can't pretend
This happens every day,
My Pony.

Bethune painted his self-portrait which he gave to
Marian Scott, the Montreal artist, who later
donated it to McGill University. On McGill's day of
tribute to Bethune, on November 25, 1971, it was
presented to the government of the People's
Republic of China.

Boasting that his paintings would be accepted in an exhibition, he painted "Night Operating Theatre." It did appear in the exhibition. He was equally attracted to literature. Two of his favourite authors were D. H. Lawrence and Katherine Mansfield, (both of whom were tubercular). He once advised a young doctor: "It distresses me you should be reading that fellow Maugham. Beware of the facile exponents of laisser faire. There is an odor of decadency in all his works—a sweet and faintly putrid aroma, producing in the mind, illusions, shapes, forms and colors unlife-like, sentimental and enervating. He should really know better since he is a doctor of medicine. . . . Cultivate the satirists but shun the cynic. Irony is the salt of life and will take you to your grave a merry if not a happy man."

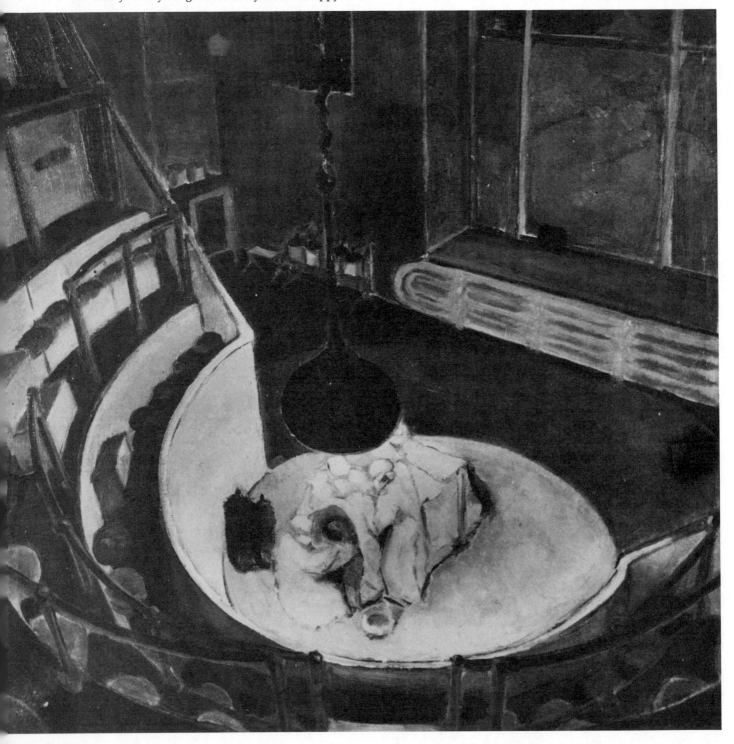

His painting and poetry, no less than his work as a surgeon and inventor, revealed his passion for self-expression. He regarded himself as an artist, as one whose role was to reflect reality not only when he stood before a canvas but in every aspect of his life. He resented artificiality. He preferred to drive into the country to pick wild flowers than to buy them at a florist's shop. When he bought a radio, he startled a friend by throwing away the cabinet, stating that it was a false exterior.

He tried to translate his beliefs into his behaviour toward others. Since nature was open and frank, so would he be. He would not practise artifice. Instead he would react directly and sincerely to people. As a virtually lone practitioner of such a philosophy he was often misunderstood. The sometimes ludicrous and often awkward situations that resulted merely intensified his determination. They also increased his anger and contempt for those who slavishly obeyed society's dictates. Such an attitude seldom won him friends; it never made him popular. Once when some guests arrived early while he was showering, he shocked them by answering the door nude and dripping water. They fled in anger and disgust.

He had a full range of emotions and attitudes. As frequent as his shocking public displays of contempt for what he despised, he privately revealed a profound sense of compassion. Having agreed to operate on a child considered inoperable by another doctor, he failed to save her life. As she lay dying, she implored Bethune to kiss her. Fully aware of the danger of infection, he leaned over and kissed her on the mouth. The contradictions in his nature that led to the turmoil in his life often tormented him. He once confessed to Frances: "I want to be saved from myself."

If his highly unusual personal behaviour made him a pariah to most of his professional colleagues, it recommended him in Montreal's thriving Bohemian community. A prominent surgeon who wore turtleneck sweaters, a porkpie hat, who drove an open roadster, who painted and wrote poetry was an attractive rarity. As he found himself being ostracized by polite society, he opened his downtown apartment to writers, artists and poets for festive parties that became the talk of Montreal. It was in this setting that he discovered politics—the politics of dissent.

Until this time he had been indifferent to the organization of the state, to laws and to government. To the limited extent that he thought at all about politics he was a conventional tory. He had been too absorbed in his own world, too self-centred even to feel the Depression that was strangling Montreal. Now for the first time, he entered into discussions and heated arguments that centred on problems that had never before concerned him. Typically, he joined these debates partly out of curiosity and partly for the sheer enjoyment of verbal jousting.

Bethune loved children. He persuaded Fritz Brandtner to direct free art classes for poor children on Saturday mornings in Bethune's Beaver Hall Hill apartment. The paint and other materials were supplied by Bethune.

Bethune had begun to collect art when he lived in London. In Montreal, where he was well known in the artistic community, he continued to buy paintings which covered the walls of his apartment.

Gradually, he felt himself drawn in by a growing sense of conviction.

Almost every shade of political opinion was represented by those who gathered in his apartment. Yet to him the most articulate and appealing were those which advocated change. Destroy the old. Create a tabula rasa. *Construct anew. This was the political reflection of Bethune's personal philosophy.*

Rarely does political conversion occur overnight, even in a person as instinctive as Bethune. Slowly he began to sense the importance of politics. It was the third side of the triangle that linked medicine and economics.

In the summer of 1935, after selling his car to finance the trip, he went to the Soviet Union to attend the sessions of the International Physiological Congress. It was the road to Damascus! He returned deeply impressed with Soviet medical organization.

Back in Montreal he made no attempt to conceal his admiration for a system that provided treatment for all patients without regard for their ability to pay. When his favourable comments attracted the attention of the Communist Party, he was asked by Louis Kon to head an *organization called "The Friends of the Soviet Union." He described his reactions to their proposal in a letter to his friend Marian Scott.*

Oct. 8, 1935

I was approached today by the Executive Committee of "The Friends of Soviet Russia" with the offer of the chairmanship of that association for the coming year.

It would appear that Sir Andrew MacPhail had spoken about or recommended me. Why, I can't say for since my trip, my expressions have not been entirely complimentary in some quarters (depending of course on my audience!—enthusiastic to the reactionaries, minimizing to the radical.)

Now, it is rather a question to me whether or not I can conscientiously take such a position. I explained my attitude frankly to Mr. K——saying definitely that though in theory I am entirely in agreement with the

Bethune was especially fond of his sister Janet's three children: Betty, Ruth and Joan. He painstakingly produced this letter for Betty on a large sheet of paper and mailed it to her.

ideology of this modern religion, yet I was disturbed and rather deeply disturbed, in some of its aspects in practice. In short, that I did not believe that communism as practiced in Russia today was a suitable technic for the Anglo-Saxons (predominately Anglo-Saxon, at heart) of this country. Their attempt to discover some method of herd living suitable for their new concepts of equality and justice in a machine age. But that basically—not imitatively, in detail, I was in deep sympathy with Russia. To my surprise he agreed with me.

I added that I was profoundly distrustful of social democracy and of the C.C.F., in their non realization of the absolute inevitability of the use of force and force alone as the only true persuader.

Moneyed people will *never* give up money and power until subjugated by physical forces stronger than they possess. Democracy will come again, as it will come again in Russia, only after the people are conditioned, as they are being conditioned, to their new manner of living, but democracy *at first* is shiftless, careless, ignorant and willful. Only when the course is set can it be permitted to guide the ship.

Well, what shall I do? Do you think I can conscientiously take this job? I don't think I know enough. I feel very ignorant. Yet I feel a tremendous impulse *to do, to act*. I hate to be thought one of the intelligentsia who talk and talk and talk and believe their words. You feel their hearts are cold and it's only an intellectual conundrum. A game.

You must remember my father was an evangelist and I come of a race of men, violent, unstable, of passionate convictions and wrong-headedness, intolerant yet with it all a vision of truth and a drive to carry them on to it even though it leads, as it has done in my family, to their own destruction—as it did my father.

Beth

His response to Louis Kon was negative.

October 28, 1935

I am extremely obliged to you for your kindness in lending me "Moscow Dialogues." I am finding it extremely interesting as the philosophy underlying communism had never been explained to my satisfaction, outside the rather idealist and grandiose flourish of the "right yeoman" etc. etc. I hope you will let me keep it a little longer.

Now in regard to the other matter of the chairmanship—I will be perfectly frank with you so you will understand my position exactly.

I do not feel able to accept for two reasons. The first is that I am not, as yet, perfectly convinced that communism is the solution to the problem. If I were, I assure you, I should not only accept your offer but would become a member of the Communist party. What stands in the way of my acceptance? This—my strong feeling of individualism—the right of a man to walk alone, if that's his nature—my dislike of crowds and regimentation. Perhaps all these fears are illusionary and do not necessarily conflict with the practice of communism, even though they seem to be solved in its theory—I am afraid.

This being so I must read more, think more about this problem. In short I am not yet ready.

Second, such being the case, to jeopardize the only position—economic and professional—I possess, by even associating with a communistic-leaning Association such as yours would be senseless. If I felt as strongly and as purely towards communism as perhaps I should, such jeopardization of my means of livelihood would not be an obstacle in any way. But the ironic and ludicrous picture of a half-hearted convert, reluctantly being burnt at the stake for his half-hearted, feeble convictions, rises in my mind.

So it all hinges on this—I am not ready as yet to throw in my lot with you.

Yet I belong to the League for Social Reconstruction even though I feel that they are following a will-of-the-wisp and theirs is not the right way. At the same time I am filled with despair towards the smugness and passivity of the oppressed workers and bourjoise [sic] of this continent, but until they accumulate in their hearts a far greater certainty of their own doom than they at present possess, then it is useless to impose on them, for without the will to rebellion, it seems they must go still farther down into the abysss before they will rebel. The last election shows they are not ready.

I would be glad to address your Union on some impressions of my recent trip to the U.S.S.R.

Yours sincerely,
Norman Bethune

Bethune photographed here by the distinguished artist Charles Comfort.

He was not ready to throw his lot in with the Communists—not yet. He was still straddling two worlds, but the time was coming. His leanings became more evident in an address to the Montreal Medico-Chirurgical Society just before Christmas. He called his talk "Reflections on Return from 'Through the Looking Glass'."

20 December 1935

My position as the last speaker of this evening was of my own choosing. I had decided to take up the opposite position to that of my fellow Lenin graduates. I felt fairly sure they would be unanimous. If they depreciated Russia, I would praise her and if they praised, I would diminish her. This would not be done in a spirit of pure perversity, but from a concern for truth which appears to me to consist, not infrequently, in the conjunction of apparently irreconcilable aspects of reality. Whatever one says about Russia is true—relatively true and not in any absolute terms, of course.

All accounts of returned travellers from strange lands and foreign shores are essentially self-disclosatory and unwittingly autobiographical in character. Criticism becomes a critique of the critic. This is traditionally true of all returned travellers, from those Biblical gentlemen who reported Palestine to be a land flowing with milk and honey—when it was nothing of the sort—to Marco Polo, Christopher Columbus and Baron Munchhausen. What you are hearing tonight is an account of four men in terms of one country.

Now, I did not go, like these others, to Russia to attend a physiological congress. I went to Russia for much more important reasons than that. I went to Russia primarily to look at the Russians, and secondarily, to see what they were doing about eradicating one of the most easily eradicable of all contagious diseases, namely, tuberculosis. I happen to possess some very definite ideas on how this might be done, given the necessary courage and currency. I shall not say anything tonight about what they are doing in this way. I will also say nothing about the congress, since I only attended one session—the opening one—being far too busy swimming in the Neva, walking about unhindered in the streets, looking into windows, making the round of the picture galleries and markets and shops—a combination of Walter Winchell, Peeping Tom and Innocent Abroad.

The title of my talk would lead one to suppose that I was about to draw a comparison between Looking-Glass Land and Russia. It would be easy enough to parody that fairy-tale or write, with one's tongue in one's cheek, an article entitled "Malice in Blunderland." Derision and denial are interesting psychological phenomena, and are essentially protective in nature. It is easier to deride than praise. But it should be remembered that in calling Russia a land of topsy-turvy, as it has been called, a reasonable doubt may arise that it may not be the things one sees upside down in Russia, but that this disturbing optical illusion may also be obtained by an observer standing on his head and seeing normal things in their proper position. Certainly, over the portals of Russia should be inscribed "Abandon old Conceptions all Ye who enter Here." To seek

comparison of the White Knight, the White Queen, the Red King, Humpty Dumpty, the Mad Hatter, Tweedledee and Tweedledum, would be entertaining and occasionally true. As an example, Stalin, who is universally acknowledged to be the greatest living statesman, might be given the role of the Walrus, and Lenin as the Carpenter and the NEP men as the Oysters who were taken for such a disastrous walk down the Beach in 1921. Also, to take without benefit of context some of the sayings of the characters in "Through The Looking Glass" as being applicable to Russia today would also be interesting; such as, Russia might be compared to the Looking Glass room which Alice found looking so like her own drawing room, only the things went the other way, and the books were like her books, except the words went the wrong way. Tweedledum and Tweedledee might be parodied as Diddleyou and Diddleme, the ridiculous, contradictory, fat little men of the Intourist Agency. That it's "Jam tomorrow and Jam yesterday but never Jam to-day", might be taken as the complaint of those workers who are impatient of what they may think is the slow progress of improvement in living conditions, and the White Queen's remembrance of things which happened the week after next, as an example of the unlimited optimism and the faith that the Russians have in their own future. And it would also be true of Russia today to use the White Queen's reply to the protest of Alice, who said: "Oh, I can't believe that." "Can't you", said the Queen, "Try again; draw a long breath and shut your eyes." Alice laughed—"One can't believe impossible things." The Queen: "I dare say you haven't had much practice. Why I sometimes believe as many as six impossible things before breakfast." Then there would be much truth in Alice's delighted exclamation, when she found the fire in the fireplace was real. "So I shall be as warm here as in the old room, warmer, in fact, because there will be no one here to scold me away from the fire." And when she looked down from a little hill and saw the whole country as a huge chessboard and life itself as a game of chess, which was being played all over the world, and said: "I shouldn't mind being a Pawn if only I might join, although, of course, I should like to be a Queen best." To this the White Queen replied: "That is easily managed, you can be the White Queen's Pawn, if you like, and you are in the second square to begin with, and then when you get to the eighth square you will be a Queen and we shall be Queens together, and it will all be feasting and fun." And that statement would be the faith and hope of communism in a nutshell.

Isadora Duncan, in the story of her life, describes her confinement: "There I lay, a fountain spouting blood, milk and tears." What would a person think, watching for the first time a woman in labour and not knowing what was occurring to her? Would he not be appalled at the blood, the agony, the apparent cruelty of the attendants, the whole revolting technique of delivery? He would cry "Stop this, do something, help! police! murder! Then tell him that what he was seeing was a new life being brought into the world, that the pain would pass, that the agony and the ugliness were necessary and always would be necessary to birth. Knowing this, then, what could he say truthfully about this woman as she lies there? Is she not ugly—yes; is she not beautiful—yes; is she not pitiful, ludicrous, grotesque and absurd—yes; is she not magnificent and sublime—yes. And all these things would be true. Now, Russia is going through her delivery and the midwives and obstetricians have been so busy keeping the precious baby alive, that they haven't got around as yet to cleaning up the mess, and it is this mess, this ugly, uncomfortable and sometimes stupid mess, which affronts the eyes and elevates the noses of those timid male and female virgins suffering from frigid sterility of the soul, who lack the imagination to see behind the blood the significance of birth. Creation is not and never has been a genteel gesture. It is rude, violent and revolutionary. But to those courageous hearts who believe in the unlimited future of man, his divine destiny which lies in his own hands to make of it what he will, Russia presents today the most exciting spectacle of the evolutionary, emergent and heroic spirit of man which has appeared on this earth since the Reformation. To deny this is to deny our faith in man—and that is the unforgiveable sin, the final apostasy.

Even before this controversial lecture, he had acted under the nurturing influence of the Soviet medical system. In the late autumn he brought together a group of doctors, nurses and social workers to plan a medical care system within the Canadian context that would provide benefits similar to those available in the Soviet Union. Known as "The Montreal Group for the Security of the People's Health," they met on a regular basis in Bethune's apartment throughout the winter and spring of 1936.

In April Bethune again accepted an invitation to appear before the Montreal Medico-Chirurgical Society. The address, later published under the title, "Take the Private

Profit Out of Medicine," was much more startling than his "Reflections." This was a direct attack upon the Canadian medical establishment.

Take the Private Profit Out of Medicine

Symposium on Medical Economics

Discussion
Montreal Medico-Chirurgical Society
April 17, 1936
Norman Bethune

GENERAL APPROACH:

Tonight there has been shown the most interesting case ever presented to this Society. It is the case of "The People versus the Doctors". We are acting both as defendant and judge. This behooves us to apply our minds with the utmost objectivity to this question. This case is an ethical and moral problem in the field of social and political economics, and not medical economics alone. Medicine must be envisaged as embedded in the social fabric and inseparable from it. It is the product of any given social environment. The basis of any social structure is economic. The economic theory and practice in this country is termed capitalistic. It is founded on individualism, competiton and private profit. This capitalistic system is undergoing an economic crisis,—commonly called the depression. This is not a temporary illness of the body politic, but a deadly disease requiring systemic treatment. Systemic treatment is called, by the timid, radical remedies. Those palliative measures as suggested by most of our political quacks are aspirin tablets for a syphilitic headache. They may relieve, they will never cure.

Medicine is a typical, loosely organized, basically individualistic industry in this 'catch as catch can' capitalistic system operating as a monopoly on a private profit basis. Now, it is inevitable that medicine should undergo much the same crisis as the rest of the capitalistic world and should present much the same interesting and uncomfortable phenomena. This may be epitomized as "poverty of health in the midst of scientific abundance of knowledge of disease". Just as thousands of people are hungry in a country which produces more food than the people can consume (we even burn coffee, kill hogs and pay farmers not to plant wheat and cotton), just as thousands are wretchedly clothed though the

THE COMMERCIAL APPEAL, MEMPHIS,

ANESTHETISTS HEAR DR. NORMAN BETHUNE

Surgeon Discusses New Method At Convention Here

Intravenous evipal anesthesia, developed in Germany five years ago, is the most pleasant anesthetic for thoracic surgery, Dr. Norman Bethune, chief surgeon of the Sacred Heart Hospital at Montreal, told the Mid-South Post Graduate Nurse Anesthetists' Assembly in convention session yesterday.

"The fast induction of the dissolved white crystals in the veins makes the anesthesia especially effective with fractures, dislocations, abdominal operations and amputations," he said. "If a patient begins to count when the anesthetic is being given, he will be asleep before he can count to 15 at a moderate speed."

The effects of the anesthesia wears off in a half hour, according to Dr. Bethune, and there is no masking, no struggling and no ill effects afterwards.

Other speakers on yesterday's program were Miss Emma Easterling, Vicksburg, Miss., who spoke on "Preparation of the Patient for Anesthesia"; Dr. Gilbert J. Thomas, Minneapolis, "Choice of Anesthetics in Surgery for Kidney and Prostatic Diseases"; Dr. Frederick A. Coller, Ann Harbor, Mich., "Water Losses by Surgical Patients in Relation to the Anesthetist"; Miss Blanche G. Petty, Little Rock, "The Patient's Viewpoint"; Dr. R. H. Jaffe, Chicago, "The Anemias with Special Reference to Their Significance in Anesthesia"; and Dr. C. R. Crutchfield, Nashville, "Spinal Anesthesia."

Mrs. Jennie Houser, chief anesthetist at the General Hospital, was named president of the Tennessee State Anesthetists' Association early last night to succeed Mrs. Louise Gilbertson, of Memphis. Mrs. Gertrude Alexander Troster, with the Crisler Clinic was elected vice president; and Jean O'Brien, of Campbell's Clinic, secretary-treasurer. The directors, all of Memphis, are Jewel Fink, Eleanor Burkhead, Irene Dixon, Pauline McClelland, Alice Little, Mrs. Lucy Gaffney, Bessie Caldwell and Grace Skinner.

Today's session will be featured by the election of officers of the Mid-South Assembly of Anesthetists, and addresses by Miss Grace Skinner, Memphis; Mrs. Gertrude Alexander Troster, Memphis; Miss Margaret A. Price, New Orleans; Dr. Claude S. Beck, Cleveland; and Dr. C. R. Straatsma, New York. Sessions are held at the Peabody.

UNPAID TAX STATUS

(Continued From Page One)

killed the authority by which the tax was impounded and hence released the grower from any tax which had accumulated.

"Frees It," Says Author

Senator Russell of Georgia,

Surgeon Startles Medical Assembly

Dr. Norman Bethune, the Montreal surgeon who startled the Mid-South Medical Assembly with his proposed socialized medicine, is shown on the left. Next to him, from left to right, are Dr. C. H. Sanford, Memphis, chairman of the program committee; Dr. C. R. Crutchfield, Nashville, incoming president, and Dr. H. King Wade, Hot Springs, retiring president.

SURGEON ADVOCATES

(Continued on Page Three)

operation because we have hundreds who can not pay anything. If medicine was socialized as it is in Russia, the doctors could be paid by a tax on everyone. They would receive salaries commensurate with their ability, as officers in the army and navy. True, we never would make much money, but persons should not enter the profession to get rich."

Dr. Bethune pleaded for a re-examination by medical men of their position under the present economic system.

Elementary Obligation

"There is little hope for a great improvement of the health of the people until the practice of medicine is liberated from its debasing aspects of private profit and taken as an elementary obligation of the state," he said.

He said that the government was "exploiting the medical profession by its non or reduced payments in taking care of the chronic unemployed or unemployable," and asked that the profession become more politically minded in realizing the inseparability of health and economic security.

"Let us abandon our so-called splendid scientific isolation and grasp the realities of the present social crisis. A change is coming and already the craft of Aesculapius is beginning to feel beneath it the great surge and movement of the world where high-

Ickes Refuses to Pose With Talmadge

SPRINGFIELD, Ill., Feb. 12.— Photographers seeking to make a picture of Secretary Ickes and Governor Talmadge shaking hands at Abraham Lincoln's tomb fared 50 per cent today.

Talmadge, critic of the New Deal, agreed to pose with the Roosevelt cabinet member, but Ickes replied emphatically:

"I will not."

only right in one out of three. He termed the tuberculin test as "old stuff."

"with a fluoroscope I can tell in 60 seconds whether a person has tuberculosis," he said. It is an X-ray device with which a physician can detect lung cavities without the necessity of a photograph.

Dr. Bethune admits that his scheme for fighting tuberculosis would require a large sum. "But think of the money being spent on the dole and many of those on relief have tuberculosis. The lower you go in the social scale the more tuberculosis you will find. The disease now is costing this country $300,000,000 a year."

Proposes a Clinic

For Memphis, he would have a clinic with equipment costing $13,500; $48,000 more a year for technicians' salaries and supplies; sanatoriums with 2,000 beds, $5,200,000; yearly cost for an estimated 2,600 patients, $1,778,500, plus $90,000 a year for their dependents. "At least

FOUR ESCAPE DEATH AS PLANE CRASHES

Desert Wind Forces Ship Down In New Mexico

ALBUQUERQUE, N. M., Feb. 12. —(AP)—A private cabin biplane, caught in a stiff desert wind, was demolished today in a forced landing in which the four occupants were shaken and injured, one critically.

A veteran New Mexico flier said it was a "miracle" B. C. Skinner, owner and pilot, and his three companions were not killed. Buffeted by the wind over Enchanted Mesa 50 miles west of Albuquerque, they landed at Acomita.

Miss Vivien Skinner, 22-year-old daughter of the pilot, Dunedin, Fla., manufacturing company official, suffered internal injuries and fractures. L. B. Keller, 34, employed by Skinner, and his niece, Miss Beatrice Keller, 22, and the pilot were badly shaken and bruised.

They were flown here by Maj. A. D. Smith, division superintendent of the Transcontinental and Western Air Line, after an emergency radio call from the Acomita field. All were taken to a hospital.

"We struck a bad squall over Acoma (famous 'sky city' of the Pueblo Indian tribe)," Skinner said. "It sent us into a dive and be-

manufacturers can make more clothing than they can sell, so millions are sick, hundreds of thousands suffer pain, and tens of thousands die prematurely through lack of adequate medical care, which is available but for which they cannot pay. Inability to purchase is combined with poor distribution. The problem of medical economics is a part of the problem of world economics and is inseparable and indivisible from it. Medicine, as we are practising it, is a luxury trade. We are selling bread at the price of jewels. The poor, which comprise fifty per cent of our population, cannot pay, and starve; we cannot sell, and suffer. The people have no health protection and we have no economic security. This brings us to the point of the two aspects of this problem.

THE PATIENTS' PREDICAMENT:

There are in this country three great economic groups, 1st: The comfortable, 2nd: The uncomfortable, 3rd: The miserable. In the upper bracket are those, who are comfortably well off, rich or wealthy, In the mid bracket are those, who are moderately uncomfortable and insecure; and in the lower, those vast masses, not in brackets but in chains, who are living on the edge of the subsistence level. These people in the lower income class are receiving only one-third of the home office and clinic services from physicians that a fundamental standard of health requires. Only 55 per cent, as shown by the Committee on the Cost of Medical Care, of as many cases are being hospitalized as an adequate standard would prescribe, and only 54 per cent of as many days are being spent in hospital as are desirable. The only exception are those surgical cases hospitalized, which is approximately normal for both rich and poor. In short, one has to suffer a major surgical catastrophe to have even approximate adequate care. The Committee's report also showed, that 46.6% of people, whose income is less than $1,200 a year received no medical, dental or eye care whatsoever in a year. If this is combined with those whose incomes are $10,000 or more (13.8% of such persons received no similar care), we are faced with the appalling fact, that 38.2% of all people, irrespective of income, receive no medical, dental or eye care whatsoever. What is the cause of this

He always loved to shock. In February 1936 he went to Memphis, Tennessee to address some of the most conservative doctors in the United States. After presenting a technical paper on anaesthesia, he delivered an impassioned presentation of his belief in socialized medicine. The newspaper heading reveals the reaction of his listeners.

alarming state of affairs? 1st: Financial inability to pay is the major cause; 2nd: Ignorance; 3rd: Apathy; 4th: Lack of medical service. So we see that in the United States with a population of 120 million people in 1929 only 48 people out of 100 had the care of a physician during the year; only 21 people out of 100 visited the dentist once a year; only 1 in 17 had hospital care; only 1 in 26 had their eyes examined, and only 1 in 9 had health examination, vaccination or immunization. Yet morbidity figures for this group of people show, that they suffered 344.5 illnesses per 1,000 persons in the same year. If Canada is taken, as it well may be, as part of the American scene, the figures for this country would not show very much variation.

THE DOCTORS' DILEMMA:

Enormous accumulation of scientific knowledge has made it practically impossible for any one man to have an entire grasp of even the facts, much less their application, of the sum total of medical knowledge. This has made specialization imperative and group practice a necessity. Individual specialization predicates concentrated centres of population. The general practitioner, unsupported by specialists, knows that he cannot give the people their money's worth, yet the financial cost of specialization bars many from proceeding to such fields. The necessity to make money after a difficult financial struggle to pay for medical education drives the young doctor too often into any form of remunerative work however uncongenial it may be. There he is caught up in the coils of economics, from which not one in a thousand can ever escape. The fee-for-service is very disturbing morally to practitioners. The patient is frequently unable to correctly appraise the value of the doctor's service or dis-service. Perrot and Collins, in 1933, in an investigating of 9,130 families in America, found the depression poor had a larger incidence of illness than any other group. Also that 61% of all physicians' calls to such a class were free, that 33% of calls to the moderately comfortable were free, and that 26% of calls to even those comfortably well off were not paid for. If $3,000. net be taken as an adequate income, 40% of all physicians in the United States made less money than that. If $2,500. net be taken, 33% of all physicians had inadequate incomes. If $1,600. net be taken, then 18% of doctors had inadequate incomes, and 5% of all physicians were unable to meet their professional expenses from gross receipts. The very interesting comparison with the salaries of physicians attached as full time workers in the army, the navy and hospitals and public health services showed, that only 13.2% had incomes below $3,000.

However, quite apart from this, it was the opinion of the Committee that the existing medical system with all its ramifications could not supply service in quantity or value to the fundamental standard of service prescribed. The tremendous expansion of the Public Health Services is urgently needed, and instead of $1 out of the $30 per capita, which is the cost of medical care, at least $2.50 would be desirable. However, our politicians in this regard have raised the cynical indifference of their attitude towards Public Health, especially the indigent, to the dignity of a doctrine.

WHERE DO WE GO FROM HERE?

Permit a few categorical statements. Dogmatism has a role in the realm of vacillation.

1.) The best form of providing health protection would be to change the economic system which produces ill-health, liquidate ignorance, poverty and unemployment. The practice of each individual purchasing his own medical care does not work. It is unjust, inefficient, wasteful and completely out-moded. Doctors, private charity and philanthropic institutions have kept it alive as long as possible. it should have died a natural death a hundred years ago, with the coming of the industrial revolution in the opening years of the 19th century. In our highly-geared, modern industrial society there is no such thing as private health—all health is public. The illness and maladjustments of one unit of the mass effects all other members. The protection of the people's health should be recognized by the Government as its primary obligation and duty to its citizens. Socialized medicine and the abolition or restriction of private practice would appear to be the realistic solution of the problem. Let us take the profit, the private economic profit, out of medicine, and purify our profession of rapacious individualism. Let us make it disgraceful to enrich ourselves at the expense of the miseries of our fellow-men. Let us organize ourselves so that we can no longer be exploited as we are being exploited by our politicians. Let us re-define medical ethics—not as a code of professional etiquette between doctors, but as a code of fundamental morality and justice between medicine and the people. In our medical society let us discuss more often the great problems of our age and not so much interesting cases; the relationship of medicine to the State; the duties of the profession to the people; the matrix of economics and sociology in which we exist. Let us recognize that our most important contemporaneous problems are economic and social and not technical and scientific in the narrow sense that we employ those words.

2.) Medicine, like any other organization to-day, whether it be the Church or the Bar, is judging its leaders by their attitude to the fundamental social and economic issues of the day. We need fewer leading physicians and famous surgeons in modern medi-cine and more far-sighted, socially-imaginative statesmen.

The medical profession must do this—as the traditional, historical and altruistic guardians of the people's health; let us present to the Government a complete, comprehensive programme of a planned medical service for all the people, then, in whatever position the profession finds itself after such a plan has been evolved, that position it must accept. This apparent immolation as a burnt offering on the altar of ideal public health will result in the profession rising like a glorious Phoenix from the dead ashes of its former self.

Medicine must be entirely re-organized and unified, welded into a great army of doctors, dentists, nurses, technicians and social service workers, to make a collectivized attack on disease and utilizing all the present scientific knowledge of its members to that end.

Let us say to the people not—"how much have you got" but—"how best can we serve you". Our slogan should be "we are in business for your health".

3.) Socialized medicine means that health protection becomes public property, like the post office, the army, the navy, the judiciary and the school. 2nd: supported by public funds; 3rd: with services available to all, not according to income but according to need. Charity must be abolished and justice substituted. Charity debases the donor and debauches the recipient; 4th: its workers to be paid by the State with assured salaries and pensions; 5th: with democratic self government by the Health workers themselves.

Twenty-five years ago it was thought contemptible to be called a Socialist. To-day it is ridiculous not to be one.

Medical reforms, such as limited Health Insurance schemes, are not socialized medicine. They are bas-tard forms of Socialism produced by belated humani-tarianism out of necessity.

The three major objections which the opponents of socialized medicine emphasize are: *1st: Loss of initiative.* Although the human donkey probably needs, in this state of modern barbarism, some sort of vegetable dangled in front of his nose, these need not be golden carrots but a posy of prestige will do as well.

2nd: Bureaucracy. This can be checked by democratic control of organization from bottom to top. *3rd: The importance of the patient's own selection of a doctor.* This is a myth: its only proponents are the doctors themselves—not the patients. Give a limited choice—say of 2 or 3 doctors, then, if the patient is not satisfied, send him to a psychiatrist! Sauce for the goose is sauce for the gander—the doctor must also be given his own selection of patients! 99% of patients want results not personalities.

4.) Our profession must arouse itself from its scientific and intensely personal preoccupation and becoming socially-minded, realize the inseparability of health from economic security.

Let us abandon our isolation and grasp the realities of the present economic crisis. The world is changing beneath our very eyes and already the bark of Aesculapius is beginning to feel beneath its keel the great surge and movement of the rising world tide which is sweeping on, obliterating old landscapes and old scenes. We must go with the tide or be wrecked.

5.) The contest in the world to-day is between two kinds of men: those who believe in the old jungle individualism, and those who believe in cooperative efforts for the securing of a better life for all.

The people are ready for socialized medicine. The obstructionists to the people's health security lie within the profession itself. Recognize this fact. It is the all-important fact of the situation. These men with the mocking face of the reactionary or the listlessness of the futilitarian, proclaim their principles under the guise of "maintenance of the sacred relationship between doctor and patient", "inefficiency of other non-profit nationalized enterprises", "the danger of Socialism", "the freedom of individualism". These are the enemies of the people and make no mistake. They are the enemies of medicine too.

The situation which is confronting Medicine to-day is a contest of two forces in Medicine itself. One holds that the important thing is the maintenance of our vested historical interest, our private property, our monopoly of health distribution. The other contends that the function of Medicine is greater than the maintenance of the doctor's position, that the security of the people's health is our primary duty, that we are the servants, not the masters, of the people, and that human rights are above professional privileges. So the old challenge of Shakespeare's character in Henry IV still rings out across the centuries: "Under which King, Bezonian, stand or die!".

Now there was no turning back. When a provincial election was called for the summer of 1936 the activities of Bethune's group were intensified.

On the eve of that election, the Manifesto of the Montreal Group for the Security of the People's Health was delivered to election candidates in Montreal, to the Premier of Quebec and to hospital, health and religious authorities.

The Manifesto was a thorough indictment of the

Bethune en route to Spain.

contemporary medical system. To replace it, Bethune and the Montreal Group outlined in extreme detail the structure for a system of socialized medicine.

Caught up in the frenzy of last-minute preparations, exhausted by months of debate and perhaps, naively optimistic, Bethune was unprepared for the public reaction. The hostility of many who regarded the scheme as Communist-inspired was expected. What was not was the mindless indifference of most who read the Manifesto. Few took it seriously.

The long meetings, the endless gathering of statistics and the assembling of arguments which Bethune presented in speeches to medical groups in Canada and the United States had moved him closer to a political decision.

The reception given the Manifesto was a delayed endorsement of a step he had quietly taken a few months earlier. He had made his decision to throw in his lot with the Communist Party.

He was angry now. Montreal and Canadian society were indifferent to the calamity of the Depression and lacked the necessary energy and courage to combat it.

He wanted action. He wanted to do something tangible that could demonstrate that he was willing to act against the hostile forces that were inexorably crushing a paralysed society. His opportunity came with the outbreak of civil war in Spain. In October 1936 he resigned from Sacré Coeur and sailed for Spain.

He was no longer straddling two worlds.

Madrid Will Be the Tomb of Fascism

Melilla, an African town on the edge of a long peninsula jutting out into the Mediterranean, was the most easterly military outpost of the Spanish Protectorate of Morocco. In the early afternoon of July 17, 1936, troops from the local garrison and a unit of foreign legionnaires moved swiftly to occupy all public buildings and cut off communications with the mainland. Within hours any feeble resistance had been savagely crushed and Melilla was under martial law.

By evening the rebels had telegraphed the news of their triumph to General Francisco Franco, Chief of the General Staff, who was in the city of Las Palmas in the Canary Islands. Just before dawn the following morning, Franco issued a manifesto, explaining that the army had taken the lead in a campaign to restore order to Spain. That day, in the same manner as in Melilla, army units rose throughout the Spanish peninsula. The Spanish Civil War had begun.

Though long aware of a rumoured coup, the government in Madrid was stunned by the Melilla uprising. While the people of Madrid gathered at points throughout the capital stormily demanding decisive counter-measures, the cabinet vacillated. Finally and reluctantly, they yielded to the intense pressure of the unions and left-wing political parties which demanded arms for the people. On the morning of July 19 the Prime Minister ordered the armouries to be opened to the unions. This happened just in time to overcome the rebels in Madrid and Barcelona. Had the government acted earlier, the revolt on the mainland might have been crushed. Had it delayed a day longer, Franco might have succeeded and three years of bloody war would have been prevented.

In those first few days, Franco was justly optimistic. With the important exceptions of Madrid and Barcelona, the carefully planned rebellion had been successful in numerous towns and cities. There were many who wanted the uprising to succeed: big business, the Falange Española, or Spanish fascist movement, the conservative political parties and the hierarchy of the Roman Catholic Church. The bulk of the armed forces sided with their chief and when the uprising escalated into war, he was able to call on prearranged military aid from Germany and Italy.

Arrayed against Franco's Nationalists was a disparate, unorganized group united only by a desire to defend the legally elected government. Known as Loyalists or Republicans, it included a very few members of the regular armed forces, many intellectuals, some small businessmen, and most of the urban and rural workers

With Sorensen en route to Madrid.

Bethune with Sorensen, Carmen, (Spanish nurse) Sise and Celia Greenspan (an American laboratory technician) in front of headquarters at 36 Principe de Vergara Street. After Franco's victory, many street names were changed. Principe de Vergara was renamed General Mola after the Nationalist general who coined the term "Fifth Column".

who were the rank and file of the Socialist, Communist and Anarchist movements. Spain was not allowed to settle her family quarrel alone. From the outset European and North American interest focussed on the gathering conflict, and foreign partisans of both Spanish factions launched into a furious propaganda battle. What began as an internal struggle was rapidly transformed, largely through world opinion, into a guerre a l'outrance *between the rival ideologies of Fascism and Communism.*

In their eagerness to gain an advantage each Spanish force invited foreign intervention. Within weeks of the Melilla uprising German airplanes and crews and Italian tanks and troops began to pour into Spain to back up Franco's legions. On the Loyalist side, though later and in smaller numbers, tanks and airplanes arrived from the Soviet Union to aid the now beleaguered government forces.

The direct participation by Germany, Italy and the U.S.S.R. confirmed the belief that Spain was the battlefield on which the significant issues of the twentieth century would be decided. This was held particularly by those whose politics ranged from the centre to the extreme left and who believed that their contribution to the international crusade must be more than engaging in ideological debates with their rivals in the safety of their native land. At least 40,000 men and women from more than sixty nations made their way to Spain to serve the Republican government as members of the International Brigades.

Nearly 1,200 Canadians were to enlist in the ranks of the International Brigades in the Mackenzie-

Hazen Sise returned to Canada in 1937 after Bethune. He practised architecture, and was working with the National Capital Commission at the time of his death in 1974.

Papineau Battalion, but this organization was just taking shape in the late summer of 1936.

Before the end of July of that year Bethune was already planning to go to Spain. He was unequivocally committed to the belief that civilization was on trial: "It is in Spain that the real issues of our time are going to be fought out. It is there that democracy will either die or survive."

By late October he was en route to Madrid, where he arrived without a prearranged role. During the first several days, in the company of Henning Sorensen, a multilingual Danish-Canadian who volunteered as his interpreter, he visited hospitals in and near the Spanish capital to assess the situation. It was more than a week later, on a train returning from Valencia, that he outlined to Sorensen his plans for a mobile blood transfusion service.

Typically, this inspirational decision was the product of insight triggered by passion. In hospital after hospital he had been moved by the tragic sight of dying Republican

Henning Sorensen has had a varied career. Through his knowledge of languages he was employed by the international service of the CBC and then in the early 1960s served as a translator in the Cuban Ministry of Foreign Affairs. He has lived in Vancouver for the past dozen years.

A portrait of Bethune taken in Madrid.

soldiers lying on stretchers, their young bodies blanched by the loss of blood. Instead of taking the wounded to the blood, he knew there must be a system by which the blood could be taken to the wounded. To solve this problem would save hundreds, perhaps thousands of lives. And it would also provide the drama that gave meaning to his life—an emotional thrust that toiling as an anonymous surgeon in a military hospital would never provide.

The concept was not new; it simply had not been tried. Bethune, for whom thought and action were virtually synonymous, decided to put the scheme into practice.

Having discovered a practicable outlet for his creative energy, he immediately began to exercise his considerable organizational skills. He and Sorensen rushed to Paris and London, purchased supplies and were back in Madrid before the middle of December, accompanied by Hazen Sise, a young Canadian living in England.

Within days, the Servicio Canadiense de Transfusion de Sangre (Canadian Blood Transfusion Service) was receiving donated blood from the people of Madrid. The funds for the operation had been supplied by a Canadian organization, the Committee to Aid Spanish Democracy (CASD). Bethune described those first days in a letter to a committee chairman, the Reverend Benjamin Spence.

49

Bethune, Sorensen and Sise spent several days with a Republican alpine unit in the Guadarrama Mountains near Madrid at Christmas 1936.

Servicio Canadiense de Transfusion
de Sangre,
Principe de Vergara 36,
Madrid Dec. 17/36.

Dear Ben:

This is really the first time since my arrival in this country that I can give you definite news and detailed information.

I am glad to say that we are now completely organized and settled in for work. As I wrote you before (I hope you received my letter) unless we were able to offer the Government some definite proposal and concrete scheme our efforts would peter out —by

this I mean I would simply go into a hospital as a surgeon and that would be the end of the *"Canadian Unit."* Now it seemed better to emulate England and Scotland and establish ourselves as a definite entity. England has the "English Hospital," Scotland has the "Scottish Ambulance."

So with this in mind and after making several blind starts (such as the two days we spent at the front with the International Brigade) Sorensen and I left for Paris to collect apparatus and car.

No cars are for sale in Spain. I had in mind a Ford station car, as a compromise between a truck and a car. It must carry about $1^{1}/_{2}$ tons of cargo, could be used as an ambulance if needed for such and yet it would be handy enough to transport 4 people in comparative comfort.

I couldn't buy this car in Paris. I had to go to London. Here I was able to pick one up for one hundred and seventy five pounds sterling and with alterations such as luggage rack on top, built in boxes etc. made a good type of transportation for our purpose so I bought complete equipment for a mobile blood transfusion service.

The idea of mobility was always kept in mind so such apparatus as refrigerators, auto clave, incubators etc. all were purchased to run by gasoline or kerosene and to be independent of electrical power.

The refrigerator is Electrolux run by kerosene and very efficient. The auto clave (for sterilization of solutions, bottles, etc. is run by gasoline, the incubator by kerosene and the distilled water still by kerosene.

So our four major pieces of apparatus run to about one ton in weight (the auto clave weighs about 450 lbs itself). They take up the major part of the interior.

Then in addition we have 175 pieces of glassware of all varieties and kinds—vacuum bottles, blood flasks, drip bottles, containers etc. We have 3 complete direct blood transfusion sets of the latest English model (Froud syringe) microscope haemocytometers, complete set of chest instruments, 2000 sets of type 2 and 3 blood serum for testing blood groups, hurricane lamps, gas masks etc.

In all, our equipment consists of 1,375 separate pieces. We have enough chemicals to make up solutions for intravenous injections of physiological serums, glucose and sodium citrate to last us for three months, I estimate.

These chemicals are packed in water-tight tin cases and each is weighed out separately so that by adding each package to a given amount of distilled water the proper strength of solution is obtained.

Now we are installed in a 15 room flat formerly occupied by a German diplomat (Fascist, now in Berlin) very magnificent and palatial at the above address. Just above us are the S.R.I. [Socorro Rojo

With Sise, a nurse and members of the alpine unit.

Internacional] head offices. We are working under their protection. They are the best organized and powerful health organization in Spain and much superior to the International Red Cross (this organization is very suspiciously Fascist between you and I) or the weak Spanish Red Cross.

The S.R.I. was formed before the revolution to care for the political prisoners and their families who suffered Fascist oppression and since the revolution has gradually taken over the majority of the sanitary services of the country. Their work in the rescue of orphans and evacuation of abandoned areas is tremendous. They run about 1,000 orphanages, camps, hospitals, creches etc. in Spain. All their leaders are party people—as everywhere in Spain the people who lead the major services are Communists—they do the hard and dirty work.

Now as to our organization. Through the press and daily over the local radio we broadcast appeals for blood donors. As a result we have thousands of volunteers and are busy grouping them and card indexing them. We have now 800 and in a few days will have over 1,000. There are about 56 hospitals in the City. We have surveyed the entire situation and have a list of them containing the information as to size, capacity, addresses, under what organization, telephone, chief surgeon, type of service etc. A large map of the City (4×5 ft.) in our office (the former library, the walls entirely lined by 8,000 books, gold brocade curtains and Aubusson carpets!) gives at once the route to the hospitals.

We collect the blood every day from a selected group of donors types I, II, III, IV. We are running about 1 gallon daily just now. This is stored in our refrigerator. On call from the hospital the blood flasks are transferred to heated vacuum bottles and carried in knapsacks with additional bottles, warm physiological serum and glucose solution plus a complete sterilized tin box containing:

Towel	
Forceps	
knife	
syringe	We have
catgut	15

group testing serums	complete sets of these

So on arrival we're ready to start work at once. We go to the man and decide what he needs—either blood or physiological serum, or glucose or a combination of these. If blood is needed on account of acute exsanguination we "group" him at once with our serum. This is done by a prick of the finger, a glass stick and serum and takes 2 minutes, then after grouping we give him the blood of the type needed (type I, II, III, or IV).

If in doubt we can always give IV as this is called the "Universal" donor. We are not sure how long the citrated blood will keep good in our refrigerators but we are experimenting and hope for several weeks.

We have plans to branch out and give the service up in the Guadarrama Mountains up to a distance of 100 miles from the City later and might need another car but this won't be for several months yet.

Now as to personnel—I, myself am of course director, Henning Sorensen is Liaison officer, Hazen Sise is driver and general utility man (he is a Canadian, the son of Paul Sise, president of the Northern Electric Co. of Montreal, a talented young architect) then we have 2 Spanish medical students, a Spanish Biologist and Mrs. Celia Greenspan of New York (wife of M. Greenspan the journalist) as technician. We have a staff of 4 servants, a cook, 2 maids and laundry man, also a military armed guard for our door. We are all well and happy.

About one quarter of the City is badly damaged and abandoned except by troops. 300,000 people, mostly women, children and aged have been evacuated. Between 7-8 thousand civilians have been killed by bombardment in the last month and many more thousand wounded.

Morale is excellent. Madrid won't fall but will be the tomb of Fascism!

Junker machines (3 motor bombers) came over yesterday at 6 p.m. accompanied by 24 pursuit planes; they dropped several tons of bombs. I took some photos of a hit hospital in the afternoon. Their 100 and 250 kilo bombs make an awful mess!

Just now there is a lull but Franco has declared he will not leave one stone standing in Madrid. Well let him try.

The water is still good. No epidemics have broken out as yet. The electric light is on but the gas is very low and reserved for hospitals. Coal is practically gone and meat is scarce, no milk, butter, sugar but plenty of vegetables and fruit (oranges and apples).

Well, we are here "for the duration" as we used to say in 1914. I can only say how grateful I am for the wonderful backing of the committee and the people of Canada.

The $1,800.00 I came over with—$1,000.00 went to the Oviedo Miners for Anti Tetanus Serum and the $800.00 was spent in travelling and living expenses for Sorensen and myself in Spain and back to London (incidentally I would have been lost in these early days without his Spanish and French). The $3,000.00 received in Paris and the additional $4,000.00 in

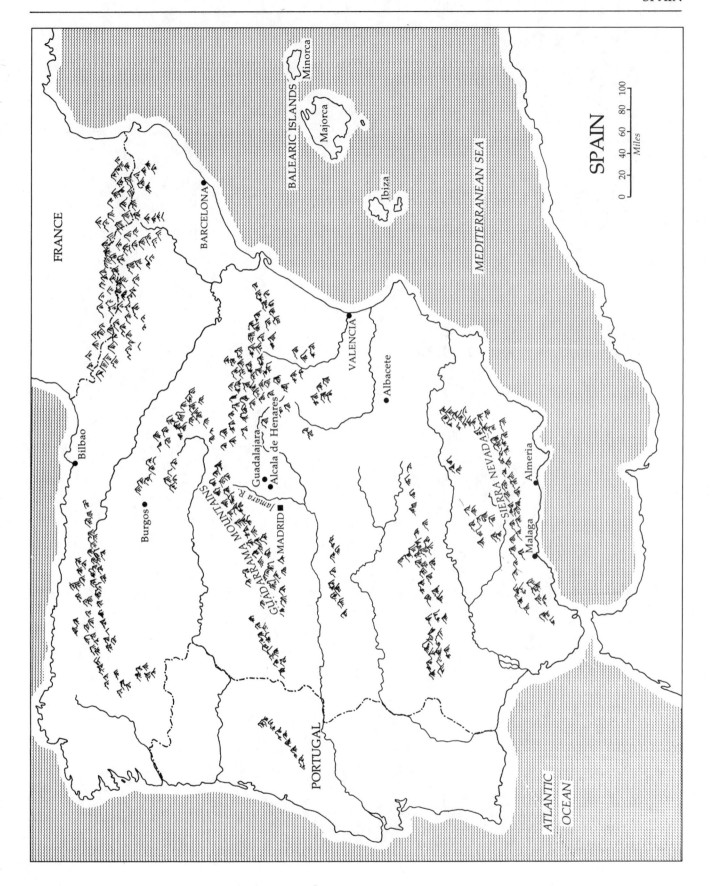

SPAIN

Miles

0 20 40 60 80 100

FRANCE

BARCELONA

BALEARIC ISLANDS

Minorca

Majorca

Ibiza

MEDITERRANEAN SEA

VALENCIA

Albacete

Bilbao

Burgos

GUADARRAMA MOUNTAINS

Guadalajara

Alcala de Henares

Jarama R.

MADRID

SIERRA NEVADA

Almeria

Malaga

PORTUGAL

ATLANTIC OCEAN

London went into the car and equipment ($1,200.00 in duty (*refundable*) leaving a balance of cash in hand now sufficient to keep the unit in this country under *present conditions* for 3 months more. Of this cash on hand, *$2,000.00* is in American Express orders and the balance ($500.00) in Spanish Pesetas and the dollar is fixed by the Government at *11 pesetas* or roughly 9 cents. Prices are spiked and there is no inflation.

I am enclosing a photo but will send you a better one next week. This was taken on our arrival last week. I enclose also samples of our stationery. A *Medal* is being struck for our donors with a *Star* for each donation. Will send you next week a photo and a badge also.

This letter is going out with a member of the Scottish Ambulance which is returning to Scotland to be re-organized.

Best of luck to everybody and a Merry Christmas.

Your comrade
Norman Bethune

P.S. This unit is causing considerable interest among the Foreign Press but I am keeping back the story until next week, when I have informed the Press Censor (an Austrian Comrade—!) it may be released as you will probably hear about it before this letter reaches you.

N.B

In January, he sent another summary of recent events.

Madrid Jan. 11-37

Dear Ben:

We have had a very hectic ten days as you may know and I haven't really had the time to sit down and write you a letter but as an Englishman is leaving today for Paris I felt I should take advantage of this and let you know the news.

Frank Pitcairn—author of "A Reporter in Spain," promised to write an article on our unit for the "Daily Worker" of London whose correspondent he is. But as he hasn't turned up today—he stays with us—I expect he has left for another front.

Professor J.B.S. Haldane who stayed with us for two weeks, has returned to London and has promised to

Bethune had learned to ski well in the Laurentians north of Montreal. He borrowed these skis from the alpine battalion and was photographed at the Navacerrada Pass in the Guadarrama Mountains, 26 December 1936.

send "The Clarion" an article on us. I think these would be better than one I might write myself.

As you know we have withstood the heaviest attack and the most serious effort of the Fascists to take the City since the first and second weeks of November. Their losses have been terrific—at least 5,000 (our papers say 10,000) Germans have been killed and Franco has taken the Moors away from Madrid and replaced them with fresh German troops. They thought they had a walk-over and advanced in exactly the same massed formation as they did in 1914-1915 in France. Our machine guns simply mowed them down. Our losses were 1 to 5 of theirs.

The International Brigade has suffered badly of course as they are shock troops but large re-inforcements of French, German, English, Polish, Austrian and Italians—with some Americans and Canadians are arriving.

We have been having 2 & 4 raids a day for 2 weeks now and many thousands of non-combatants, women and children, have been killed. I was in the Telephonic Building the other day when it was shelled. However, it is very modern and strongly built. No great damage was done—a handful of people were killed only.

You simply can't get these people to take shelter during shelling and bombing!

Our night work is very eerie! We get a phone call for blood. Snatch up our packed bag, take 2 bottles (each 500 c.c.)—one of group IV and one of group II blood—out of the refrigerator and with our armed guard off we go through the absolutely pitch dark streets and the guns and machine guns and rifle shots sound like as if they were in the next block, although they are really half a mile away. Without lights we drive, stop at the hospital and with a search light in our hands find our way into the cellar principally. All

the operating rooms in the hospitals have been moved into the basement to avoid falling shrapnel, bricks and stones coming through the operating room ceiling.

Our bag contains a completely sterilized box of instruments, towels etc. so we can start work at once. The man is lying most frequently on a stretcher so we kneel down beside him, prick the finger and on a slide put 1 drop each of Serum type II and type III. If his red blood cells are agglutinated by II and not by III—he is a type III. If agglutinated by II he is a III, if by both he is a type I, if neither, he is a group IV.

So now we know what blood he can take safely. If I, III or IV he gets our bottle of blood group IV (the

"I will use the latest Russian-American methods of collecting blood, storing it at suitable temperatures in vacuum bottles and transmitting it to any hospital needing it within 25 miles . . . . We collected and gave 10 gallons of blood during January. Expect to increase this to 25 gallons during this month."

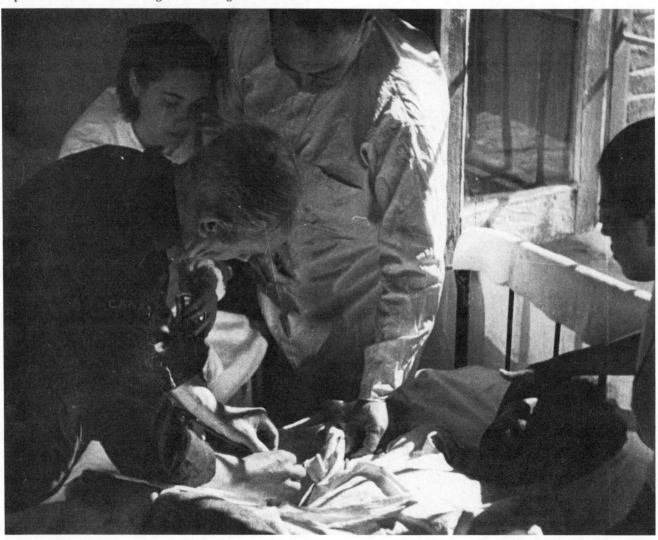

"We have succeeded in unifying all remaining Spanish transfusion units under us. We are serving 100 hospitals and casualty-clearing stations in the front lines of Madrid and 100 kilometres from the front of the Sector del Centro . . . . This is the first unified blood transfusion service in army and medical history. Plans are well under way to supply the entire Spanish anti-fascist army with preserved blood. Your institute is now operating on a 1,000 kilometre front."

universal blood). If he is a II he gets blood group II. He could also take IV but as these "Universal Donors" are about only 45% of the people, we must use II's when we can. Then the proper blood is warmed in a pan of water and we are ready to start. The man is usually as white as the paper, mostly shocked, with an imperceptible pulse. He may be exsanguinated also and not so much shocked, but usually is both shocked and exsanguinated. We now inject novo-caine over the vein in the bend of the elbow, cut down and find the vein and insert a small glass Canula, then run the blood in. The change in most cases is spectacular. We give him always 500 C.C. of preserved blood and sometimes more and follow it up with saline of 5%

glucose solution. The pulse can now be felt and his pale lips have some color.

Yesterday, we did three transfusions—this is about the average daily, besides the blood we leave at hospitals for them to use themselves. We collect $1/2$ to $3/4$ gallon daily, mix it with Sodium Citrate (3.8%) and keep it just above freezing in the refrigerator in sterile milk and wine bottles. This blood will keep for about a week. We are working on the use of *Locke's Solution* to preserve the red blood cells longer and are making up Bayliss' *Gum Solution*. (Gum Arabic in Saline). Bayliss was (or is!) an English Physiologist who brought out this gum solution for shock during the war of 1914-18.

The International Brigade Hospital needs male and female French and German speaking nurses—not English speaking at present although these may be needed later. Brain surgeons also.

Well, this is a grand country and great people. The wounded are wonderful.

After I had given a transfusion to a French soldier who had lost his arm, he raised the other to me as I left the room in the Casualty Clearing Station, and with his raised clenched fist exclaimed "Viva la Revolution." The next boy to him was a Spaniard—a medical student, shot through the liver and stomach. When I had given him a transfusion and asked him how he felt—he said "It is nothing"—Nada! He recovered. So did the Frenchman.

Transfusion work should be given in Casualty Clearing Stations when they come out of the operating room of the 1st hospital behind the lines and *before* they are sent back to rear hospitals. But as Madrid is the front line, our work is mostly here although we go out 25 kilometers to other parts of the line.

I am sending you the engine plate of a German fighting plane—a Heinkel.

I sent you last month 25 posters and will send more.

"The new name of the Canadian Medical Unit is *Instituto Hispano-Canadiense de Transfusion de Sangre*. I have been appointed Director-in-Chief as a grateful tribute to Canadian workers and have been give the military rank of Comandante."

At the headquarters of Dr. Duran Jorda in Barcelona. Duran Jorda had developed a transfusion service that was technically superior to Bethune's but he was on the Aragon front which was relatively quiescent in 1936 and 1937. The inscription on the ambulance is in the Catalan language.

These posters are wonderful artistic efforts. The whole city is covered with them. They stress as you see—*Anti-fascism not* Anarchism, Socialism or Communism. More and more every day all parties are becoming united under the realization of this war against international fascist aggression.

I am enclosing some radio speeches. Use them when you think fit. Either singly or I would suggest *together* in the press or journals.

Well I will close now. We all feel enormously encouraged by your grand support. You may rest assured and give our assurance to the workers of Canada that their efforts and money are saving many Spanish, French, German and English lives. *We will win*—the Fascists are already defeated. Madrid will be the tomb of Fascism.

Salud, Companyeros!
Norman Bethune

P.S. I nearly forgot to mention the reason you received so little news of me in December was I gave

If the electrical system in the refrigerator failed, the bottled blood was cooled in streams.

letters to the Foreign Propaganda Chief who was arrested a week ago as a suspected spy. None were sent out! Except one I gave to an English woman going out to Paris. There are too many Fascist spies here.

N.B.

Madrid is the centre of gravity of the world and I wouldn't be anywhere else.

Please send us—Periodicals and papers.

We have seen no papers nor journals since arrival. Was Roosevelt elected?

Please send—Montreal Gazette, Montreal Star—Toronto Star, New Masses, New Frontier, etc.

N.B. We really know nothing of the outside world.

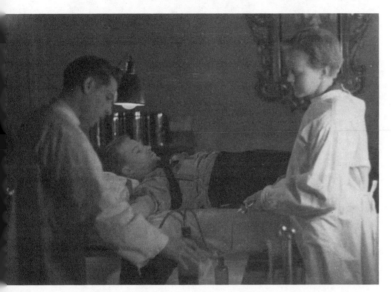

One of the four Spanish doctors who worked with Bethune, Dr. Antonio Culebras, is extracting blood. The donor is Allen May, a Canadian who joined the unit in 1937. Assisting is Jean Watts, a Canadian journalist.

The perimeter of the area served by Bethune's unit was soon extended beyond Madrid. Accompanied by Sise and Tom Worsley, an Englishman, Bethune drove to Barcelona in early February.

Reports of a massive Republican defeat at the coastal city of Málaga made him decide to take a truckload of bottled blood to aid the victims. A few miles outside the city of Almería, he encountered the first pitiful survivors of the combined Nationalist-German-Italian attack. Envenomed by his loathing of an enemy who considered unarmed civilians fit targets, he vividly recorded the tragic flight from Málaga to Almería. This was published in a pamphlet entitled "The Crime on the Road: Málaga-Almería."

A working-class residential area of Madrid, Cuatro Caminos was a constant target for savage aerial attacks by Nationalist bombers. The bombing of a hospital in this area inspired Bethune's poem, "I Come from Cuatro Caminos"

> I come from Cuatro Caminos,
> From Cuatro Caminos I come,
> My eyes are overflowing,
> And clouded with blood.
> The blood of a little fair one,
> Whom I saw destroyed on the ground;
> The blood of a young woman,
> The blood of an old man, a very old man,
> The blood of many people, of many
> Trusting, helpless,
> Fallen under the bombs
> Of the pirates of the air.
> I come from Cuatro Caminos,
> From Cuatro Caminos I come,
> My ears are deaf
> With blasphemies and wailings,
> Ay Little One, Little One;
> What hast thou done to these dogs
> That they have dashed thee in pieces
> On the stones of the grounds?
> Ay, ay, ay, Mother, my Mother;
> Why have they killed the old grandfather?
> Because they are wolf's cubs,
> Cubs of a man-eating wolf.
> Because the blood that runs in their veins
> Is blood of brothel and mud
> Because in their regiment
> They were born fatherless
> A "curse on God" rends the air
> Towards the infamy of Heaven.

The evacuation en masse of the civilian population of Malaga started on Sunday Feb. 7. Twenty-five thousand German, Italian and Moorish troops entered the town on Monday morning the eighth. Tanks, submarines, warships, airplanes combined to smash the defenses of the city held by a small heroic band of Spanish troops without tanks, airplanes or support. The so-called Nationalists entered, as they have entered every captured village and city in Spain, what was practically a deserted town.

Now imagine one hundred and fifty thousand men, women and children setting out for safety to the town situated over a hundred miles away. There is only one road they can take. There is no other way of escape. This road, bordered on one side by the high Sierra Nevada mountains and on the other by the sea, is cut into the side of the cliffs and climbs up and down from sealevel to over 500 feet. The city they must reach is Almeria, and it is over two hundred kilometers away. A strong, healthy young man can walk on foot forty or fifty kilometers a day. The journey these women,

children and old people must face will take five days and five nights at least. There will be no food to be found in the villages, no trains, no buses to transport them. They must walk and as they walked, staggered and stumbled with cut, bruised feet along that flint, white road the fascists bombed them from the air and fired at them from their ships at sea.

Now, what I want to tell you is what I saw myself of this forced march—the largest, most terrible evacuation of a city in modern times. We had arrived in Almeria at five o'clock on Wednesday the tenth with a refrigeration truckload of preserved blood from Barcelona. Our intention was to proceed to Malaga to give blood transfusions to wounded. In Almeria we heard for the first time that the town had fallen and were warned to go no farther as no one knew where the frontline now was but everyone was sure that the town of Motril had also fallen. We thought it important to proceed and discover how the evacuation of the wounded was proceeding. We set out at six o'clock in the evening along the Malaga road

Assisting refugees fleeing from Málaga.

and a few miles on we met the head of the piteous procession. Here were the strong with all their goods on donkeys, mules and horses. We passed them, and the farther we went the more pitiful the sights became. Thousands of children, we counted five thousand under ten years of age, and at least one thousand of them barefoot and many of them clad only in a single garment. They were slung over their mother's shoulders or clung to her hands. Here a father staggered along with two children of one and two years of age on his back in addition to carrying pots and pans or some treasured possession. The incessant stream of people became so dense we could barely force the car through them. At eighty-eight kilometers from Almeria they beseeched us to go no farther, that the fascists were just behind. By this time we had passed so many distressed women and children that we thought it best to turn back and start transporting the worst cases to safety.

It was difficult to choose which to take. Our car was besieged by a mob of frantic mothers and fathers who with tired outstretched arms held up to us their children, their eyes and faces swollen and congested by four days of sun and dust.

"Take this one." "See this child." "This one is wounded." Children with bloodstained rags wrapped around their arms and legs, children without shoes, their feet swollen to twice their size crying helplessly from pain, hunger and fatigue. Two hundred kilometers of misery. Imagine four days and four nights, hiding by day in the hills as the fascist barbarians pursued them by plane, walking by night packed in a solid stream men, women, children, mules, donkeys, goats, crying out the names of their separated relatives, lost in the mob. How could we chose between taking a child dying of dysentery or a mother silently watching us with great sunken eyes carrying against her open breast her child born on the road two days ago. She had stopped walking for ten hours only. Here was a woman of sixty unable to stagger another step, her gigantic swollen legs with their open varicose ulcers bleeding into her cut linen sandals. Many old people simply gave up the struggle, lay down by the side of the road and waited for death.

We first decided to take only children and mothers. Then the separation between father and child, husband and wife became too cruel to bear. We finished by transporting families with the largest number of young children and the solitary children of which there were hundreds without parents. We carried thirty to forty people a trip for the next three days and nights back to Almeria to the hospital of the

In Almería, discussing the refugee situation.

Socorro Rojo International where they received medical attention, food and clothing. The tireless devotion of Hazen Sise and Thomas Worsley, drivers of the truck, saved many lives. In turn they drove back and forth day and night sleeping out on the open road between shifts with no food except dry bread and oranges.

And now comes the final barbarism. Not content with bombing and shelling this procession of unarmed peasants on this long road, on the evening of the 12th when the little seaport of Almeria was completely filled with refugees, its population swollen to double its size, when forty thousand exhausted people had reached a haven of what they thought was safety, we were heavily bombed by German and Italian fascist airplanes. The siren alarm sounded thirty seconds before the first bomb fell. These planes made no effort to hit the government battleship in the harbor or bomb the barracks. They deliberately dropped ten great bombs in the very center of the town where on the main street were sleeping huddled together on the pavement so closely that a car could pass only with difficulty, the exhausted refugees. After the planes had passed I picked up in my arms three dead children from the pavement in front of the Provincial Committee for the Evacuation of Refugees where they had been standing in a great queue waiting for a cupful of preserved milk and a handful of dry bread, the only food some of them had for days. The street was a shambles of the dead and dying, lit only by the orange glare of burning buildings. In the darkness the moans of the wounded children, shrieks of agonized mothers, the curses of the men rose in a massed cry higher and higher to a pitch of intolerable intensity. One's body felt as heavy as the dead themselves, but empty and hollow, and in one's brain burned a bright flame of hate. That night were murdered fifty civilians and an additional fifty were wounded. There were two soldiers killed.

Now, what was the crime that these unarmed civilians had committed to be murdered in this bloody manner? Their only crime was that they had voted to elect a government of the people, committed to the most moderate alleviation of the crushing burden of centuries of the greed of capitalism. The question has been raised: why did they not stay in Malaga and await the entrance of the fascists? They knew what would happen to them. They knew what would happen to their men and women as had happened so many times before in other captured towns. Every male between the age of 15 and 60 who could not prove that he had not by force been made to assist the government would immediately be shot. And it is this knowledge that has concentrated two-thirds of the entire population of Spain in one half the country and that still held by the republic.

Mounting bitterness derived from repeated exposure to wanton destruction intensified Bethune's faith in the cause of Republican Spain. He continued to believe that he had joined an international crusade that would ultimately obliterate the savage and malign force of Fascism. This idealism is evident in his description of a visit to a field hospital. It appeared in the Toronto Communist newspaper, The Daily Clarion *under the title, "With the Canadian Blood Transfusion Unit at Guadalajara."*

July 17, 1937

The hospital stood at the top of the hill on the right as we crossed the bridge coming into the town of Guadalajara. It was about eleven—the clear, cold-bright day of March 12. In the Ford was Henning Sorensen, Geysa, and Calebras, my Spanish assistant. I was driving. In the back we had a refrigerator and ten pint bottles of preserved blood packed in a wire basket. We had left Madrid at ten and had made the 54 kilometres in less than an hour, rolling along that fine paved Zaragosa road at well over seventy most of the time.

At Alcala de Henares we had looked for one of our hospitals but found they had moved over night up to the front, leaving behind, in their hurry, their refrigerator. We picked it up and were taking it to them.

All the roads showed the evidence of the battle ahead. We passed truck after truck loaded with young soldiers standing in the swaying cars with bayonets fixed, singing and shouting as we shot past. No more could be seen the old signs they used to paint on the side—no more C.N.T., U.G.T., F.A.I., C.P.—now just the great red five-pointed star of the people's united army.

Tanks ahead—a string of them—like great dinosaurs, you didn't realize until you tried to pass them how fast they were moving on their seeming-clumsy caterpillar wheels—25, 30, 40, 45 miles an hour—we catch up and pass with a wave of our hand to the unseen driver. Gasoline trucks, bread wagons, donkey carts, mule trains all moving up. Yes, a drive was on. How important? Who are those steel helmeted troops—a shout in German—the famous Thaelmann Battalion going into action. It must be important. They are the feared "shock troops" of the International Brigade.

The wind was piercing cold as we crossed the plain. Blowing straight down from snow-covered peaks of the Guadalarama [sic] range on our left, glittering so near, it made us turn up the collars of our warm brown coats and thank again below our breath, the generous Syndicate of Tailors of Madrid who had presented us with them the week before. The front left window of the car was broken and had been for a week—hit by the swinging pole of a mule train—no time to lay the car up now for repairs.

Fifty, sixty, seventy, eighty kilometers an hour—God, what a swell road! At this rate we could be in Franco's line in half an hour's driving!

Sharp left turn at the top of the hill and there was the 500 bed hospital. No more red crosses now. Last week the fascist planes tried to bomb it so down came the cross—too easy a mark to hit—500 wounded helpless men, too good a chance to miss.

The sure sign of an engagement were the long rows of blood-drenched stretchers, propped up on end, leaning against the walls, waiting to be washed.

All was bustle and hurry.

"Yes, go straight up." So up we go to the operating room. Here three tables are at work, the close air

Despite the protests of Sorensen and Geza Karpathi, his photographer, Bethune drove through a hail of bullets at the battle of Guadalajara. Finally they abandoned the ambulance and crawled through a field to safety. The following day they returned to retrieve the ambulance.

heavy with the fumes of ether. Casting a glance, a nod, a salud to the chief surgeon as we cross the room to the white enamelled refrigerator standing against the wall. The row of empty blood bottles on the top tell the story—three, five, seven empties and inside, only three unused.

"Better leave them six now; must come back tomorrow." "All right?"—the chief surgeon looks up for a second from the table. Nods his head and smiles.

"Where are the tags?"

"Here," says a nurse and pulls a handful of blood-stained bottle tags from her apron. A glance at each—on the back is written the name, the battalion, the wound, the date of the recipient. "Let's go." Out of the door, down the long corridor filled with stretcher-men, doctors, nurses and walking wounded to Dr. Jolly's department. His fine, open New Zealand face breaks into a smile as he sees us. We are old friends from early days in Madrid.

"Where's the refrigerator?"

"We have it in the car outside."

"Good, bring it in, we need it. There's a rush on."

The room is packed with wounded. They sit on the floor with blood-stained bandages on head, arms and legs, waiting to be dressed.

"Sorry, I must go now. Just operated on an Italian captain, poor fellow. Shot through the stomach. Hope he will live. André wants to see you. He's used up all his blood."

We feel fine. We feel like a successful salesman who has just placed a big order for goods. This is great! Isn't it grand to be needed, to be wanted!

So we bring the refrigerator in and set it down and plug in. Inside we put our remaining four bottles of blood. Here comes André, Jolly's assistant. A young French doctor just out of medical school, his fantastic black, short-cut beard making him look like a young pirate. He shakes our hand and bursts into rapid machine-gun French.

"Can you leave me another two needles? I need another syringe. I broke one last night. Can you give me some more grouping serums?"

"Sure." His thanks are effusive.

"I want to write my thesis for my master's degree in

the University of Paris on blood transfusion at the front. Will you Canadians help me?"

"Sure." More effusions, more French. Dr. Jolly calls him from the operating room.

"I must go now, but there's a wounded man upstairs from the International Brigade and we can't make out what nationality he is. He can't speak English, French, Italian, Spanish or German. He's been hit by a bomb, lost one hand. We had to amputate the other and he's blinded in one eye. He needs a blood transfusion. We have to operate but I'm afraid he can't stand the shock. Will you give him a blood transfusion?"

"Let's go."

"Where's the man you can't make understand?" The pretty Spanish nurse shakes her dark head with a sad smile.

"Oh, there's lots of those."

"He's lost both hands and he's blind."

"Oh, I know, here, come, this ward."

Yes, it must be him. He's a big fellow with a great bloody bandage on his head. Must be six feet anyway, close to 200 lbs. His swollen face is covered with caked blood. Half an hour from the line. Still has his old shirt on. It's covered with stiff blood. Where hands used to be are two shapeless bundles of bloody bandages.

"Sorensen, come here."

At the name, the man turns his head slowly and from his swollen lips a question painfully comes. I can't understand, but Henning breaks into a rapid strange speech. "Why, he's Swedish. No wonder they can't understand him."

Yes, he needs a transfusion. Two tourniquets still in place to check the blood flow from both torn radial arteries. Must have lost a couple of quarts from the look of his face and feeble pulse. Five minutes and we're ready—blood heated to body temperature, grouped, syringe all sterilized. I look at the label "Blood number 695, Donor number 1106, Group IV, collected Madrid 6th March." Yes, it's O.K. No haemolysis. Let's go—needle in, syringe working smoothly—five minutes and it's finished.

"Feel better?"

Translation. A twist from his bruised lips is his reply.

Henning bends over him with the anxious, distressed air of a father for his only child. They talk. I clean the syringe and pack the bag. Then back.

"What's the pulse?" Yes, one hundred and stronger, color better. He'll do.

"Come," to Sorensen. He tears himself away with reluctance, a backward glance at the door, a word, a reply.

"What did he say?"

With Sorensen and members of the International Brigades. Bethune was responsible for supplying blood to Republic Army units. He also responded to requests from the International Brigades, including the Canadian unit, the Mackenzie-Papineau Battalion.

Sorensen, quiet, mournful and low: "He said, 'ten days ago I was in Sweden. I have been in Spain three days. This was my first engagement, and now I am no more use to my comrades. I have done nothing for the cause.' "

"Done nothing!" We look at each other with amazed eyes. "Done nothing!" What modesty, what courage, what a soul!

Yet that is the spirit of the International Brigade; of ten thousand determined unconquerable men, with no thought of themselves, with no thought of sacrifice, but simply and with a pure heart ready to lay down their lives for their friends. "Greater love hath no man more than this!"

These are your comrades in Spain.

To them—salud!

The importance of propaganda was obvious to Bethune. When Station EAQ, a short-wave station that beamed its signal to North America, invited him to broadcast, he enthusiastically accepted. The following, "Madrid: Peaceful Amid War" (January 2, 1937), was one of several radio speeches that he made.

Madrid is, paradoxically enough, the most peaceful city in Europe.

It is a city at equilibrium within itself, a city without the intense class antagonisms and discords that are called disorder in any other city. That is due to its homogeneous society—the workers, the small shop-keepers and the petit-bourgeois all molded into one class with one idea—winning the war against the Fascist aggressor.

So, as in a family or clan in which there is internal peace although the family or clan may be fighting against its external enemies. No police are needed to maintain the law. Every member, every citizen, is under the strict necessity of order—self-imposed and conscious.

Private property is respected—confiscated property belonging to the people at large, is equally respected. On large magnificent mansions, which once belonged to the late so-called nobility, one may see signs such as these: "Citizens, this property belongs to you, respect it". Note the wording of the sign—not "Belongs to the State"—the State as an institution superior to and above the people, but—"belongs to

you"—belongs to me. So, if you or I damage it, we are damaging our own property.

There is absolutely no looting. This is clear from one manifest fact—the things which are looted in a war are first of all articles of necessity such as clothing and food. Later come the luxuries—jewels, fur coats, etc. Now the people of Madrid are wearing the same clothes as they wore before the rebellion in spite of the large quantities of fine clothes left by fleeing Fascists and members of the so-called upper classes.

Buying of necessities and clothing is brisk in the shops. I was in a large departmental store today and saw a woman of the so-called middle classes buy a tricycle for her boy of 10 and a large doll for her daughter of 5.

We were heavily bombed from the air today about 12 noon. Twelve huge Italian tri-motored bombers came over the city and bombed not positions of military importance, but a poor quarter of the city called Cuatro Caminos. This is a district some miles behind the front line, inhabited by the poorest people living in one or two story mud and brick dwellings. The massacred victims were mainly women, children and old people.

Standing in a doorway as these huge machines flew slowly overhead, each one heavily loaded with bombs, I glanced up and down the streets. People hurried to "refugios"; a hush fell over the city—it was a hunted animal crouched down in the grass, quiet and apprehensive. There is no escape, so be still. Then in the dead silence of the streets the songs of birds came startlingly clear in the bright winter air.

What is the object of these bombings of lowly civilian habitations? Is it to produce panic in the city? Because, if so, it is a completely cruel, useless and wanton endeavour. This people cannot be terrified. They are being treated by the Fascists as if they were soldiers bearing offensive arms. This is murder of defenseless civilians.

No one can realize what utter helplessness one feels when these huge death-ships are overhead. It is practically useless to go into a building—even a ten-storey building. The bombs tear through the roof, through every floor in the building and explode in the basement bringing down concrete buildings as if they were made of matchwood.

It is not much safer to be in the basement of the lower floors, than in the upper stories. One takes shelter in doorways to be out of the way of falling masonry, huge pieces of facade and stone work. If the building you happen to be in is hit, you will be killed or wounded. If it is not hit, you will not be killed or wounded. One place is really as good as another.

Red Moon

And this same pallid moon tonight,
Which rides so quietly, clear and high,
The mirror of our pale and troubled gaze,
Raised to a cool Canadian sky,

Above the shattered Spanish mountain tops
Last night, rose low and wild and red,
Reflecting back from her illumined shield,
The blood-bespattered faces of the dead.

To that pale disc we raise our clenched fists
And to those nameless dead, our vows renew,
"Comrades, who fought for freedom and the future world
Who died for us, we will remember you."

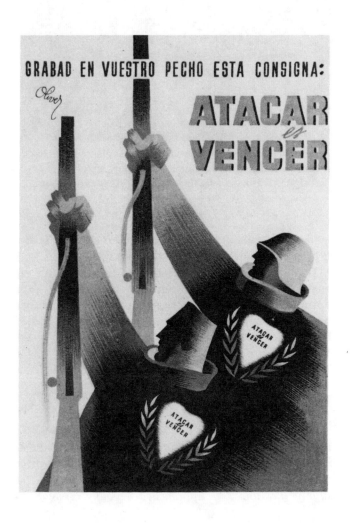

After the bombs falls—and you can see them falling like great black pears— there is a thunderous roar. Clouds of dust and explosive fumes fill the air, whole sides of houses fall into the street. From heaps of huddled clothes on the cobblestones blood begins to flow—these were once live women and children.

Many are buried alive in the ruins. One hears their cries—they cannot be reached. Burst water and gas mains add to the danger. Ambulances arrive. The blackened and crumpled bodies of the still-alive are carried away.

Now observe the faces of, not the dead, but those who still live. Because it is the wished-for effect on them which is the motive for these massacres, not just the killing of a few hundred innocent civilians and the destruction of property, but the terrorizing of hundreds of thousands who escaped this death. They stand and watch or work themselves at the rescue. Their lips are set and cold. They don't shout or gesticulate. They look at each other sorrowfully, and

"We are well and happy and believe we are doing good. What more can one ask."

Bethune bought a French truck in Marseilles which was specially fitted with a generator and refrigerator in Barcelona. This truck was used to ferry refugees to Almería.

when they talk of the fascist assassins, their faces express fortitude, dignity and contempt.

These people have endured from the arrogance of wealth, the greed of the church, the poverty and oppression of centuries. This is just one more blow, one more lash of the whip. They have stood these blows, these lashes before and they will stand them to the end. They cannot be shaken.

For some time he had been considering the most effective means of describing the work of his unit to people in North America. When he was able to convince the CASD to supply the funds, he approached a young Hungarian

photographer Geza Karpathi (later to become the screen actor Charles Korvin), and an American news correspondent Herbert Kline. Together they produced the now classic film Heart of Spain *that told the story of Bethune's blood transfusion service.*

Enthusiasm and propaganda without adequate weapons rarely win wars against a better armed and numerically superior enemy. In the spring of 1937 Franco and his foreign allies gradually pushed back the Republican forces. By now Bethune's unit was carrying blood to most sections of the front in a nearly continuous round-the-clock routine. It was a magnificent effort both in its conception and execution which has subsequently been regarded as one of the most significant military-medical innovations of the Civil War. At the time Bethune's achievements were impressive enough for the Spaniards to grant him the rank of major.

Unfortunately, the strain of months of work and tension began to wear Bethune down and when he was caught in a bureaucratic snare, he exploded. The carefully developed relationship with the Republican government was endangered when the latter decided to assume control of the unit. Bethune retaliated by dashing off a cable to Canada demanding the recall of himself and the other Canadian personnel.

April 12, 1937
Madrid

Government decrees all organizations in Spain whether Spanish or Foreign must come under control of Ministry of War. No independent organizations allowed. The Sanidad Militar have taken over control Canadian Unit. Our positions now nominal. Fortunately transfusion service is well established and can carry on without us. Ninety percent capital equipment expenditure paid out. Strongly urge you act immediately. Authorize me by cable as Chief to first withdraw Canadian personnel, second hand over to Government refrigerators and equipment, third agree to provide two hundred dollars monthly six months for maintenance institute, fourth return Canada with such Canadians as desire with film for antifascist propaganda. Our work as Canadians here is finished. Remember Kleber and the International Column. Only future cables signed Beth Bethune are from me continue collection funds. Many schemes more urgent now than Blood Transfusion. Will inform you later Salud.

CASD officials rejected his proposal to bring the members of the unit back to Canada. Instead, they ordered Bethune to come home. He would be far more useful and less dangerous to the cause in Canada, where a fund-raising lecture tour was being prepared for him.

The decision embarrassed but failed to disappoint Bethune who was emotionally as well as physically exhausted by the war. It was time to leave.

Shortly before his departure he wrote a letter to a Canadian friend that was later published with the title "An Apology for Not Writing Letters." It was an attempt to blend his recent commitment to Marxism with his continuing dedication to art.

This is an attempt at an explanation why I, who think of you so often, with love and affection, have not written—or so briefly—since my arrival in Spain.

I had thought to say simply (that is, shortly)—I have been too busy; I am a man of action; I have no time to write. Yet as I look at these words, I see they are false. They simply aren't true. In fact, I have had plenty of time to write you, that is if I had cared to write, but, in truth, I did not care. Now why is this? Why have I not written to those of you who, I know, without illusion, would like to hear from me? Why is it I can not put down one word after another on paper and make a letter out of them?

I will try and be truthful. It is difficult to be truthful, isn't it?

First of all, I don't feel like writing. I don't feel the necessity of communication. I don't feel strongly the necessity of a reconstruction of experience—my actions and the actions of others—into the form of art which a letter should take. As an artist, unless that re-construction take a satisfactory form which is truthful, simple and moving, I will not, nay, I can not, write at all. I feel that unless I can re-construct those remembrances of action into reality for you, I will not attempt it. To me, a letter is an important thing—words are important things. At present, I don't feel any necessity to communicate these experiences. They are in me, have changed me, but I don't want to talk about them. I don't want to talk about them yet.

Besides, I am afraid to write you. I am afraid of the banality of words, of the vocal, the verbal, of the literary re-construction. I am afraid they won't be true.

Only by a shared physical experience—tactile, visual or auditory—may an approximately similar emotion be felt by two people without the aid of art. Only through art, can the truth of a non-shared experience be transmitted. To share with you what I have seen, what I have experienced in the past six months, is impossible without art. Without art, experience becomes, on the one hand, the denuded, bare bones of fact,—a static, still-life,—the now-many-ness of things; or, on the other hand, the swollen, exaggerated shapes of fantastically-colored romanticism. And I will do neither. I refuse to write either way. Both are false—the first by its poverty, the second by its excess.

So I despair of my ability to transpose the reality of experience into the reality of the written word. Art should be the legitimate and recognizable child of experience. I am afraid of a changeling. I am afraid it would have none of the unmistakable inherited characteristics of its original, true, parental reality.

I can not write you, my friends, because this art of letters is a second, a repeated form of action. And one form of action at a time is enough. I can not do both—but successively, with an interval of a year, or ten years. Perhaps I can do both. I don't know. I don't think it matters very much.

I think that art has no excuse, no reason for existence except through the re-creation—by a dialectical process—of a new form of reality, for the old experience—transmitted through a man's sensorium—changed and illuminated by his conscious and unconscious mind. Exact reproduction is useless—that way lies death. The process of change from the old to the new is not a flat circular movement—a turn and return on itself, but helical and ascending.

The process of creative art is the negation of the negation. First there is the change, that is, the negation, of the original, the positive reality; then the second change (or negation), which is a re-affirmation, a re-birth, through art, of the original experience, to the new positive, the new form of reality.

Let us take an example from painting—a moving object such as a tree swaying in the wind, a child at play, a bird in flight—any form of action, seen and perceived. This is the positive, the thesis. Reduced from the dynamic positive in time and space to a static form, by representation, (in this case, by paint on canvas) it becomes the negation of action, the denial of action. This is the antithesis. Then by the miracle of creative art, this static thing, (of necessity static, owing, to the medium employed) is vivified, transformed into movement again, into life again, but into a new life, becomes positive again, becomes the negation of the negation of the negation, the synthesis—the union of life and death, of action and non-action, the emergence of the new from the old within the new.

Now the same thing applies to the literary art, the plastic arts, music, the dance or what not—any art form. And unless that fresh emergent form, with its core of the old, is a new thing, a dynamic thing, a quick and living thing, it is not art. It arouses no response except intellectual appreciation, the facile response to familiar, recognizable objects, or admiration for technical skill.

And because I can't write you, my friends, as I should like to write you, because my words are poor, anaemic and hobbling things, I have not written. Yes, I could write, but I am ashamed to write—like this:

"We were heavily shelled today. It was very uncomfortable. Fifty people were killed in the streets. The weather is lovely now although the winter has been hard. I am well. I think of you often. Yes, it is true I love you. Good bye."

I put them down and look at these words with horror and disgust. I wish I could describe to you how much I dislike these words. "Uncomfortable"—good God! what a word to describe the paralyzing fear that seizes one when a shell bursts with a great roar and crash near by; "killed", for these poor huddled bodies of rags and blood, lying in such strange shapes, face down on the cobble-stones, or with sightless eyes upturned to a cruel and indifferent sky; "lovely" when the sun falls on our numbed faces like a benediction; "well" when to be alive is well enough; "think" for that cry rising from our hearts day by day for remembered ones; "love" for this ache of separation.

So you see, it's no good.

Forgive me if I talk more about art. It must seem to you that I know either a great deal about it or nothing at all. I really know very little about it. I think it is very mysterious, very strange. But it seems to me to be a natural product of the subconscious mind of man, of all men, in some degree. Arising into the realm of deliberate thought, its life is imperilled. A theory of art reminds me of a medieval chart of the then-known world—curious, fantastic and wonderfully untrue. A theory of art is an attempt of the rational mind to impose its discipline and its order on the seeming chaos and seeming disorder of the emotional subconscious. If this is attempted—and it has frequently been attempted, a certain form of art,

"It is in Spain that the real issues of our time are going to be fought out. It is there that democracy will either die or survive."

ordered and neat, arises. By its subjection to the conscious mind, to the deliberate directional thought of the artist and his theory, it lives for a while and then languishes and dies. It can not survive its separation from the great breeding ground of the unconscious. The mind (that alien in the attic) by its dictatorship, destroys the very thing it has discovered.

Most great artists of the world have been,—thank Heaven—"stupid" in the wordly sense. They didn't think too much, they simply painted. Driven on by an irresistable internal compulsion, they painted as they did, as they must paint.

A great artist lets himself go. He is natural. He "swims easily in the stream of his own temperament." He listens to himself. He respects himself. He has a deeper fund of strength to draw from than that arising from rational and logical knowledge. Yet how beautifully the dialectical process comes in again,—modified by thought, his primitive unconsciousness, conditioned by experience, reacts to reality and produces new forms of that reality. These particular forms of art arise, satisfy for their time, decay and die. But, by their appearance, they modify and influence succeeding art forms. They also modify and influence the very reality which produced them. Art itself never dies. Art itself

71

is a great ever-blooming tree, timeless, indestructable and immortal. The particular art forms of a generation are the flowers of that immortal tree. They are the expressions of their particular time but they are the products also of all the preceeding time.

The artist needs, among other things, leisure, immense quietness, privacy and aloneness. The environment in which he has his being, are those dark, sunless, yet strangely illuminated depths of the world's subconscious,—the warm, pulsating yet quiet depths of the other-world.

He comes up into the light of every-day, like a great leviathan of the deep, breaking the smooth surface of accepted things, gay, serious, sportive and destructive. In the bright banal glare of day, he enjoys the purification of violence, the catharsis of action. His appetite for life is enormous. He enters eagerly into the life of man, of all men. He becomes all men in himself. He views the world with an all-embracing eye which looks upwards, outwards, inwards and downwards,—understanding, critical, tender and severe. Then he plunges back once more, back into the depths of that other-world,—strange, mysterious, secret and alone. And there, in those depths, he gives birth to the children of his being—new forms, new colors, new sounds, new movements, reminiscent of the known, yet not the known, alike and yet unlike; strange yet familiar, calm, profound and sure.

The function of the artist is to disturb. His duty is to arouse the sleeper, to shake the complacent pillars of the world. He reminds the world of its dark ancestry, shows the world its present, and points the way to its new birth. He is at once the product and the preceptor of his time. After his passage we are troubled and made unsure of our too-easily accepted realities. He makes uneasy the static, the set and the still. In a world terrified of change, he preaches revolution—the principle of life. He is an agitator, a disturber of the peace—quick, impatient, positive, restless and disquieting. He is the creative spirit of life working in the soul of man.

But enough. Perhaps the true reason I can not write is that I'm too tired—another 150 miles on the road today, and what roads!

Our first job is to defeat fascism—the enemy of the creative artist. After that we can write about it.

Good bye. I do think of you with love and affection. Forgive me when I do not write.

Salud
Norman Bethune

MADRID, May 5, 1937.

They Call Me A Red

THE SPEAKING TOUR

Bethune arrived in New York on June 6, where he rested briefly before beginning a speaking tour to raise funds for the transfusion service. For nearly three months he travelled across Canada and the United States describing his work in Spain and showing the film Heart of Spain.

At the outset he was ordered by the Committee to Aid Spanish Democracy to conceal his political affiliation. Since its inception the Committee had rigorously projected itself as a liberal, anti-fascist organization with its most radical members slightly to the left of centre. The entire Committee, including its Communist members, feared that any taint of communism attached to the tour would turn away many potential donors of funds. Reluctantly Bethune abided by this restriction until late July when he defiantly announced to an audience in Winnipeg that he was a Communist.

This revelation seemed to have little appreciable affect on the crowds who gathered to hear Bethune's graphic portrayal of the horrors of war. Repeatedly he turned to his theme of the Canadian government's refusal to grant the transfusion service the status of an humanitarian agency. Their failure to do so forced him to pay duty on the station wagon at the French border. His favourite target in these frequent attacks was Prime Minister Mackenzie King. The following is from a speech in Kirkland Lake in July:

I appeal to you to give money to further the cause of the Loyalists in Spain. When I went there I did not know which way to turn. People were dying in the streets and finally I thought the best thing to do would

The first speaking engagement was in Toronto on June 14, where Bethune addressed five thousand people on the lawn of the Ontario Legislative Buildings. Earlier in the day in an interview he gave this response to William Strange, who had asked him if he were a Communist. "Look here, let's get this thing straight. You can call me a Socialist if you like. I am a Socialist in the same way that millions of sane people are Socialists. I want to see people getting a square deal, and I hate Fascism. The clenched fist is used as a People's Front salute. It's used in Spain by everybody who is against the Fascists. That's really all it means — Anti-Fascism. Why, Premier Blum of France uses it, and he's no Communist. I should describe it as a reply to the raised hand salute of the Fascist."

be establish a blood transfusion station . . . (Allan May, of the Toronto Globe, who accompanied me to Spain, said that I should establish my post among English doctors.) I asked Ottawa for permission to recommend the use of a Canadian ambulance and I was refused by Mackenzie King, the same man who a little later was photographed shaking hands with the biggest murderer in the world today—Hitler.

However I did not need the permission and I established my post. Before I left I had 1,200 donors in Madrid and I could send blood to any hospital within a 150-mile radius of Madrid within three hours.

My friends, everybody in Spain is a Red, because they believe in the truth. Truth is propaganda and as we believe in the truth we are Reds. Then they are black who do not believe in the truth and tell false stories about the Spanish Loyalists.

On July 20 he told a banquet given in his honour in the St. Charles Hotel in Winnipeg: "I have the honour to be a Communist. I didn't care then what the system was called, but I knew that what we wanted was the thing those Russians had got." Later he said: "They call me a Red. Then if Christianity is Red, I am also a Red. They call me a Red because I have saved 500 lives."

During a rare break in the tight speaking schedule he sits with the son of his friend, the artist Paraskeyva Clark, on the shore of Lake Ontario near Toronto.

By the end of the tour in mid-September he had raised thousands of dollars. He had made it possible for the transfusion service to continue in Spain. But it would function without Bethune, who had no wish to return to Madrid. Nor was he willing to remain in Montreal. It would have been awkward, if not impossible, for a professed Communist to remain on the staff of a Catholic hospital.

Bethune, the restless wanderer, was on the move again. He could not go home. He would have to find a new cause. He chose China. Throughout July, he read the daily newspaper reports of the relentless Japanese invasion of China. When he revealed his new interest to Tim Buck, the Canadian Communist leader consulted Earl Browder, his American counterpart. Browder, a former Comintern agent in China, was interested and promised financial support. Bethune went to New York in October.

I Am Content;
I Am Doing
What I Want
To do

On the night of September 18, 1931, a bomb was detonated on a railway line near the Manchurian city of Mukden. Within hours Japanese troops seized control of the city and other strategic centres in this most northerly Chinese province. While the enraged but impotent Chinese government was appealing to the League of Nations to take action against the aggressor, Japan methodically assumed control of the entire area. In 1932, renamed Manchukuo under a puppet Chinese ruler, it formed a powerful Japanese beachhead for the planned conquest of the remainder of China.

Initially there was little Chinese resistance. General Chiang Kai-shek, the leader of the Kuomintang government in Nanking, was too preoccupied with his obsession of eradicating the last of his internal enemies, the Communists. In 1930 he had launched an "extermination campaign" to destroy what he contemptuously referred to as the "red bandits." These were Chinese Communists under the leadership of Mao Tse-tung who had grouped in the Chingkang mountains on the Hunan-Kiangsi border.

The brilliant military tactics of the Communist general Chu Teh ruined Chiang Kai-shek's first campaign. During the next four years, virtually ignoring the Japanese menace, Chiang doubled, then redoubled his forces in a determined effort to root out his resilient foes. His fifth and final campaign was so formidable that the entire Communist force of more than one hundred thousand men, women and children was forced to retreat. What followed, a trek of more than six thousand perilous miles over mountains and through deserts and swamps as they continually fought the harassing Kuomintang troops, was one of history's epic events, the Long March. More than a year later, with perhaps fewer than twenty-five thousand survivors, Mao formed a new base in Yenan, a mountain village in Shensi province.

Convinced that Mao's escape would be short-lived, Chiang Kai-shek ordered General Chang Hsueh-liang to ferret out the broken remnants of the Long March. Chang was commander of the large Manchurian army forced from its homeland by the Japanese conquest.

Months passed without news of the capture of Mao nor of the destruction of Yenan. Finally, in December 1936, Chiang flew to Sian, the headquarters of Chang Hsueh-liang, to prod the Manchurian general into action. To his complete surprise, Chang refused to continue his campaign against the Communists. Instead he urged Chiang to agree to a ceasefire and the establishment of a united front against the real enemy, the Japanese.

The shocked Kuomintang leader refused and was promptly arrested by Chang Hsueh-liang. His life was spared, ironically, by the intervention of a Communist official, Chou En-lai, called to Sian by Chang Hsueh-liang. Chou persuaded him that Chiang's agreement to end the internal conflict would be of far greater value than his execution. Fortunate to escape with his life, Chiang gave in and promised to direct his entire military effort against the Japanese.

The "Sian Incident" was not a well-kept secret. When the Japanese realized its implications, they tried to shake the Kuomintang leader from his commitment but Chiang refused to renege. After repeated warnings the Japanese prepared to attack. The incident that sparked the war was a clash between Japanese and Chinese troops at the Marco Polo Bridge near Peiping (Peking) on July 7, 1937.

The Japanese invasion force was well-equipped, superbly trained and incredibly savage. Employing terrorist tactics referred to as the "Three-all" campaign (Loot all, burn all, kill all), they systematically ravaged the heavily populated areas. The most horrifying example was the "Rape of Nanking" where Japanese troops wandered through the defenceless capital city indiscriminately murdering, raping, plundering and burning.

By contrast, the Chinese defenders were without adequate weapons, poorly trained and badly led. In the initial stages of the war the Kuomintang troops fought heroically but ineptly and were swiftly driven back by the Japanese.

To gain his release from Sian, Chiang Kai-shek had agreed to the formation of the United Front. By this accord, Mao Tse-tung's forces, regrouped as the Eighth Route Army, were given the responsibility to defend two areas in north-central China. Called Border Regions, they were Shen-Kan-Ning (parts of Shensi, Kansu and Ningsia provinces) and Chin-Ch'a-Chi (parts of Shansi, Chahar and Hopei provinces).

The tactics employed by the Communist forces were those they used so successfully against their erstwhile enemy, the Kuomintang, during the extermination campaigns. Always avoiding pitched battles and superior enemy forces, they concentrated on rupturing the Japanese transportation and communication systems. Their success lay in their ability to strike swiftly before escaping into the surrounding countryside with which they were so much more familiar than the foe. As a result, the Japanese were forced to commit much larger forces to the region than they had planned. In this way pressure was eased slightly from the Kuomintang forces.

If the Chinese government had failed to raise world opinion against the Japanese invasion of Manchuria in 1931, they could expect even less foreign concern in 1937. Most Europeans and North Americans remained absorbed by events in Spain. China was too distant. Although western governments failed to respond to the Chinese dilemma, there were organizations, mainly leftist, willing

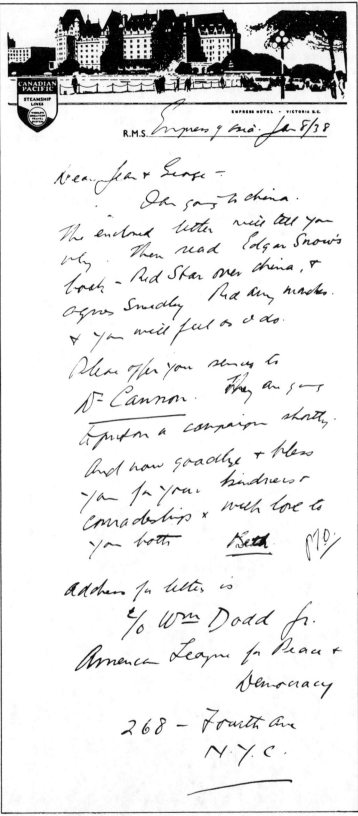

On the eve of his departure for China, Bethune sent this New Year's card, January 1937.

to offer support. It was on these that Bethune was to place his hopes for financial aid in setting up a medical mission in China.

He was in New York during the last two months of 1937 preparing for the trip. With funds donated by two organizations, the China Aid Council and the League for Peace and Democracy, he began to collect medical supplies. Most of the money was raised by Dr. Lewis M. Fraad, a young New York doctor who planned to follow Bethune to China. After a farewell New Year's Eve party in Manhattan, Bethune left the following day for Toronto. One week later, he embarked at Vancouver on the S.S. Empress of Asia bound for Hong Kong. With him were Jean Ewen, a Canadian nurse who spoke Chinese, and an American surgeon, Dr. Charles H. Parsons.

Their only plan of action was to make themselves available to the Chinese authorities of the United Front to serve in any useful capacity. Unable to find a liaison official in Hong Kong, they flew to Hankow, the temporary Chinese capital. When Bethune insisted on joining the Communist Eighth Route Army in Yenan, Parsons returned in protest to America. Jean Ewen stayed with Bethune.

Bethune described his activities in China in letters, which he sent to several Canadian and American friends. This letter, later published under the title of "From Hankow to Sian," outlines his often harrowing attempt to reach the Communist forces.

Bethune, Jean Ewen, a friend of Jean's and Dr. Parsons before departure in Vancouver, January 8, 1938. He wrote an old friend that day: "You see why I *must* go to China. Please read *Edgar Snow's* book, Red Star Over China. *Agnes Smedly*, Red Army Marches, *Bertram's* First Act in China. I feel so happy and gay. Happier than since I left Spain. Goodbye and bless you."

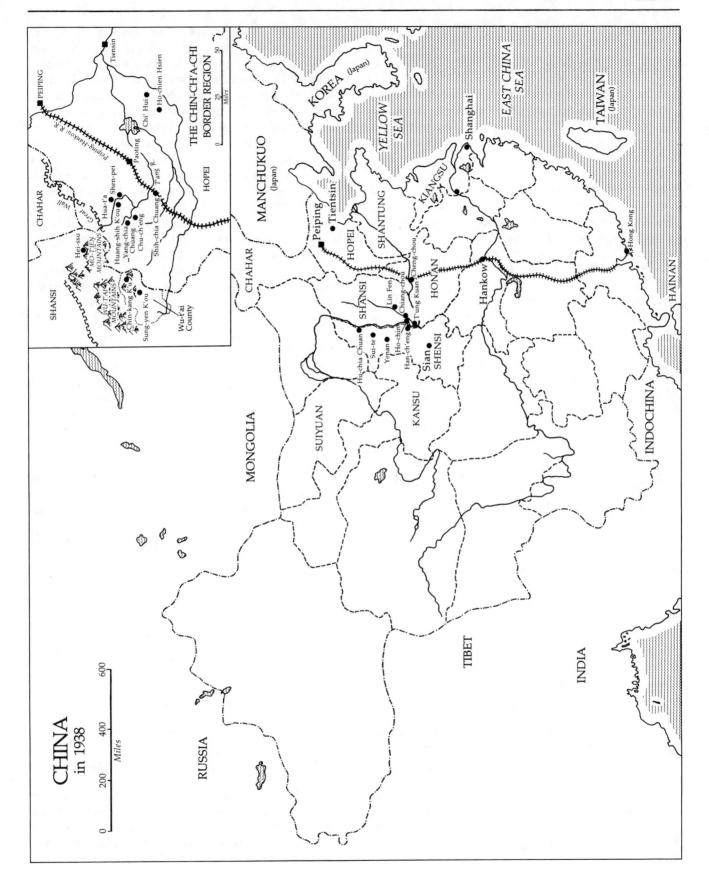

CHINA
in 1938

Miles
0   200   400   600

THE CHIN-CH'A-CHI
BORDER REGION

Miles
0   25   50

PEIPING
Tiensin
Ho-chien Hsien
Chi' Hui
Paoting
Shen-pei
Hua-t'a
Huang-shih K'ou
Yang-chia
Chuang
Chu-ch'eng
Shih-chia Chuang
Tang R.
Hei-ssu
MO-T'IEN MOUNTAINS
WU-T'AI MOUNTAINS
Chin-kang Ku
Sung-yen K'ou
Wu-t'ai County
SHANSI
CHAHAR
Great Wall
Peiping-Hankow R.R.
HOPEI

RUSSIA

MONGOLIA

MANCHUKUO
(Japan)

CHAHAR

SUIYUAN

KOREA (Japan)

YELLOW SEA

EAST CHINA SEA

TAIWAN (Japan)

Peiping
Tientsin
HOPEI
SHANTUNG
KIANGSU
Shanghai
SHANSI
Lin Fen
Chiang-chou
Cheng-chou
Tung Kuan
HONAN
Hankow
Hong Kong
Hu-chia Chuan
Sui-te
Yenan
Ho-chin
Han-ch'eng
Sian
SHENSI
KANSU

TIBET

INDIA

INDOCHINA

HAINAN

From Hankow to Sian

I really don't know where to start to tell you of our exciting experiences since we left Hankow on the 22nd of February. I think I wrote you on leaving but whether I posted the letter in Hankow or in Tungwan I have forgotten. However, I will start from Hankow and retrace our steps.

We arrived at Chengchow at 11 p.m. travelling third class with one of the soldiers of one of our divisions, who was returning to rejoin his unit. His name was Chow Tsang Cheng, 27 years of age, 11 years in the Army. A fine lad, intelligent and as merry and gay as a cricket. I gave him my jack-knife from Madrid, which pleased him very much.

When we arrived at Chengchow we found the train for Tungwan completely filled, so after a stroll up the main street to see the damage which the Japanese had done the week before, we stretched out on the wooden bench of an open shed and, wrapped in our warm sheepskin coats, spent a comfortable night. The damage the bombing had done was bad enough but, as usual, the much proclaimed accurate marksmanship of the Japanese was pretty bad. About this markmanship more later, from personal experience! Here their objective was the railway station and round house. They missed both by a hundred yards!

Next morning we left at 11 for Tungwan. This railway is called the Lunghai line. The line we were on yesterday was the Peiping-Hangkow railway. The train was jammed with refugees fleeing west. After an hour's slow travelling the air raid warning was sounded by the engine, and we all scampered out of the cars and lay down in the fields about a hundred yards away. The engine was uncoupled and went forward. We could see the bombers flying very high, but they did not bother us. They were flying south. It is certain they did not visit Hangkow, for we have since heard that Hangkow has not been bombed since the week of the 14th, when eleven Japanese were brought down at a cost to us of six of ours. This was a wonderful victory for the Chinese, as not a single foreign aviator was flying for them. Incidentally there are no more than a dozen foreign flyers here, the most of them being Americans.

We travelled all day, all night and arrived at Tungwan at 3 p.m. the next afternoon. There we saw for the first time the great Yellow River. We went to the Army barracks and were much impressed with the cleanliness, order and fine discipline of the men. At nine o'clock two Japanese prisoners were brought in. No one could speak their language, but Chow was able to write it. They were deserters who were tired of the war. They said that many of the comrades felt the same. Slept in the office on the floor, six of us. Up at 6:30 a.m. Hot tea, after washing. Breakfast of rice, turnips and pork at nine. Ten porters, with wheel barrows took our luggage (15 cases) down to the river, which we crossed in a junk. Carried ashore by porters, naked to the waist, wading in the ice cold water. The river here is 400 yards wide with a current I would estimate at eight miles per hour. The junks are carried down stream by this current as they cross for as much as a quarter of a mile. They then have to be towed back above their starting point to recross.

As we boarded the train the air raid warning sounded. Immediately there was a great exodus to the hills and the river bank, but we pulled out and did not wait to see what happened. This railway is called the Tung Kau line and runs north through the centre of Shansi to Chang Chia Kou, north of the Great Wall. It is held by the Japanese beyond Tai-Yuan. The train is filled with troops. We were in the postal car which was very comfortable, as we could spread our luggage out and use the boxes as seats. At night it was rather draughty as the entire sides and roof were perforated with bullet holes, the train having been heavily machine-gunned the trip before.

We are going up the east bank of the Fen river. Two ranges of mountains accompany us, one on either side. This is the loess country. These loess are curious low hills or mountains of light, brownish-ochre sand. The hills are cut in terraces which rise, one after the other, as regular as a stair case. I thought at first these terraces must have been made by man, so regular are they, but when one sees them for hundreds of miles, and often far from human habitation, one realizes that they are a natural formation. We travel very slowly. The weather is fine and warm with a clear blue sky. At every station there are vendors of food, hot millet soup, noodles, tea, friedhard, wheatrolls and steamed buns, and hard-boiled eggs. Many trains are coming down, packed with refugees, sitting on the tops of the carriages, on the engine, anywhere to have a foothold. The river on our left looks very low. There are literally thousands of ducks flying overhead. The land parched, practically treeless, except for a few low cedars.

On Saturday, the 26th, we arrived at the station of Linfen at 3 p.m. There we learned for the first time that the Japanese were only a short distance away and the city was being evacuated. The station itself was jammed with humanity—civilians, men, women and children, carrying all they possessed, their bedding, rolls, a few pots and pans, wounded soldiers, arms, hands and heads wrapped in bloody, dusty bandages. Flat cars loaded with mules, rice and munitions. At four o'clock the Japanese bombers came over and machine-gunned us. We took to the trenches dug in the sand about the station. Only four men were wounded. The Headquarters of the Army was moved and no one seemed to know where it was located. A train on a siding loaded with stores was preparing to leave. Back to Tungwan! With a heavy heart we climbed aboard a box car filled with bags of rice to the roof and slept fitfully till 3 a.m., when we were awakened by the silence. Our train had gone off and left us on a siding, having brought us only 25 miles. We were the last train from Linfen.

The name of this station was Goasi. Here we stayed all day, while our Commander, Major Lee, was making arrangements with the surrounding villagers to unload the trainload of rice, reload it into carts and start off on the 200 mile march back to the Yellow River. A fine hot day. We lay in the sun and looked up the railway line, expecting the Japanese any hour to come around the bend. No soldiers, no one but a hundred or so wounded men walking down the line. We have 400 bags of rice—very precious. It must not be captured. We walked up to the village close by. It is practically deserted except for a few old people. Jean Ewen asked an old woman why she was staying. Her reply was "What is the use, I can not be worse off than I am now." All day long we hear explosions down the line. We hear the Japanese planes overhead but are not bombed. Buy a quarter of a pig—$1.40. The Commander tells us that we are not going back to Tungwan, but that we will cross the river into Shensi and make for Yenan, about 300 miles west, crossing two rivers and a range of mountains.

On the 28th we left Goasi with 42 carts, pulled by 3 mules apiece, two in the lead and one between the shafts. We were forced to abandon half the rice and the winter uniforms. It was a brilliant fine day. I walked ahead of our caravan for two hours enjoying the clear dry air. Every town we would come to the gates were closed and no one would answer our call, so we were forced to go around the walls, to pick up the road beyond. At about 4 p.m., having been on the way for four hours, I, who was walking alongside the leading cart, saw two bombers going south about half a mile to our left. As we watched them I saw the second of the pair who was trailing the leader, begin violently to waggle his wings. I recognized the signal and knew that we had been seen and were in for it! We must simply have made the Japanese mouth

With Ewen en route to Yenan. Ewen had nursed in a hospital in Shantung in the early 1930s. She spoke Chinese well and acted as Bethune's interpreter until they reached Yenan.

water—42 carts stretched out over a quarter of a mile, not an anti-aircraft gun within two hundred miles and not a Chinese pursuit plane in the entire Province! We were sitting birds asking to be knocked off! And this they proceeded to do to the best of their ability. They were flying at a height of about one thousand feet. They turned sharply off their course, and while one stayed high the other came down to 500 feet and flew our line looking us over very closely. We were all lying out on the flat ground, not a tree or a stone to protect us. There were fifty of us, drivers, men and boys, with five old rifles between us.

After passing down the line, the bomber turned and flew back to the head, then diving on us so that he was only 200 feet above us, dropped four bombs on the leading section. His aim was so bad that even at that height he missed the leading carts by fifty feet. I would be prepared to bet that had I been in the plane I could have hit those carts with a baseball! As a matter of fact, he was as close to us lying out in the field as he was to the target he was trying to hit. After bombing the leading carts he returned and repeated the performance on the last section with another four bombs. Here his aim was a little better—the bombs dropping about 20 feet away. Jean, who was riding on the last cart, had a narrow escape, a soldier lying beside her getting a piece of bomb in his back and the driver a fractured arm. These three were lying on the ground 150 feet away from the carts. The bombs explode immediately on striking and make only a small hole in the ground. In this way they are more effective, as the steel sprays out flatly instead of burying itself in the ground. I observed wounds on the legs of the mules and horses reaching no higher than two feet from the ground, which were received at a distance of 100 feet away. One is really not safe unless one is in a trench. Our total casualties were 15 mules killed and an additional 12 wounded. Three of these had to be shot. Four of our men were wounded. Jean Ewen showed great pluck and fortitude under her first baptism of fire and immediately after the bomber had passed started to dress the wounded and arrange for their transportation to the nearest village a quarter of a mile away, so that by the time I had walked from the head of the line to the rear where the men had been wounded, she had already applied dressings to the most serious ones.

The wounded driver was only concerned about his mules and wept to hear that all three had been killed. Our Commander paid promptly for the killed animals—100 dollars each (a Chinese dollar is about 30 cents). No wonder the peasants welcome them—this is one army that does not take advantage of the poor and defenceless.

After cutting out the dead and wounded animals from the carts we resumed our way, our caravan now reduced to 20. We travelled all night, riding on top of the rice bags—our precious rice—and slept as best we could. The night was cold, dark and overcast. At 5 we reached the bank of the river Fen and turned in on top of a hard kang (brick sleeping oven) for some more much needed sleep. Up again at 10. Breakfast of hot sweet fermented rice water with an egg beaten up in it—very good.

On the south bank of the river opposite lies the city Kiangchow, I can see the twin spires of a Roman Catholic Mission church—typical French architecture—rising high above the roofs of the one and two storied tile-roofed houses and looking very incongruous and out of place. We hear that the Japanese have taken Linfen and are coming down the railway rapidly. We have met no soldiers on the road. We are the rear of the rearguard—we, and the hundreds of walking wounded whose infected wounds are covered with dirty blood-stained, sand-caked bandages that have not been changed for a week or more. We hear the Japanese planes bombing the railway line ahead of us. Their cavalry cannot be far behind us. The river here is two hundred yards wide and, it being low, reaches only

up to the waist—but at that is too deep for our mules and low carts. We must unload.

The Ferry junks and the cable overhead line was burned by Chinese to obstruct the Japanese advance. They certainly obstructed our retreat! While our Commander is making arrangements for our stuff to be taken over, I crossed over, being carried piggyback. The current is about six miles an hour of brown muddy water. I was much amused to see the efforts of 20 Chinese coolies trying to get two camels on their feet who had obstinately lain down in the shallow water and refused to move. The crowd alternately burst into roars of curses and laughter, all to no avail. To the best of my knowledge they are still there, unless the Japanese have some secret of how to move camels!

I climbed up the hill, through the city, to the church. The city is practically deserted except for a few shopkeepers and beggars. These two classes are all that remain—the propertied and the propertyless. The first will await the coming of the Japanese with some fear and trembling, but their goods are more important than their fears. They are the typical bourgeoisie the whole world over. They regard this war as just another battle between professional soldiers. They are politically illiterate. Their only concern is their individual welfare. The poor beggars could not be worse off under any other master. This also applies to the poorer peasants. If they leave they will starve, so they remain.

At the mission, the compound of which was completely filled with the families of the church members taking refuge, I had a very pleasant talk in mixed French and English with Father T. Van Hamert, O.F.M., missionaire apostolique, Shansi meredional, a bearded Dutchman, and with Father Quint Pessers, O.F.M., Praef. Apostolique. They opened a bottle of red wine and gave me a good cigar. They told me that the mayor and the police had fled the city two days before, and that they were expecting the Japanese in 36 hours. What would happen to them? Would the Japanese respect the French flag on the church spire? A shrug of the shoulder. Yes, some missionaries had already been killed. They would stay and try to protect their parishioners. I admired their courage. In discussing the Japanese atrocities (the rape of Nanking and the brutal murder of 8,000 men, women and children will go down in history as an unforgivable crime of the Japanese army), they were of the opinion that the Japanese officers had little or no control over their men, and that this would be the main danger. Both were calm and smiling as I bid them goodbye. Their last words to me were, as we parted, "I hope we meet again on earth, if not, then in Heaven."

The next day our rice was carried over the river on the backs of porters. The river had risen during the night so that it was now up to the breasts of our porters, who, completely naked except for a folded jacket on their shoulders, carried us over sitting on chairs carried by four men. I was standing on the north bank waiting to cross, when I heard a great shout of laughter from the opposite side. I looked up to see Jean go over backwards, turning a perfect summersault in three feet of water. One of her bearers had slipped or stumbled. Of course this accident delighted the crowd!

We left Kiangchow at 1:30 p.m., feeling glad to get the river between us and the Japanese, as we heard this morning that the enemy are only 25 miles away and their cavalry even less. It is a cold, heavy day with a bitter wind. We push ahead with two carts, leaving the commander behind to superintend the transport of most of the rice sacks, as not enough mule carts can be found, the army which is ahead of us having commandeered the supply. The villages we pass through are deserted, no workers in the fields, all the culverts torn up. We covered 60 li (20 miles) by 7:30 that evening, walking all the way. Stayed the night at a little village called Chi-Shan. With my jack-knife I opened the carotid artery of a wounded mule with a broken leg (his ears and tail blown off by an aeroplane bomb the day before) and who had been left in agony for a day by the side of the road. The soldiers refused to shoot it, saying that the owner might claim damages. I took a chance on that and put the poor beast out of its misery. Off the next day early. No soldiers to be seen but the poor walking wounded.

Of the hundreds of wounded we have seen in the past few days, we have not seen a single case of a serious leg wound, only one head injury (a bullet through the jaw). The wounds are all of the hands and arms, many of them being multiple. All the other wounded have either died, been killed or captured. In the four days since leaving Linfen we have not encountered a single army medical officer or seen an ambulance. We have seen only two wounded beings carried by stretcher-bearers and one man in a bullock cart who had a great wound in the thigh, which had not been dressed for ten days. Our first-aid bags became rapidly exhausted, but we were able to buy in the larger towns small quantities of gauze, cotton and some crystals of potassium permanganate. With these and our morphine tablets the wounds of all we came across in each day's march were dressed. These exhausted, dust-covered, gray-faced men and boys, abandoned by their officers, endured without complaint the heat of the day, the bitter cold of the long night (none had blankets or bedding rolls) the pain of their undressed, suppurating wounds, lack of food (to many we gave money to buy rice) all of this without complaint. It was marvelous to see such fortitude. I only wished that I had some of their medical officers in front of me to tell them what I thought of them. None of these men were of the Army. I was to learn later from Professor Messer of the League of Nations' Commission in Sian that the only seriously wounded he had seen in military hospitals in China was in the Army. All other hospitals were filled only with those men who could make their way back to the rear by their own efforts.

As I walked along ahead of the carts, I saw a young lad ahead of me stopping to rest every once in a while. On coming abreast of him I noticed that he was very short of breath. He was only a child of 17. There was a great old dark blood stain on the front of his faded blue jacket. I stopped him. He had been shot through the lung a week previously. There was no dressing on a badly suppurating wound of the upper right anterior chest wall. The bullet had gone through the lung and came out at the back. There was fluid in the pleural cavity up as high as the third rib in front. The heart was displaced three inches to the left. This boy had been walking in this condition for a week. If I had not seen it myself I would not have believed it possible. We put him up on our cart where he lay coughing painfully as the mule cart moved slowly along over the rough road, enveloped in clouds of dust. We only made 20 miles that day.

The sensation of having no one between us and the Japanese is a decidedly draughty one! We know that they are gaining on us as their cavalry is capable of doing twice our distance in a day. It is a race between them and us who will reach the Yellow River first. Not until we cross that great stream will we be out of danger. What a humiliating thing it would be to be captured before even joining the Army, after having come half way cross the world to do so!

On the 3rd of March we came to the city of Ho-Chin. It was filled with the provincial troops of General Yan Shi San. We have caught up to the Army!

That night our Commander arrived, having walked day and night from Kiangchow, a distance of 75 miles. He was able to trace us by following the print of my rubber soles in the sand! We heard that the American Presbyterian Hospital left the city a month ago. A week later 500 wounded men arrived from the north. There was no hospital of any kind for them to go to. I went to see the only doctor in the city. He is a combined doctor, dentist and druggist. That is to say he is a quack. His shop was filled with wounded waiting dressings. He is charging $1.00 a dressing. He charged me $4.00 for a small roll of gauze worth 50¢.

There seems no organization whatever among the troops. We learn that some refuse to obey their officers. Some of the officers have been accused of cheating the soldiers over their pay. Their pay in the field is $6.00 per month, with food and uniforms. It is said that some of these troops have not been paid for months.

Walked in the town. Live carp in water buckets for sale; black pigs with big floppy ears; barkless dogs, white paper windows; lousy k'angs.

My birthday—48 last year in Madrid. Dressed six wounded soldiers (arms and hands) nothing but neglected minor injuries—all others have died on the way back.

On March 4th we left Ho-Chin for the village of Shan-Chien-Chen on the east bank of the Yellow River. We hear that the Japanese have burned the village we passed through the day before yesterday. At 9 p.m. in the pitch dark we march down to the river banks. Here was an unforgettable sight. Lit by a dozen fires five thousand men were collected with trunks, carts, mules, horses, artillery and great piles of stores waiting to cross the river into Shensi. The light of the fires was reflected back from the steep wall-like mountain side. The river rushes between two high cliffs. The swift current (12 miles an hour) carries great floating ice flows, which clash against each other far out on the dark surface. The whole scene is wild and fantastic. Lying on top of rice bags we finally sleep at midnight. The man next to me has a hand grenade in his belt, and as he turns in his sleep it sticks into my back.

At 5 we are awake, a cold overcast dawn. There are only four junks. It will take four days to carry us all over. We hear that the Japanese are only ten miles away. The Chinese officer in charge of the ferry puts us on the first junk to leave the bank. The boat is about fifty feet long and twenty-five feet wide. There is 100 on board with field artillery, mules and baggage. As we are swept down stream we see that the wounded (about 1000 of them) are being collected in one spot and are being sent over first. We go down with the current for half a mile, then with long sweeps manage to get out of the main stream. A naked boy leaps overboard and with a pole-anchor slows down our progress. Then the men on the sweep slowly manoeuver us to the bank, assisted by a back wash current behind a bend. Many troops on the west bank, which is to be strongly fortified with good trenches, dugouts. Several batteries of field guns. Machine guns on mule back. Troops in dusty-faded uniforms the color of the soil, which has stained them for months. Equipment good. Many automatic rifles, both light and heavy machine-guns, stick hand grenades.

We march to a nearby village and occupy a deserted house. Open two cans of chipped beef for our midday meal. The last sight I remember as we crossed the river was the great red horse belonging to Chu Teh, which he had loaned to Captain Carlson, the U.S. Military Attache, who had been inspecting the north Shansi front some time ago. Carlson rode the horse down and it had been left in charge of our Commander to return to Chu Teh, who was reported to be very fond of it. It had been captured from the Japanese and was a

Bethune and Ewen would have seen this ancient pagoda long before they entered Yenan. Crowning the highest hill above the town in the valley below, it remains today as the symbol of the town and of the Communist resistance against the Japanese and the Kuomintang.

grand, big animal with a fine red colour. We hear that the Japanese are in Ho-Chin, the city we left yesterday. Well, we beat them to it!

The river is rising. The high bitter wind makes the shallow broad beamed junks unmanageable. I am afraid that many men will be captured tomorrow on the east bank when the Japanese come down to the river. Ho-Chin is only 5 miles away. This afternoon many Chinese troops crossed from west to east from Shensi into Shansi. That is very encouraging. We are expecting a battle on the river bank. It is raining and cold.

March 6th was cold. A high wind filling the air with dust. The Japanese cavalry arrived on the east bank across from us at 4 p.m. I had gone down to the river with a party of men who were carrying back our supplies from the beach. We were machine-gunned, the bullets striking the water a hundred yards away. We scrambled up the bank into a trench and from there could plainly see the enemy on the opposite side. Walking along the trench out into the river bank we were forced to leave it finally and make a dash across a piece of open land. Here they fired on us again. We threw ourselves down on the ground, the bullets kicking up the dust uncomfortably close. I raised my head and, to my horror, saw that we were lying in front of one of our field-guns 50 feet away. As soon as the Japanese turned his attention elsewhere we spent no great amount of time in getting out of that particular spot.

I will say this for the Japanese, their accuracy of range was excellent, as the distance was about 1000 yards and the light by no means good. They were firing up at us. We hear that the Japanese force is 20,000 and consists of four to five hundred cavalry, several batteries of field guns and infantry. Most of our supplies have got across, but no news of the Red horse of Chu Teh.

We moved into a cave tonight, much more comfortable than a house. Dressed many wounded men. Have seen no army doctors. Two of our men have left to get mules and carts. A cold night with two inches of snow the next morning on the ground. We pity the poor troops lying out on the ground without protection. Our cave is fine and warm. Nothing to eat in the village but millet.

In the morning the Japanese artillery arrived on the opposite bank and shelled the west bank all day, the noise of the explosions echoing back and forth between the mountains. Ours reply. This goes on for three days. A Japanese shell blows the top off a house 300 feet away, but they can't hurt us in our cave, which is dug in the side of a hill and 40 feet underground.

We have found supply of drugs. Bottles of Tinc. Camph. Co., Digitalis, Adrenalin, silk sutures, syringes, ampules of cocaine.

Woke the next morning to hear one of our Chinese singing the Marseillaise. A fine clear day with a sharp soapstick enema—cure! During the convulsion the mother rushed outside the cave and called the child's name loudly. This to bring back his soul which had temporarily left the body (reminds me of the Scotch "bless you" when one sneezes).

On the 9th we set off for Sian on foot—225 miles away. Lee, Jean and I set the pace. Jean is out to show some of our sceptical young comrades that she can take it! It is a fine warm day, and the country looks very well with the wheat up about four inches. Shansi, which is denuded of trees, never looked as good and prosperous as this province, which is more fertile (at least in the southern part) and with much more trees. We keep the Yellow River on our right. Lee, a former rickshaw man in Shanghai, arrives at Hanchang comparatively fresh. He has legs like trees. He is a splendid chap about 32 years of age and was on the Great Trek, so that a mere 25 miles a day is nothing. The only English he knows is "damn fool."

As we came in sight of the city of Hanchang, I for one was not sorry. We enter the city at five in the afternoon, through the west gate of the high city wall. We passed many students on the road from the University of Linfen. The students (3,000 of them) all were scattered west and south, some had been killed, some had died in the mountains of cold. Many were eager to go to the University at Yenan in Shensi run by the Army.

In the city of Hanchang we stayed a week, waiting for trucks to come from Sian. To describe all our week here would be too long. I was besieged with civilian

This photograph of the young Mao Tse-tung was taken by Bethune in Yenan in April 1938.

This official painting of the meeting with Mao Tse-tung was completed in the aftermath of the Cultural Revolution. Lithographs of it appear everywhere in China.

patients, pulmonary tuberculosis, ovarian cyst, gastric ulcer. Here was a Chinese military base hospital in a temple. After a few days the chief surgeon and the entire nursing staff offered to come with us up to Yenan. Of course we could not take them!

On March 19th we left for Sian 200 miles away. We made this in two days, and here we are now. The first thing we did was to go to the bath house. The ineffable bliss of a hot bath—the first bath in a month! We found that we had been lost and no one knew whether or not we were alive or dead, or captured. We are now waiting to go north to Yenan in four days' time.

After a week in Sian collecting supplies they set out for Yenan, reaching it on the evening of the last day in March. Near midnight they were summoned to meet Chairman Mao Tse-tung. With Ewen acting as interpreter, Bethune met Mao in the Communist leader's cave dwelling.

Bethune was able to convince Mao that he would be most useful in the Chin-Ch'a-Chi Border Region. While the expedition was being prepared Bethune and Ewen worked in the Yenan hospital.

At the beginning of May, Bethune and a military escort

left Yenan by truck. With him was Dr. Richard Brown, a Canadian surgeon from an Anglican mission. Having learned of Bethune in Hankow, Brown volunteered to work with him until his furlough ran out. He also brought to Yenan medical supplies that Bethune had stored in Hong Kong.

In this letter Bethune described the first day of the trip. Agnes Smedley, to whom he refers, was an American journalist and author.

May 3

We are now enroute to the front, having left Yenan yesterday. This city is approximately 100 miles north of Yenan. We came here by truck. The only truck that will stand up to these mountains and roads is a really big job like a Dodge. Our medical stuff, now collected at last—valuable lesson learnt, never to be separated from your baggage in China—completely filled the truck, and with a dozen soldiers and guards, we were heavily loaded. The road from Yenan to Yen Chuan is pretty bad, from Ching Chien to Suiteh is good (I mean good for this part of the country). All roads are packed dirt with a hard surface. The only reason that better time can not be made on them than is now possible, is that they are not graded and scraped down. There is one very long and high mountain between Ching Chien and Suiteh, called Jui Li San (the 9 "li" mountain). The country gets steeper the farther north one gets, there are 8 rivers to ford—no

In Yenan he addressed the students of K'ang-Ta (Yenan Military Academy and Anti-Japanese Aggression University). The willingness of the Communists to drive out the Japanese impressed many students who made their way to Yenan from all parts of China to join the Communist forces.

This part of Shensi province is covered in loess soil, a fine silt. For centuries people have built cave dwellings which are relatively cool in the summer and warm in the winter. When Bethune arrived they were serving as the Yenan hospital.

bridges. In the rains, this road will be impassable to cars. At Yen Ping are two oil wells—one at least, is working. Kerosene is made here. All the way up, along the road, are open seams of coal. This coal is a high grade of anthracite. It is simply dug off the open seam and carted away on donkey back.

At (or rather near) Yen Chuan, is a military hospital of 300 beds. This is the hospital that I have written to the American Committee about and had Smedley send a cable asking for $1000 a month for our Unit to operate as a model hospital. In view of the fact that there has been no word from the Committee—I have not received a line from this Committee since I left America—I was forced to tell the Medical Service of the 8th R.A. that it seemed useless to expect financial support of our Unit from America, but that in spite of this, we were entirely at their disposal and would go anywhere they cared to send us, but that, of course, we had no money of our own, refused, in addition, to work with or under the direction of Smedley, and would have to be supported by the 8th R.A. This the Chief of Staff assured us would be fine. Acting on this, we drew $100 on April 12. That is Jean Ewen and I received from the 8th R.A. $50 each for our current living expenses, on that date. You must understand that this step was taken with extreme reluctance, on our part, but we were absolutely broke, no word had

90

Ho Tzu-hsin, a seventeen-year-old and veteran of the Long March, was assigned to Bethune as his *hsiao-kuei* (little devil). When he finally learned to boil an egg to Bethune's satisfaction, this photograph celebrated the occasion. He remained with Bethune until his death. Today he is frequently released from his duties as a factory worker to describe his experiences with Bethune to groups of students and workers.

come from America in spite of our telegrams, cables, and letters from us, written weekly at least.

We have not, at any time after the outfitting of this Unit—the last items which were added in Sian—needed much money, but Yenan is an expensive place to live. We needed money not only for food, but there are always other expenses; developing and printing the photograph films cost $4 to $5 a week. Charcoal is expensive—$3 a small load. This is used not only for cooking, but for heating our cold caves. There is always 4 to 6 for dinner, of the foreigners in the city. I am only mentioning these housekeeping facts, to give you an idea of the conditions here.

Well, since the model hospital was off (it must be carefully kept in mind that all schemes, even the tentative ones proposed were fully discussed with responsible officials) the Chief Medical Officer of the Medical Service of the Front (Dr. Chiang) decided last week we should go to Shen Mu, in the extreme north, near the Great Wall, as soon as our American Supplies arrived. All the American material arrived safely and in good condition. Nothing was lost. You can imagine our joy! We embraced the panniers! But before the stuff arrived in Yenan, we got word that it had come to Sian, so Jean was sent down to bring it up personally. The stuff arrived but no Jean! I sent her two telegrams but received no reply—the last one saying that Brown and I were leaving for the front in 4 days' time and to return. We left word in Yenan, that when she arrives she is to follow us.

At Ching Chien we met the Chief Medical Officer of the Front, who told us that owing to the changed military situation—owing to the Japanese withdrawing from a large part of the territory they held in Shansi, that the wounded were coming into Shensi by another route, and that he intended to send us to Pan Tang. This town now has 600 wounded according to last reports, and no doctors above the rank of dresser.

We, that is Brown and I, have agreed to go to Pan Tang at once. At the same time we told him of our desire to go to Wutaishan. He has asked us to "clean up" the hospital at Pan Tang first and that later, if they need help in Wutaishan, that he will send us there. This "cleaning up" process will probably take a month.

So that is the situation at present.

Our address for books, magazines and papers (you seem determined not to send any letters) is Dr. Ma Haidah, Yenan, Shensi, China. He will forward. If you change your mind about giving additional medical assistance to the 8th R.A., send all money direct to Mao Tse-tung, at Yenan. The 8th R.A. and nobody but the 8th R.A. should be the recipient of money from abroad, directly.

Six days on foot to Pan Tang. Off tomorrow, all our supplies on pack ponies.

Salud,
Norman Bethune

P.S.   This Dr. Richard Brown, is a fine fellow—speaks Chinese like a native. Unfortunately, he only has 4 months leave from his hospital. When he leaves, Dr. Haidah will come north to replace him. But I could use a half dozen more Canadian or American doctors. Where is Dr. L. Fraad? Send him over immediately. Send a spare tube for the X-ray and a generator.

Bethune and Dr. Brown flank a Chinese in a military hospital. Bethune wrote: "With me is a Canadian missionary—Dr. Richard Brown, of Toronto. We call it the Canadian-American Medical Unit, but that's just to let the Americans get their money's worth—all three of us are Canadians!" (The third was Ewen.)

From Sui-te they continued north to the base hospital at Hu Chia Ch'uan. Here Bethune wrote a lengthy report to the military authorities in Yenan describing his activities to date, making recommendations for improvements in existing conditions and listing required paraphernalia for expected volunteers from America.

Hu Chia, Ch'uan, Northern Shensi,
May 17, 1938

Letter to Yenan:

The following is a brief, introductory report on medical conditions in this hospital, with some recommendations for your consideration.

We left Yenan on Monday, the second of May. At Er Shi Li Pu, we stopped to pick up some supplies and to leave others. Of the supplies we asked for, Dr. Sung gave us only a small part. We asked for 50 lbs. of ether, and received 10; for 25 lbs. of gauze, none; for 10 lbs. of refined salt, for intravenous use, a handful; for a small barrel of Plaster of Paris, for fracture work, none. I may say that all these supplies were out at Er Shi Li Pu, as we saw them there. In view of the amount of work that we were asked to do, and the long distance we were to be away from supplies, and especially as there was an increasing amount of supplies coming to Er Shi Li Pu, this refusal was very regrettable. At the same time it should be remarked that the people there leave valuable drugs unpacked. We were never able to see an inventory of supplies on hand. It is suggested that shelves be erected, all drugs and supplies unpacked and put on them, that inventory be made, stock books kept. In addition, the place is over-staffed.

At Chang Chien, we met Dr. Chiang, who joined us on our trip north. Ten days before he had asked us to go to Pan Tang, where he said there were six hundred wounded. He informed us that the hospital in Pan Tang had been moved to Hu Chia Ch'uan and we were to proceed there. After a 2 day stop at Mi Shih to repack our supplies, we set off with 13 mules, on May 6th, arriving here on the 11th.

At Yen Chuan, there are no wounded, only sick; at Mi Shih, only 20 or 30, of the 8th Army wounded. We were not asked to see these. At Chia Hsien all the wounded belong to the Shansi Provincial Army, and none to the 8th R.A.

In this hospital, instead of the 600 we expected to find there are only 175 wounded of the 8th R.A. Of these 35 are very serious. All have old neglected wounds of the thigh and leg—most of them incurable except by amputation. Three of the 35 are lying naked on straw-covered k'angs, with only a single cotton quilt. The others are still in their old, unwashed cotton-padded winter, dirty uniforms. They are, without exception, all anemic, underfed and dehydrated. The surgical care they receive is to dress the wounds—discharging sinuses leading down to the diseased bone. They are dying of sepsis. These are the cases we are asked to operate on. They are all bad surgical risks.

May 22, 1938

The first three days were spent in preparing an operating room and post-operative ward. This was difficult on account of the lack of material—such as cotton cloth, pails, gauze, etc. Mattresses had to be made to cover and enclose straw as otherwise it becomes wet and unusable. There was only enough cotton cloth to make 10 mattresses. The patients were evacuated from two adjacent rooms, opening one into the other and these were used as operation and recovery rooms, after as thorough a cleaning as it was possible to give them. Sheets, towels, gauze squares, mops, masks, glove cases, all were cut from our remaining cotton cloth, sewn and sterilized in the autoclave.

We had, after examination of the 35 serious cases, divided them into classes 1, 2, or 3 depending on the emergency of the case. Class 1 required immediate operation, principally on account of abscess formation complicating bone infection. Class 2 could wait a short time, and Class 3 were those in which operation time was not important. All these cases are completely bedridden . . .

The important question of proper training of the doctors and nurses will be taken up later.

This hospital is filled with men walking around on crutches. These cases have minor injuries of the thigh, leg or arm. Yet the joint above the injury is frequently flexed at 45 degrees. This means mismanagement. Such flextures should never be allowed to develop. If from the time of injury splints were properly applied, then later passive and active movements of the joint undertaken, at least 20 men here would be walking without crutches, or have a useful arm.

There is enough work here to keep an orthopedic surgeon and team of masseurs and rehabilitation experts busy for 6 months.

2. Much of the disabilities in patients here are

preventable. They can be—and must be—prevented at the time of injury or shortly after. Where? At the front. Proper debridement of wounds within 24 hours after injury, the immediate application of splints to injuries of bones (if Thomas splints can, for one reason or another not be used, on thigh and leg fractures, then wooden splints must be employed).

We have frequently heard since coming to the 8th R.A., that we must forget much of our training in other armies, since the 8th Route Army is very poor in equipment and in trained personnel of its medical service, and that it does the best that it can under the circumstances. We quickly agree. We have seen many instances of the devotion to duty of the personnel of the medical service under the most primitive conditions possible. But that phase is passing, and more and more assistance is coming. The change in the conditions necessitates a change in organization. The principal change in organization is in the training of personnel. We must not hide the fact that their training is inadequate. How can this be improved?

The other 2 questions which arise are the obtaining of more medical supplies and the establishment of additional hospitals. So we see three important problems:
1. Improvement in the training of personnel of the Medical Service.
2. Obtaining more supplies and equipment.
3. Establishment of special hospitals—especially for orthopedic cases.

And in connection with this last problem, the great question of rehabilitation and re-education of the soldier no longer fit to fight, but useful in other work.

We must take, in discussing these problems, both the short, immediate view point and the long range view.

The following suggestions are put forward with the full knowledge that our experience in the 8th Route Army has been short, and that our lack of knowledge of political aspects of these problems is profound. You will bear this in mind, that the following ideas are projected tentatively and humbly, for your consideration.

Training of Personnel
1. Training of personnel by auxiliary medical (foreign) units. Example training of the staff of this hospital by the members of the Canadian-American Medical Unit. Other examples—training of the 8th Army personnel by Chinese Red Cross Units. It is our opinion that this should be undertaken at all times. Difficulties—language, inadequate preliminary training of doctors and nurses, length of time necessary, lowered efficiency of the Unit employing

untrained or partially trained personnel, destruction of equipment by untrained personnel, unfamiliar with its use. We, in our short time here have encountered all these troubles (our autoclave, for the sterilization of towels, sheets, gauze, etc., has already been ruined).

Just as experts in other branches of the army have to be sent for special training, so there should be a selection of the best and brightest of the personnel made, and they should be sent to foreign (mission) hospitals, in China, for an intensive two to three months' course in surgical nursing, the elements of surgery, antiseptic and aseptic technique, application of splints, etc. Dr. Richard Brown, of this Unit, has offered to take back with him to his hospital, three nurses or doctors from the 8th Army. Application should be made to the Baptist Hospital in Sian, to the Union Mission Hospital in Hankow, for the placement of others. We do not think that the selection of hospitals should be confined to Mission Hospitals, but that any modern hospital will do. It is quite possible that these Mission Hospitals will give free board, a small living allowance (say $5.00 a month). These men, returning to the 8th Route Army, should be "seeded" throughout the medical service and will be able to instruct others. Such a scheme would raise, in a very short time, the medical standard of the service. This will do for nurses, but for doctors, other plans should be made.

2. Obtaining additional medical and surgical supplies. All future supplies for the medical service must come from sources other than those bought and paid for by the 8th R.A. In other words, the medical service must cease to be an expense to the 8th R.A. treasury. This, we are firmly of the opinion, can be hoped for now.

There must be a ten-fold increase of all medical supplies. This hospital lacks most of the elementary equipment—pails, basins, towels, soap (most of the patients haven't had a bath for 9 months, their skins are ingrained with dirt), sheets, (there was not a single sheet under a patient—they were lying on dirty straw) cotton coverlets (of the 37 seriously wounded, only half had adequate covering to keep them warm at night), change of clothing (all patients here except the 3 completely naked, were lying in their old, dirty winter uniforms), mattress covers (unprotected straw rapidly becomes filthy and causes infection), pillows (there were no pillows here before we made a dozen), bed rings (most of the patients have bed sores), socks, etc. Bed pans, urinals are unknown.

There is a great demand for large bottles and corks for solution.

There are no splints of any kind here except a few

short lengths of wood for fractured arms. No leg splints.

No bandage rollers, no safety pins. No sterilizer for gauze and cotton—sterilizing is done by suspending package of gauze over boiling water in a big iron pot for an hour. This, of course, does not sterilize properly.

Instruments consist of a dozen pairs of short dressing forceps, 6 scissors, 10 probes. There are 3 irrigating syringes. One enema syringe.

In regard to drugs, as is common in China, it is overstocked in non-essentials. In regard to essentials, it is understocked. There are dozens of bottles of drugs—unused and unusable—example: 10 bottles of Sodium Hydroxide, but no alcohol; pounds of Tincture of Digitalis, but no Castor Oil; no Dakins solution, no vaseline, only 10 ampules of Morphine, no cod liver oil, no Lysol, no Bichloride of Mercury.

All the above points to a lack of organization and central experienced control. Remedy: 1. Draw up a list of standard drug equipment for each medical unit in the Army, whether regimental, brigade, division, field hospital or base hospital.

2. Stop doctors writing prescriptions by having all units supplied by standard, uniform, concentrated stock mixtures. Most stock mixtures can be concentrated 1 to 10 and even more. All it will be necessary to do then will be to add water. But don't carry around diluted stocks. Stop buying expensive mixtures, such as cough medicine when they can be made up at a small percent of their cost.

Immediately prepare a pharmacopoeia for the army, have it printed and supplied to all units. Forbid writing prescriptions for each patient as at present. And supply all units with one dozen, concentrated stock mixtures such as a stimulating cough mixture, anti-diarrhoea, two tonics, anti-constipation mixture, rheumatic mixture, headache, sleeplessness. Then 2 lotions, 3 salves, two eye drops, a gargle, 3 antiseptics. But standardize everything. Send such a list of drugs needed to all places, so as to prevent them from sending unsuitable material. Send such lists to all sympathizers and raisers of money in China, so that the money sent will be for what we need. Keep careful inventories of supplies at Er Shi Li Pu. Have all medical units sent to Er Shi Li Pu, a weekly list of their stock on hand and their requirements for the future. Take away half the drugs at present in the hospitals and replace with stock mixtures, standard to the entire army.

Write a Manual of Medical and Surgical Instruction—in mimeograph form—of about 50 pages, giving instruction in the use of these stock mixtures, in the

En route to Chin-Ch'a-Chi with Dr. Brown and soldiers. Young Ho is on top of the truck. When the truck was stuck, Bethune jumped out of the cab and, up to his ankles in the mud, began to push. The Chinese were amazed. They were accustomed to foreigners who let the Chinese do the dirty work.

care of patients (most of the nurses don't know how to properly lift or turn a patient) in the principles of asepsis, application of splints, etc. Distribute this booklet to all medical units. Start self-criticism classes in medical units. Demote some doctors to the rank of nurses, raise others. Start classes of instruction to patients, in hygiene, etc., while in hospital.

Apply to the International Red Cross of Hankow, for the 50% grant towards the supply of artificial legs. Approximately 500 such legs are needed at once.

Establish a Centre for the fitting of legs. This Centre should be in the Rehabilitation and Re-Education Hospital. Here all men with amputations should be collected together for special training.

Let the Foreign Relations Committee (a memorandum on this projected Committee was submitted to you before Dr. Bethune left Yenan) take upon itself the preparation of an appeal (using some of the material in this letter) for circulation in China and abroad. Dr. Brown, on his return from Shansi and Wutaishan, is eager to go on a lecture trip to the large cities in China to raise money for the medical service of the 8th Army. Canada and America must increase their contributions. Too much of the money subscribed abroad is being sent to the International Red Cross of Hankow (Dr. Maxwell). It is not the question of the mis-use of this money (there is not the slightest idea that it is not being properly used), it is only the question that if this tremendous sum of money and supplies is being distributed in an equitable manner. The proposal might be made to the I.R.C. to set aside a Sinking Fund for the establishment of a Civil Hospital in Suiteh, for Northern Shensi and Inner Mongolia. This city has everything needed—isolation, running water, coal, uncared-for population. Here might be the Amputation Centre and Rehabilitation Hospital for Discharged Soldiers.

The idea behind the thought about the I.R.C. is merely that we are not perfectly sure that it has any plans for dispersal of monies and supplies beyond the immediate present. We know that the Mission Hospitals have been put on their financial feet and are better off now, as a result of the war, than they have been for ten years, but, although the Mission Hospitals are doing their part in the war very well, there are, after all, only about 150 operating in uncaptured territory. But whether or not the I.R.C. has long range plans for the future, and whether or not these plans include the Special Regional Area, should be ascertained. If they do not, then the presentation of the need of this District should be made—if it can be made in such a way that the Special Regional Government has control of such institutions, and the expenditure of such money. The sum of money to be asked for should not be less than one quarter million dollars.

3. Establishment of Special Hospitals; there is a great need for an Orthopedic Hospital. At present, these cases are our greatest problem—the length of time taken for their proper care, the experience necessary to do this—all make them special cases. Unfortunately, they comprise the majority of wounded. With them also the problem of transportation is ever present. We understand it costs $80.00 to transport a wounded man from this hospital to Yenan. So this hospital must be closer to the front.

Owing to the changing nature of this front, it would seem impossible, at present, at least, closer than Chia Hsing, on the Yellow River. Later on, it can be placed on the railway in mid Shansi. We think that a special appeal should be made to America and to England for an Orthopedic Unit to be sent out from those countries. Each should have their own x-ray Portable machine (run by gas engine). These Special Units are, of course, in addition to the Mobile Operating Units, such as ours here. In the meantime we will carry on, although our place is closer to the front in attempting to prevent such cases from occurring, as they do now, with such appalling frequency.

Our Plans for the Immediate Future, of the Canadian-American Mobile Medical Unit
We (that is Dr. Brown and Bethune are working in the closest co-operation both in practical everyday work, and in Round Table discussions with Dr. Chiang. Some of our conclusions are as follows:

1. It is unpractical to think that this Unit of 2 surgeons can go into hospitals such as this and do all the work which needs being done. In this hospital alone, there is enough work to keep us both busy for six months. We can't do it for two important reasons: 1. the present nursing staff cannot give, with their limited experience and equipment, the proper after-operation care, even though we do operate. 2. the operations are the least important part of treatment—after-care the most important. So, the most we can do here is to operate only on such cases as require the smallest amount of after-care; amputations and minor cases.

2. The great need to get to the front and, by instruction, prevent many such cases as we see here from getting into such conditions.

3. The very short time that Dr. Brown has left before he must return to his own hospital, and the necessity that he should inspect the entire front (including partisan territory, such as Wutaishan) to be in a position to describe, from first hand information, the medical needs of the 8th Route Army. His report will be a most valuable piece of work, for publicity.

4. It would be unwise to split the Unit at present, until a doctor can be found or trained to replace Dr. Brown. Dr. Bethune, with his ignorance of the language, in addition to a partially trained Chinese, would be placed in a position in which his work would be seriously hampered. In the interval before Dr. Brown leaves, every effort will be made to find Dr. Bethune an assistant.

5. It is planned to form a permanent Mobile

Operating Team, after Dr. Brown's departure—and in the meantime, to train such a team. It will be composed of the following:

1. Personnel— Dr. Bethune, Surgeon
   Chinese doctor, Asst. Surgeon
   Chinese nurse, Operating Room Nurse
   Chinese nurse, Post-Oper. Ward Nurse
   Chinese, quartermaster
   Chinese, secretary
   4 Hsiao kwei
   3 grooms for horses
   Cook

2. Equipment—The present American equipment, supplemented by additional medical supplies.

3. Cost—(to be entirely borne by the American and Canadian Committees).

Cost Monthly (in Chinese currency)

Salaries—14, at $1.00 a month	$ 14.00
Food—at 10¢ a day, 25¢ for foreigners	49.50
Transportation	100.00
Gauze, cotton, towels, etc.	200.00
Instrument replacement	50.00
Drugs, anaesthetics, etc.	100.00
Splints	500.00
Total	$ 999.50
Add for emergency—25%	250.00
Total	$1250.00

With the above plan in mind, we are leaving this hospital on a tour of the various Divisional Hospitals in Shansi. We may go to Wutaishan. If so we will return for more supplies—and if Bethune does not, then Brown will.

We leave on the 27th of May. Our first stop is Hsing Hsin, in Shansi. An Operation Room is being prepared for us there now, in the Divisional Hospital.

We will close this report with a list of the medical and surgical supplies needed, as far as we have seen them, up to the present.

Note: This unit themselves possess more instruments than the rest of the entire medical service in the 8th R.A. combined. Yet the instruments of the Unit, brought from America, are no more than adequate to do general surgery.

This list will give enough to go on with. All the above supplies can be purchased immediately with the assurance that they are desperately needed. This list will undoubtedly be added to the future. Do not be afraid that all this material will not be used to save lives. Delay means life or death.

Additional list. Not of necessities, but of things to make our patients in hospital happier.

1. Radios. (battery sets, there must be hundreds of these discarded in America, alone, since the appearance of the batteryless sets. They should have good batteries, spare tubes, and one charger to every 4 or 6 radios. These chargers must be run with a "kicker"—preferably on kerosene, not gas) 6

2. Gramophones. Records in Chinese —to be bought or donated in China...............24

3. Books—plenty of illustrations—to be bought in China...........1000

4. Games, foreign or Chinese ....lots

5. Colored pictures, posters to hang on the walls of the wards ...hundreds.

Anything else that occurs to you to brighten their lives.

> With greetings,
> *Dr. Norman Bethune*
> *Dr. Richard Brown*
> (Canadian-American Mobile Medical Unit, 8th Route Army

P.S. Please send us Dr. Ma Hai Teh as soon as possible . . . .

Note to Canadian and American "detail men", re equipment:

Personal: When in the army, at arriving at Sian, all personnel of medical units from abroad should immediately adopt the uniform of the 8th Route Army. These uniforms are made by tailors in all towns and cities, and can be obtained in 24 hours, made to measure. The material is of thin blue cotton. The jacket is a regulation army jacket with a high collar. The shirt (if any) is not exposed. Four pockets—the lower 2 are patch. All 4 are fastened by buttons. The trousers are made either straight or riding. The cap is the same material and is rather small, peaked and high—more like the French Army style. No insignia of rank are worn in the 8th Army. All wear the same uniform—men and women alike. These uniforms cost $5 a piece for the summer ones. The winter uniform is the same except that it is padded with cotton. They cost about $10. A padded long coat (or better still, sheepskin lined) is worn in the winter. Don't bring furs from America.

A good pair of khaki riding britches may be brought. Also bring gloves—both summer unlined and winter lined. There are no gloves made in China fit to wear. Bring underwear—2 suits of winter (heavy) and summer. Socks—there are no socks in China that an American can get into. They are all too small. Bring 2 wool flannel winter shirts, and 2 white or colored cotton shirts for summer. Civilian attire should be worn until arrival at Sian. This should consist of 1 good raincoat and a warm (preferably Camel hair) overcoat. Boots (or shoes). The 8th R.A. wear cotton slippers or sandals. These are quite all right for Americans if their longitudinal arches are O.K. Don't bring rubber soled golf shoes. A pair of "sneakers" is useful however, also bedroom slippers. High riding boots (1 pair) laced, will be useful.

Women should bring 1 tweed skirt, 2 or 3 thin wool or silk plain blouses. Thin and thick underwear. Both men and women will find a soft leather or Grenfell cloth windbreaker good while travelling.

Each member should have a small tin dust-proof trunk, measuring approximately 24 x 18 x 12. They may have 2 of these, each. Larger than this is difficult to strap on mule back. Each may bring a leather attaché case for personal things and correspondence. Portable typewriters—Hermes portable (I am using one now) are good. Bring plenty of spare ribbons—I have only one left. In Hankow can be bought the kind of paper this letter is written on. About 1000 sheets should be brought north. Fountain pen, Venus pencils (hard), pencil sharpener. Gillette razors and a thousand blades, diary, mending kit, a small first aid box (gauze, bandage, merchurochrome, adhesive) camp cot, sleeping bag and canvas cover (the kind we bought from Abercrombie and Fitch, N.Y.) are excellent. Folding camp canvas chair (not the kind that when folded are square or rectangular but more compact—A. and F. have them)—bring me one of these when you come. Small tool kit—hammer, screwdriver, saw chisel, nails and screws. One camel hair blanket each.

Instead of the tin trunks, the oblong, compressed fibre panniers we bought from A. and F. are a good substitute. On consideration, I think they are better. They are an ideal size for the mule pack. The only drawback is the awkwardness of carrying them by hand, by the single strap. Around the inner edge of the lid should be a strip of leather or rubber to make them comparatively dust proof. The typewriter should have a dust proof cover also.

Things you can buy in China (in the big cities like Hankow)—soap, all varieties of drugs, talcum powder, cosmetics. Things you can't buy—socks, underwear, books, boots and shoes (or of poor grade) rain coats, hats, cameras, films. In Hongkong, on the contrary, the supply of goods is O.K. Cameras and films should be bought there.

We have found the Coleman kerosene lamp we bought from A. and F. a great treasure. Don't bring things that have to be run on gas—oven kerosene is expensive—we paid $15 for 5 gallons in Suiteh. However, a cigarette lighter would be useful—I have often regretted I didn't bring one. One should bring lighter fluid and flints. Chinese matches are small and reasonably efficient and can be bought everywhere. Webb straps of all lengths; collapsible, canvas water bags (A. and F.) big size; aluminum canteen; inter-fitting aluminum cooking utensils (A. and F.); knives and forks; folding metal camp stove with telescope stove pipes; folding metal oven (you will get awfully tired of boiled and fried meat); frying pan with folding handle; and a compressed fibre pannier to take all your cooking and eating utensils. A. and F. have a large variety of oiled silk basin covers that tighten up. Bring a couple of dozen at least of these. One of the curses of this country is the dust and everything must be covered.

Mercks' Manual. If personnel wear glasses —3 pair. Sun glasses. Movie camera (16mm) projector (must run on its own power), developing tank, etc. Small mimeograph machine. Battery radio and battery charger, spare batteries and tubes. Tape measure. Unbreakable vacuum bottles.

I may say that we have found our equipment quite adequate and it is giving us good service. The cots and sleeping bags are fine. The cot cover should be strong or canvas. We lack cooking and eating utensils—and as we cook all our own meals this is a serious lack. A small folding table (there is one on the market that has seats for four people attached) would be a great comfort. Chinese chairs (up here, at least) are uncomfortable—nothing is as comfortable as the canvas folding chair sold by A. and F. Each member should have one—and bring one for me! Our folding operating table is fine but is 56 inches too low. Have bucket or sleeve attachments (removable) made for the next.

10. I am beginning to doubt whether or not you have received all the letters I have sent you. I have kept copies only of those written since I left Hankow—as previous to that I did not possess a typewriter. I will give you the dates: March 22, Sian; April 14, Yenan; April 17, Yenan; April 8, Yenan; April 13, Yenan; April 20 Yenan; May 3, Suiteh.

Expense accounts—to date from Feb. 22, 1938, Hankow, to May 23, 1938, Hu Chia Ch'uan.

1. February 22 to March 26 $700.00
2. March 27   714.00
3. March 29   160.85
4. March 30 to April 10   39.00
5. April 8 to May 23   50.00

These expense accounts noted above are in addition to at least 6 other I have sent the American Committee since leaving New York. I have not received from them a single acknowledgement of their receipt.

Two cables have been sent—one by Jean and I from Shanghai demanding the recall of Parsons, and the other, through Smedley, appealing for $1000 a month for medical aid. No reply has been received to either. In addition, while we were in Hankow, Smedley sent 3 cables but as far as I know (and I would have known) received no reply.

I have exhausted every means in my power to try and get a word from the American Committee. I give it up—after 5 months. You people in America can cable us—why, I can be reached by wire in 24 hours from New York, even up in this little village, in the wilds of Northern Shensi. We have a direct telegraph line to Yenan—a military line. But Yenan has a commercial wire to the outside world. Send the cable to Mao Tse-tung with a request it be sent on to me. Is this too much to ask of you? We have no money to cable you and even though we had, our experience in the past has been so disappointing that I don't feel like asking the 8th Army to give us the money to try again.

Have you received a single letter I have written? Perhaps not. Perhaps the American Committee has not received any of my letters, cables, and appeals. If such is the case, I beg of you and them to forgive the anxious, irritable and angry tone of my letters. Acting on this assumption, I am not sending this letter directly to you to prevent possible interception.

I have sent the American Committee enough material for publicity and press to fill a paper. The only reply was a letter from the mail clerk of the American League for Peace and Democracy, asking me if Yenan was my correct address. But not a line from any one else.

Well, I will close.

We are happy and content in our work.

Norman

On the following day he wrote to a Canadian friend. In this letter he complained of losing track of his nurse, Jean Ewen. Many years later she explained that on her return to Yenan from Sian, she found a telegram from Bethune warning her of the rugged conditions and advising her not to follow him and Brown. She decided to stay in Yenan where she worked in a hospital and later in another in Lan Hsien. She never saw Bethune again. She returned to Canada just before the attack on Pearl Harbor, and now lives in retirement in Burnaby, British Columbia.

The Village of Hu Chia Ch'uan, on the Sha Ma Ho,
Northern Shensi,
May 23, 1938.

We have started work here in this little village of about 50 houses. We are 20 li (6½ miles) west of the Yellow River, and about 75 miles south of the Great Wall. We came here on May 11th, walking all the way from Mi Shih—the end of the road for trucks. It took us 6 days to cover the 265 li. The country is wild and mountainous. Our best day was 75 li (25 miles). We had 13 mules for our supplies. The weather was warm and even hot. We all wore straw hats for the sun. The country is practically treeless except in the bottoms of the valleys, where a few willows grow.

There are 175 wounded here, scattered among the houses. It would make your heart bleed to see them,—lying on the hard brick k'angs, with only a little straw beneath. Some have no coverlets—none have blankets. They are crawling with lice. They have only one uniform and that they have on. It is filthy with the accumulated dirt of 9 months' fighting. Their bandages have been washed so often they are now nothing but dirty rags. Three men, one with the loss of both feet through frost bite gangrene, have no clothes at all to wear. They lie huddled up under a single cover—and this in a country so cold at night that we are glad to have our feather-filled sleeping bags to sleep in.

Their food is boiled millet. All are anemic and underfed. Most of them are slowly dying of sepsis and starvation. Many have tuberculosis.

Canada must help these people. They have fought for the salvation of China and the liberation of Asia. I know we are poor. I know Spain needs our help, but Spain never needed help as these uncomplaining people do. For five months now the American Committee in New York has been completely silent—not a word from them—in spite of my repeated telegrams and letters. I can give no explanation to Mao Tse-tung—I am ashamed. If the American Committee has ceased to function, surely the Canadian can help, in addition to supplying the personnel of the first mobile operating unit in any army in China. Cannot Canada alone raise the money to keep our Unit from being an expense to the hard-pressed 8th Army. As you will see in my reports, I have calculated the monthly expenses of our Unit to be $1250.00 (Chinese dollars) a month. At the last rate of Exchange this could be less than $400 (Canadian).

I don't know what has happened to Jean. On the 20th of April she left for Sian to bring back our American equipment which had arrived there. I asked her to wire and to keep in touch with us and to return as soon as she could as both Dr. Brown and I were anxious to get away to the front. This she promised to do. She left in good spirits, leaving her personal belongings behind. Two days after all our supplies arrived, but no Jean. Hearing that she was staying at the Sian Guest House (in spite of the request of Dr. Hai-teh not to do so, as it looked so bad not to stay in the 8th Army Barracks) I sent her 2 telegrams asking her to return immediately as we were leaving for the front. To these telegrams there was no reply, so that Dr. Brown and I decided to leave without her. This we did on May 2. We told Dr. Hai-teh that when she returned she could take her choice as whether or not to follow us or to work in Sian. On our march, both Dr. Brown and I commented that she would not have been very happy walking up and down the mountains we crossed. Up to the present she has not turned up here and as we have received no letters or telegrams since leaving, I don't know where she is.

Lord! I wish we had a radio and a hamburger sandwich.

Norman

From Hu Chia Ch'uan they moved on to Chin-kang K'u, the administrative headquarters of the Chin-Ch'a-Chi Border Region. Shortly after their arrival Bethune was named Director of the International Peace Hospital, a collection of infirmaries scattered throughout the Wu T'ai Mountains. Following an inspection tour of the area he submitted a report to Yenan on July 1.

This is the result of my tour of inspection of the rear and front hospitals. The detailed report that I give on the Hu Chia Ch'uan hospital is typical of conditions in this area.

1. Number of patients—180
2. Patients scattered throughout 25 houses of the village, some at distance of several li, an out-door department for dressings, no operating room.
3. Staff, 2 doctors and 18 nurses.
4. Technical efficiency of personnel—poor. No qualified doctor, no medical student. The doctors lack the essential knowledge of the principles of surgery, antiseptics, asepsis. Dressing of wounds consists principally of plugging discharging sinuses with gauze. This is, of course, not correct! Staff lack all ideas of the use of splints. The majority of the patients have useless knees, elbows, wrists and fingers due to neglect.
5. Hospital equipment—poor. No bed pans, or urinals, no sheets, no pillows, about 50 cotton coverlets for the more serious bed cases. No pails, 2 trays, 10 ampules of morphine, no lysol, practically no soap, no separate hand towels, no bichloride, no alcohol, a small amount of mercurochrome, no Dakins solution, no rubber tubing, no irrigation syringes, no rubber sheets or gloves. About a dozen pieces of board as total splints. No proper method of sterilizing gauze. 3 small trays, 24 pairs of dressing forceps, 6 probes, 5 lbs. of gauze and absorbent cotton.
6. Food, inadequate. There is practically no meat to be had, no eggs, no milk. Average haemoglobin 65 to 70 percent. All diets are "soft". Many patients are suffering from slow starvation. The food is deficient in vitamins with too high a proportion of carbohydrates.
7. Classification of patients. Convalescent surgical or medical 57.8%. Surgical with suppurating wounds, 42.2%.

The above classification is important because it will determine the future policy of the medical service! We must take a three year view ahead—in what kind of institutions and with what staff.

We must therefore consider the immediate needs for equipment and supplies and the setting up of two Permanent Base Hospitals in the northwest. I would place the sum of money needed to buy supplies and to bring equipment up to a reasonable standard (not, however, an American standard) as 50,000 Chinese dollars a month (approx. £1,666, U.S. $8,333). This does not include sick allowance (10¢ a head for food for the wounded) no extra food allowance, nor transportation. I have nothing in mind but the purchase of drugs, gauze, splints and instruments. The initial expenditure for the next six months should be double that figure to buy cloth, coverlets, mattresses, etc.

This was the first meeting with Nieh Jung-chen, commander-in-chief of the Chin-Ch'a-Chi Border Region. The man on the left was an interpreter. Nieh eventually became one of the Vice-Premiers of China under Chou En-lai.

The hospitals I have visited in addition to Hu Chia Ch'uan are Hsing Hsien and Lan Hsing. I noted an improvement in the Divisional Hospitals compared to Hu Chia Ch'uan. I intend to return to these hospitals after dealing with Wutaishan and clean them up surgically. A front line casualty clearing station is essential, not more than 25 li behind the Front in order to operate on the wounded the same day as they are received, particularly abdominal cases and to deal with the application of fractures.

I cannot close without telling how happy I am to be here and to feel of some practical service to my heroic Chinese friends.

By mid-July, with his furlough almost at an end, Dr. Brown was forced to leave. Despite his intention to return, he never did. Bethune sent this letter to Dr. Ma Hai-teh in Yenan. Ma is George Hatem, an American medical doctor from Buffalo, New York, who went to China in the early 1930s. After guiding Edgar Snow to Yenan in 1936 and thus enabling him to gather material for his book Red Star Over China, *Ma joined the Eighth Route Army. With the Communist victory in 1949, he directed the medical campaign against venereal disease. As a result of his work and that of his associates the Chinese claim to have eradicated this scourge. Dr. Ma lives in Peking where he continues to practise medicine.*

General Nieh's Headquarters,
(near) Wa Tai Shan,
July 13, 1938.

Dear Ma,

An A.P. Correspondent, Hanson, has just come thru from Peiping and gone south to Chu Teh with Brown who is on his way out to Hankow. He is a good little fellow but politically innocent. I have done my best with him.

I am enclosing some letters. Please send them on air mail. Get the money from Mao Tse-tung. They are important. One is a long article to the New Masses on this Region. It should get there quickly.

All is well. I did 8 operations today and two blood transfusions. I am tired, but enormously content.

Did you succeed in keeping Ewen? I don't need her. I have trained a first class staff and have a good interpreter.

Please send on all mail. Any news? I wish you were here.

> Best regards to Li teh,
> Aye
> *Norman*

You can open and read it if you like. It's addressed Eric Adams.

P.S. Please send me my x-ray outfit with all accessories. General Nieh has promised me a dynamo and small gas engine to run it. It will be valuable here. Can you get this off at once, Ma? Also Chinese dictionary and papers and magazines. I intend to stay here. I am the only qualified doctor in this region of 13,000,000 people. The hospital has 350 beds—56 new admissions—all wounded—this month so far. I am doing 10-15 operations a day. Come up and see me some time!

> N.

With Brown gone, Bethune was completely alone. His greatest needs were equipment and trained personnel. He explained this to Elsie Siff, a friend in New York.

Near General Nieh's Headquarters,
Wutaishan, Shansi July 19.38

My dear Elsie—

It seems so long since we met and parted, seven months, yet they have gone quickly enough. You have been many times in my thoughts, and always pleasant and grateful ones.

As you probably know, we, that is the nurse and I, arrived in Sian and later in Yenan, safely. Dr. Parsons fulfilled all of my forebodings, as he turned out a drunken bum. We were glad to get rid of him. Later, another Canadian, Dr. Richard Brown, a medical missionary, joined us. He and I came to Wutaishan—a month's trip, on foot and horseback, a month ago. He has gone out to raise more money and left me, once more alone. Our nurse stayed in Lan Hsing—a town about 50 miles east of the Yellow River in Shansi.

This is the centre of the Partisans. It is an organized United Front Government and has the name of Chin-Ch'a-Chi (Shansi-Chahar-Hopei Provinces) as it takes in parts of all 3 provinces. We are completely surrounded by the Japs, north, east, west and south. They hold all the towns on the railways but we still retain the enclosed country.

In this great area of 13,000,000 people and with 150,000 armed troops I am the only qualified doctor! The Chinese doctors have all beat it. I am at present ''cleaning-up'' the base hospital of 350 wounded and have done 110 operations in 25 days.

I have written and cabled that dammed Committee of Dodd's at 268 Fourth Avenue, a dozen times to send me over Louis Fraad but they never answer. I have wished for him at least a hundred times. All the ''doctors'' in the army are former nurses. I could use Fraad. I still can use him. If the Committee won't send him, will he come by himself? Ask him. We—that is the 3 of us—Brown, Fraad and myself, can have a wonderful time here. I am intending to stay, and Brown is coming back in 3 months. There are 7 other hospitals scattered around, some no more than 50 miles from Peiping. In a week's time I am going off on an inspection trip of the whole territory, staying long enough to operate at each hospital, then moving on to the next. This will take all summer. I will return here for the winter.

Here everything is needed—all drugs, surgical instruments, etc. The patients lie on straw or reed mats, no pillows, no sheets—in their old dirty uniforms. The nurses are boys of 12 to 17. In the drug room is a dozen half-filled bottles of medicines for 350 men. Send more Carbasone—it's fine. There is no malaria here but a lot of syphilis and tuberculosis. I have started blood transfusions—4 already, but I have only one syringe—my own—and am afraid of it getting broken. Send a lot of Spinocaine. But we need money. The hospital needs enlarging to 500. We need 400 coverlets and hundreds of other things which can be bought if we had the money. This is a 8th Route Army Hospital and is very poor. We can buy drugs in Peiping and Pas Ting! These cities are held by the Japs but our troops and partisans go in disguised as peasants and smuggle stuff out. If we had $1000 dollars (gold) we could fix this place up fine. Can you do something, Elsie, with that bloody Committee?

Remember me to all my friends and particularly to Irma, your sister and Procter, and Wiel, Elroy and Edith and Irma's sister.

With love,
your comrade,
Beth

He wrote to Dr. Ma the same day.

Sung-yen K'ou
Wu Tai Shan
July 19, 1938

My dear Ma—

I am enclosing a bunch of letters that I would like you to send off at once, air mail. Also a letter and a telegram to the China Aid Council in New York.

Things are going well. A combination of shouts, tears and smiles has worked wonders here. Things are organized—daily lectures to the doctors and nurses, "clean-up" squads, fly control, metal identification discs for all patients, patients' files, recreation park built with chairs for the walking wounded, specified, posted duties for all members of the staff, daily rounds. I am gradually getting the doctors to supervise the work of the nurses. There is less "passing the buck." Actually three volunteered for blood transfusions (altho I must say it was only after I demonstrated that the giving of 300 cc. of blood was a painless and harmless procedure).

Well, let me hear from you. And for Marx' sake wrap these letters and papers in strong cloth. They are arriving in shreds.

Regards to Li
Aye, *Beth*

This was the text of the cable to the China Aid Council. Bethune asked that it be sent by Chou En-lai from Hankow.

Canadian American Mobile Medical Unit working for past month in Chin-Ch'a-Chi Military District with Partisans in rear of Japanese. One hundred ten operations in twenty-five days. Desperate need money and medical surgical supplies. Cable one thousand gold Mao Tse-tung immediately for use this Region especially.

Bethune

All of Bethune's many schemes for developing an efficient sanitary service for the Eighth Route Army depended upon financial support from his American backers in the China Aid Council. Unfortunately, as his persistent complaints reveal, they let him down. Research has never been able to determine the cause of this failure. There is a faint possibility that some money may have been sent which was intercepted by the Kuomintang as the frail United Front began to crack. Whatever the reasons, Bethune's contact with North America was limited. He would never learn, for example, that Dr. Fraad's request for a passport to travel to China was refused by the American government.

In this letter to Oliver Haskell, Director of the China Aid Council he refers to one of their communications that he had received.

Near General Nieh's headquarters,
Wu Tai Shan, July 19, 1938.

Oliver Haskell, Director,
China Aid Council,
268 Fourth Avenue,
New York, U.S.A.

Dear Sir:

I received your letter—the first from the Committee in 7 months' absence—April 18, 1938, on July 14, 1938.

You give me but little particulars about matters which concern the Unit and have answered only one of the many questions and demands I have made to your Committee since leaving New York. I have sent you over a dozen letters and cables giving you the most detailed and exact information of medical conditions here. I have had from you no acknowledgement of these.

Bethune photographed with General Nieh and his first interpreter, Tung Yueh-Ch'ien. Tung was with Bethune until early 1939. Bethune's second interpreter was Lang Lin.

I thank you for sending to Mrs. Coleman [Frances] of Montreal the sum of $200. She is not the sort of person to ask for money. I request you to forward to her, unsolicited, $100 a month regularly and also any sum now in arrears since the first of the year.

I am enclosing a number of letters which may be of interest to your Committee. I wrote you (rather sent you a copy) a letter of July 10 to Mao Tse-tung, re conditions here. This was sent to Earl Browder as I had never heard from your Committee and did not know whether it was functioning.

I have not seen an American paper or magazine for three months. Please send all papers and magazines and all letters. These must be strongly wrapped and addressed to Dr. Ma Hai-teh, Yenan, Shensi, China.

I am alone as Dr. Brown has gone out to Hankow for 3 months. Nurse Jean Ewen is working in the 120th Division Hospital of the 8th Route Army at Lan Hsing, west Shansi. Dr. Brown is returning to work as my assistant. I ask you again to send over Dr. Louis Fraad. I am alone and need help.

Sincerely yours,

Norman Bethune, M/D.—FRCS.

Surgeon,
Canadian-American Mobile
Medical Unit.

On July 20, 1938 he sent Mao Tse-tung a detailed report of his work since leaving Yenan. This began with a list of the patients and the nature of their wounds. He then outlined changes that he had introduced.

1. Since my last report (July 1st), I am glad to be able to report that a great improvement has taken place in organization, cleanliness, and in construction of needed works.

Some of the improvements are—

1) An operating room has been constructed and enlarged.
2) All patients operated upon have post-operative charts kept of temperature, taken twice daily.
3) Segregation of post-operative patients in one compound, and under one doctor.
4) "Clean-up" squads to enforce disposal of refuse, food and soiled dressings; to supervise hsiao kwei's in keeping wards clean.
5) Fly control. A very difficult problem. Mosquito netting has been put on all windows and all food boxes in wards are protected by the same. More active measures are the burning of manure piles, covering over of latrines and burning of refuse in incinerator.
6) A sterilizer for instruments and dressings has been built.
7) One hundred leg and arm splints have been made.
8) Regular weekly staff conferences. These are held every Sunday afternoon, of the combined doctors and nurses. Here the problems of the week are discussed, criticisms made and suggestions for improvement come from the members of the staff themselves. In this, we have been very pleased with the response. There is a fine spirit of eagerness to improve and learn. At these staff conferences, all take and keep notes.
9) Duties of nurses have been outlined and printed and posted on the walls. Each nurse knows his expected duty.
10) Lectures to the staff. Two of these have already been given and more will be. They

are illustrated by blackboard drawings. The subjects already taken are anatomy and the treatment of wounds. Physiology, materia medica, etc., will be discussed in future lectures. These lectures are held every other day from 5 to 6 p.m.

11) Regular weekly ward rounds, seeing every patient in the hospital, are made on Sunday morning.

12) Identification discs for all patients have been made. These metal (tin) discs have printed on them the patient's name and his hospital number. All patients wear these discs. The number corresponds to that on the hospital file. This makes the location of patients easier. This system combined with a large map and file hanging on the wall of the Chief Surgeon's office, enables him to locate scattered patients with ease.

13) Complete inventories of all materials belonging to the hospital have been made. This includes drugs, surgical supplies, gauze, cotton, bandages, towels, basins, pails, etc.

14) Dressing trays have been constructed and standardized.

The projected improvements now in hand are—

1) Patients' Recreation Park. A start has been made on this, a plot of ground selected, leveled and seats (with backs) are now being built. In the ground is a cook-house which will be turned into a hall for games, writing letters, and lectures as well as a reading room.

2) An incinerator for burning soiled cotton, food, etc. is being built.

3) A de-lousing sterilizer is planned.

4) Sample hospital uniforms, pillows, coverlets, have been made and criticized, 50 of each will shortly be ready. Before being distributed, all wards will be cleaned, white washed and sterilized. One ward at a time will be taken. 50 protective oiled cotton protective sheets have been ordered to keep the new coverlets clean.

5) One dozen covered tin pails are being made for placing food and soiled dressings in away from flies. One will be placed in each ward.

6) Four stretcher racks are being built to rest stretchers on so that patients do not touch the ground. These will be placed in the Operating Room compound for patients waiting operation.

7) An illustrated booklet for doctors and nurses is in process. It will have chapters on first aid, application of splints, emergencies, drugs, anatomy, elementary physiology, treatment of wounds, etc. It will be translated by Comrade Tung into Chinese for distribution throughout the Region to all doctors and nurses. The Regional Government will be asked to print it. A further series of booklets on public health, preventative medicine, will be planned if the first one is successful.

Much still remains to be done before the "Five Weeks' Plan" of the staff to make this the finest hospital in the 8th Route Army will be accomplished. I am firmly of the opinion that it can and will be done. All are cooperating now with that in mind.

Immediate needs— A thousand % increase of drugs and surgical instruments
One thousand dollars for new bedding, etc.

Future needs— Construction of a new operating and post-operative ward. This will cost about a thousand dollars. It will contain the laundry, sterilizing room, stockroom and doctors' offices.
Enlargement of the hospital to 500 beds capacity, Centralization of arm cases, leg cases, etc. Construction of bath house.

About $5,000 dollars will be needed in all for the winter. An appeal has been made by telegraph to America for this money. I have every confidence it will be forthcoming.

With comradely greetings,
Norman Bethune, M.D.,
Surgeon, Canadian-American Mobile Medical Unit.

The failure of the China Aid Council to supply needed funds not only hampered his plans, it also injured his pride. When the Military Council in Yenan ordered General Nieh, Commander-in-Chief of the Border Region, to pay Bethune and Ewen $100.00 (Chinese) monthly, Bethune promptly replied by telegram.

Telegram to the Military Council, 8th Route Army, Yenan, August 12, 1938, in response to theirs of August 11, 1938.

Military Council,
8th Route Army,
Yenan, Shensi.

Replying to your telegram of August 11.38

(1) I refuse to accept offered $100 a month. Ewen may do as she pleases. Have no need of money personally, as all food, clothing, etc. is supplied me. If this money has been sent to me personally from America or Canada, make a Special Tobacco Fund out of it for tobacco and cigarettes for the wounded. I will draw from time to time, what little money I need, from Headquarters here.

(2) The above—ordinary expenses authorized by me last month in the Base Hospitals here were approximately $1500. This was spent on materials and labor for the reconstruction of the hospital as a Model Demonstration Hospital for the Chin-Ch'a-Chi District. A medical, surgical and nursing Training School will be opened here next week. Approximately $1000 a month will be needed in the future. This is close to my estimate in my letters of May 17 and 23, from Hu Chia Ch'uan. It should not exceed $1500 normally. Over 100 wooden splints, and many tin and metal trays, boxes, instruments, urinals, bed pans, ward furniture, have been constructed.

Fifty complete bedding, blankets and protective sheets have been made. The object is to make this hospital a model for this district. One pamphlet, illustrated, on the treatment of wounds, has been written, and will be published in a few days. Another larger book, illustrated with over 200 drawings on military medicine, surgery and nursing for the doctors and nurses of the 8th Army, is half completed and will be sent to you for publication, within three weeks.

(3) Immediate needs are $5000 worth of medicines. These may be purchased in Peiping, where contacts have been established. I am writing full particulars of this in a letter.

(4) Please inform me of the sums of money coming in from Canada and America so that I may know the financial position.

(5) All the above does not include larger projects for the construction of a permanent hospital, which would cost approximately $50,000. These plans for a permanent base hospital will be submitted to you, by

letter. What we are doing now is reconstruction with the existing materials at hand, but they are far from ideal.

(6) The need here is very great. I beg that the Military Council appeal to Canada and America for additional financial assistance.

> With comradely greetings,
> *Norman Bethune*, M.D.,
> Surgeon, Canadian-American Mobile Medical Unit.

By early August Bethune had decided that a permanent, well-equipped hospital should be built in the village of Sung-yen K'ou. It would serve both as the main base hospital for the region and as a training centre. This was the Model Demonstration Hospital to which he had referred in his telegram of August 12. He explained his plans to General Nieh. In this and subsequent letters Bethune refers to medical texts that he was writing. Unfortunately none of these has survived.

Surgical Base Hospital Sung-yen Kou,
August 13.38.

General Nieh,
Commanding Officer,
Chin-Ch'a-Chi Military District.

Dear comrade—

You may recall that I spoke to you on August 7th, about the establishment of the model hospital here and its use as a training school for the doctors and nurses of the military hospitals of the entire district. The day before yesterday, Dr. Yeh introduced the subject again and told me that you had spoken to him about this matter and had instructed him to ask me to accept the principalship of the Training School and to abandon my plans for a tour of all the front hospitals of the District.

This letter concerns this very important matter. There are two facts now apparent:

1. There is not a very high standard of technical skill among the doctors and nurses of the Sanitary Service.

2. There is a need for re-organization of the Service as well as improvement in technical training.
There are 3 ways possible.

1. The sending away of selected candidates (doctors) to Russia or to Universities in China, to be trained as fully qualified doctors. This would take 4 to 5 years. The advantages would be that the 8th Route Army would then possess its own politically reliable, fully trained medical personnel. They in turn would gradually raise the standard throughout the Sanitary Service. The disadvantages are equally obvious—the time taken and the urgent demands for even the partially trained technicians you already possess, for the needs of the moment. The changing political situation will also be the deciding factor here.

2. The sending out of the District to either modern Chinese Hospitals or to Mission Hospitals (such as the Union Mission Hospital, Hankow; or the Baptist Mission Hospital, Sian) of a certain number of doctors and nurses for a 3 to 6 months' course in surgery, surgical nursing, dispensing, etc. Arrangements for the maintenance of these doctors and nurses might, I believe, be made. These partially trained doctors and nurses, would, on their return, act as instructors to others.

3. The utilization of foreign medical units such as the Canadian-American Unit, as instructors in medical and surgical technique. This should be done by all means. The Chinese Red Cross Units (if any come here) should also be utilized in this way.

I have mentioned the 4th way, which is already in operation, namely the 8th Route Army Medical Training School, near Yenan. Since, however, there are no more than 5 or 6 fully qualified doctors in the entire 8th Army, it is difficult to understand how the essential training of the instructors makes them proficient enough to instruct others in anything else than the rudiments of medicine, surgery and nursing. This observation must not be taken in any way to depreciate the splendid work of that training school—work which I consider beyond praise—but merely as an objective fact. I have in this hospital recent graduates of that Training School. They are conscientious and hard-working but they lack clinical training and experience. They also lack the ability to direct the work of nurses, which is an essential duty of doctors.

To take up the immediate question of the establishment of a Training School here. The first point to be made is that it should be done. The second point is the plan of such a school.

It must be kept in mind that a medical training school is no different than a Military academy or a Party School. What is needed are—

1. A competent staff of instructors.
2. A definite planned course of instruction.
3. Textbooks.
4. A demonstration Hospital or ward to illustrate practical problems.

Have we here in Sung-yen K'ou these basic requirements? Can they be established?

1. The staff of the Training School. I do not consider the present staff of doctors under Dr. Yeh sufficiently trained or competent to act as instructors to others. I have had 2 months' close association with them and am only now beginning to see the results of my instruction to them. This instruction is most frequently not passed on to the nurses. There are a number of reasons for this serious defect. One is the language difficulty—I need an interpreter and so am unable to give systematic ward instruction myself. I see no effort of the doctors, especially the chiefs (Dr. Liao, Lin and Dr. Yeh) to systematically instruct the nurses. Although I have given a number of lectures to combined groups of doctors and nurses with the assistance of my excellent interpreter, Comrade Tung, such lectures are not enough, but must be followed up with ward instruction and constant supervision to be sure they are being put to practical use by the nurses. This is the duty of the doctors. I miss in them the ability to supervise and the activity to see that work is being carried out efficiently.

2. There are no textbooks to give the students who would come to the school. One pamphlet has been written and illustrated and translated. It will be printed at the Government's printing press shortly. Another larger textbook of about 200 or more pages is now in preparation and is being translated by Comrade Tung. It is essential that a textbook be put in the hands of the students. I am not aware of the textbook used in the Medical Training School at Yenan. If there is one it should be brought here at once. If not, it will be necessary to wait until the textbook I am writing is finished and published. This will take 2 months.

3. A planned course of instruction. I would be glad to draw up such a course. I would suggest it be divided into 3 parts—medical, surgical, nursing and organization. The course might be 3 weeks.

4. A Demonstration Hospital. We will have this soon—in about 2 weeks. It will be a "model" ward of 30 beds. It will be ideal for practical demonstrations. It is costing about $2,000.00. A great deal of equipment is still necessary.

To return to the major problem of the staff of the Training School. I would be glad to accept the position of Principal if it did not involve my being restricted in my movements to this hospital alone. I wish to be free to move about the District on the different fronts and to see for myself that the Sanitary Service is working smoothly and efficiently as possible. In short I do not wish to be "tied down" to this base hospital.

In regard to the other members of the staff of instructors, I frankly am perplexed. Perhaps the Yenan training school will lend us one or two of their instructors. No one man can do this job—it must be done by a co-ordinated and efficient staff, active, eager, with imagination and ideas and the ability to instruct and supervise the work of their assistants. This present staff does not possess these characteristics.

I append a confidential report on the members of the staff of this hospital from the point of technical efficiency, etc.

The general conclusion I have come to after giving this matter a great deal of thought, is, while a Training School is necessary, it should be postponed for two months until the textbook I am writing and Comrade Tung is translating is completed. During this period I will endeavor to give the doctors and nurses more technical instruction. After the completion of the book and during the period of waiting for its appearance in print, I desire to keep to our original plan that I should take a tour of the fronts in the District. That there is a great need for this is only too evident to me—example, there has not arrived from any front hospital, many wounded comrades, who have had a fracture of the arm or leg and who have had a splint on the fracture. This shows a lack of care on the part of some of the doctors at the front. This must be corrected. The best way to correct it is to go to these doctors and instruct them in the field under actual conditions.

In conclusion, I would suggest the early calling of a conference when all criticisms will be made openly and frankly in a proper Bolshevist manner. In this way, our difficulties can be solved.

> With comradely greetings,
> *Norman Bethune*, M.D.,
> Surgeon, Canadian-American Mobile Medical Unit.

A concluding note on the progress of re-organization.

It must not be thought that no progress has been made. On the contrary, I consider that we have come a great distance in the past 2 months.

Not being content with the rather loose organization of the doctors and nurses a conference was called at Dr. Yeh's office at Hopei Tsun on July 29th. All the doctors and political commissars of the 3 hospitals attended. I put forward the suggestion that to tighten up the organization, we divide all the doctors, nurses and orderlies into "teams". This would give us 5 teams composed of a doctor, 5 nurses and 9 orderlies each. To each team would be allotted a definite number of patients for which each team would be responsible. Since there are approximately 300 wounded, this would give each team 60 patients. Socialistic competitions between teams would be encouraged for neatness and cleanliness of wards, etc.

Another proposal was to keep the hospital at Sung-yen K'ou for the seriously sick (about 85) and the hospital at Ho si Tsun for the slightly wounded (about 125), and use Hopei Tsun as a convalescent camp for recovery.

Another was the fitting out of the Buddhist Temple at Sung-yen K'ou as a model ward.

All three suggestions were unreservedly accepted by the conference. The senior doctor (Dr. Lin) was given the title of Team No. 1 in charge of the seriously wounded and operated cases. The other doctors were given teams according to experience. Each doctor would be responsible for the supervision and training of the nurses and orderlies under him. Nightly reports were to be made to me by the 2 senior doctors in charge of the seriously wounded. Wounded would be seen by me at any time of the day or night on arrival. In the past it was sometimes days before I was notified!

Since the introduction of the "teams" the organization has tightened up considerably. Doctors and nurses and orderlies now know their patients and feel more responsible for them.

By the daily reports, I am able to know what is going on in the hospitals and what patients are worse or better. In the past, I not infrequently was merely informed, when I inquired about a particular patient—"Oh, he died last week!" Since I am busy with my interpreter all day long on the book we are writing, I can not have time to get around the wards, except to see the very sick and to operate on such cases as need operation.

The model ward is nearly ready. We are held up for want of cloth for sheets. We hope to open next week. We have a centralized sterilizing plant for dressings complete with drying oven, a laundry, an incinerator, a new operating room, a new drug and gauze room, a new doctor's office, new temperature charts, records,

The valley in the barren Wu T'ai mountains where the village of Sung-yen K'ou was situated. It was the site of the Model Hospital.

etc., etc. At the end of the month I will send you a complete report on this model hospital.

Nieh tried to convince Bethune that the suddenly shifting lines of a guerrilla war would make a stationary hospital vulnerable. Eventually the Military Council ordered Nieh to support Bethune, under whose direction the entire population of Sung-yen K'ou enthusiastically joined in the construction of the Model Hospital.

Only a fraction of Bethune's time was spent at the construction site. He was constantly on the move visiting other hospitals in the Border Region. He wrote the following letter to a Canadian friend during one of these visits.

August 15, 1938.

You won't find this little village on your map, it's so small—only a few hundred peasants living in their mud huts beside a clear-running green mountain stream, down at the bottom of a deep-cut valley, with steep mountains rising to the north and south. Looking up the valley to the west, I can see the range set between Shansi and Hopei, ten miles away, with the Great Wall running along its crest. We crossed this range yesterday. To the east, the valley opens out again to meet another mountain range, the tops of which are covered with clouds. If you look at your map you will find Wu Tai-shan. In Hopei, the city of Fu Ping. This little village is on the road between the two.

When I say a "road," I mean a mule path, ten feet wide and as rough as the ingenuity of nature can construct. We rode 90 li (30 miles) yesterday and it took us from 8 in the morning to 5 at night—eight hours in the saddle. The hospital is in a Buddhist Temple, among the willow and pine trees, on a little rocky elevation above the road. (Has it ever struck you how fascinated the religious mind is by nothing less than the most beautiful, the most desirable locations?) The priests are still here—regular priests, universal types, fat, obsequious, unctious and loathsome. (Do you remember the priests of Anatole France in *Penguin Island*—"pious and obese"?) Three times a day I hear their chant (remarkably like high church Anglicans), their gongs and bells. The smell, pungent and sweet, of the burning joss sticks, mixes with the scent of flowers of the open court. A few minutes later the air is filled with the revolutionary songs of the soldiers. One song, like a shout, goes like this—

Mayo Chang	We have no rifles
Mayo Paw	We have no guns
Dee ling gay	The enemy gives us
Wo-men zaw, etc.	All we have, etc.

and these sound grand after the doleful drone of "O Buddha, I have put my trust in thee." Well, all the gods that man has ever trusted, have failed him. Now he must think to save himself.

The court is filled with flowers in bloom. Huge pink water lilies, like fat slightly breathless dowagers after a good lunch, hang their heavy heads, as big as footballs, over the edges of black earthenware tubs. Geraniums, roses, bluebells, and flox, provide the colors for the ornately painted doorways. Small gauze squares, washed and now hung out to dry, are spread out on the low orange trees like huge crumpled magnolia blossoms. A few pigs and dogs are asleep. The slightly wounded sit or lie on the temple steps, their bandaged arms and legs in attitudes of awkward repose. Nurses scuttle about in their white aprons. The sun comes down out of a blue sky, warm and beneficent. Across the mountain tops pass slow, majestic parades of clouds. The golden air is filled with the cooing of doves, the wind in the trees and the murmur of the distant stream. On the four sides of the court are the wards, formerly the priests quarters and guest rooms. Here the wounded lie, on the hard-packed mud k'angs with a bit of straw underneath. They are still in their old uniforms, faded from blue to grey by a thousand suns, winds and rains. There are 75 of them. Lots are boys of 18, some are as old as 36. Most have been wounded this month. They have been carried here over steep, tortuous mountain paths, from the hills of the north and the plains of the east. Some have been carried 60 miles, with broken legs and arms, gaping wounds, infected and gangrenous. The wards are long and dark, lit only by the white-paper covered windows. The k'angs take up one side. Here the wounded lie, side by side, sometimes 15 in one row. These k'angs are really ovens, heated in the winter times, and are raised about 2 feet above the mud floors. Of course, there are no mattresses, no sheets, no pillows, just a little straw and old cotton padded coverlets. They lie, crouched up like unhappy monkeys in the zoo, regarding the world with dark, melancholy eyes or with their heads covered with towels to protect themselves from the clouds of flies. Some moan gently and persistently to themselves; there is no morphine for their pain. Others are quiet and stoical. Some are mere children—16, 17 and 18 years of age—their grave, smooth faces showing no indication that they have seen violence and death, known fear, felt the strong inward life of courage, been acquainted with despair. And when I hurt them as sometimes I must, they weep the hopeless, overwhelming tears of little children. I was trying to persuade a little boy of 18 to let me amputate his leg. It was hopelessly smashed by a bullet. No, he would not have it off. Why not? Because if he did he would never be able to fight the Japanese again. He finally consented when I assured him I would make him an artificial leg and get him a job with the General, and in this way he would be able to still fight against the enemy. He smiled as if I had given him a present for his birthday.

After his arrival in Chin-Ch'a-Chi, Bethune and Brown made an inspection tour of the immediate area and then began to treat the most serious cases. In an appeal for Canadian and American assistance he wrote: "The base hospital here is at present 350 beds and filled. It should be enlarged to 500 immediately. Brown and I have done 110 operations in 25 days. These people need everything. I am enclosing a list of their drugs in stock. Pitiful isn't it? Can you send us morphine, codeine, surgical instruments, salvarsan, carbasone (there is quite a lot of amoebic dysentery here)."

In China, Bethune was for the first time in his life, able to fit in. He summarized his feelings in a letter to the same friend.

8 p.m.—August 21, 1938.

I have operated all day and am tired. Ten cases, 5 of them very serious. The first was a fracture of the skull with the brain exposed. It was necessary to remove 4 loose pieces of bone and part of the frontal lobe. I hope he lives as he is a regimental commander. Tonight he looks very well, is conscious and without paralysis.

It is true I am tired but I don't think I have been so happy for a long time. I am content. I am doing what I want to do. Why shouldn't I be happy—see what my riches consist of. First I have important work that fully occupies every minute of my time from 5:30 in the morning to 9 at night. *I am needed.* More than that—to satisfy my bourgeois vanity—the need for me is expressed. I have a cook, a personal servant, my own house, a fine Japanese horse and saddle. I have no money nor the need of it—everything is given me. No wish, no desire is left unfulfilled. I am treated like a kingly comrade, with every kindness, every courtesy imaginable. I have the inestimable fortune to be among, and to work among, comrades to whom communism is a way of life, not merely a way of talking or a way of conscious thinking. Their communism is simple and profound, reflex as a knee jerk, unconscious as the movements of their lungs, automatic as the beating of their hearts. Here are found those comrades whom one recognizes as belonging to the hierarchy of Communism—the Bolshevists. Quiet, steady, wise, patient; with an unshakeable optimism; gentle and cruel; sweet and bitter; unselfish, determined; implacable in their hate; world-embracing in their love.

At the opening of the Model Hospital, September 15, 1938, Bethune made this speech.

Bethune, with his interpreter Tung, speaking at the opening of the Model Hospital, September 15, 1938. The stage was used for lectures. At the opposite end was the operating room flanked by a preparation and a recovery room. On either side of the stone courtyard that separated the stage from the operating room were two wings that contained the wards. Note the Spanish Republican posters that Bethune had brought with him.

Comrades: I thank you for the beautiful banners you have given to me and for the kind things you have said about me. I feel, as I know you must feel, that today is an important day in our lives and marks a milestone (I should rather say, a li stone), on the path that our hearts and wills are set upon.

The eyes of millions of freedom-loving Canadians, Americans and Englishmen are turned to the East and are fixed with admiration on China in her glorious struggle against Japanese Imperialism. This hospital has been equipped by your foreign comrades. I have the honour to have been sent as their representative. Do not consider it strange that people like yourself, thirty thousand li away, half-way around the globe, are helping you. You and we are internationalists; we recognize no race, no colour, no language, no national boundaries to separate and divide us. Japan and the war-mongers threaten the peace of the world. They must be defeated. They are obstructing the great historical, progressive movement for a socially organized human society. Because the workers and sympathetic liberals of Canada, England and America know this they are helping China in the defence of this beautiful and beloved country.

It is not many months since I arrived in the Chin Ch'a Chi Military District to work with you in this hospital. I used to think of it as "your" hospital, now I think of it as "our" hospital. For between us we have created it. We have changed each other, have we not? We have reacted each to the other in a dialectical way, I might say: modified each other; and the product of our changed relationship is this fine new hospital, the opening of which we are celebrating today. From you I have learnt many valuable lessons. You have shown me a spirit of selflessness, of working co-operatively, of overcoming great difficulties, and I thank you for those lessons. In return I may have been able to instruct you a little in the mastery of technique.

The road to victory is the mastery of technique and the development of leaders. It was the adoption of Western technique that was responsible, in part, for the transformation of Japan from a tenth-rate backward nation into a great world power in less than fifty years. Technique, in the hands of the Dictators of Finance-Capital, has made Japan the enemy of the world. Technique in the hands of the workers of China will make her a great power for world peace. Must China then copy Japan? Yes, in many ways. We must learn from our enemies; we must imitate them in their mastery of technique and surpass them in that mastery. We must use that technique for the happiness and prosperity of the millions and not for the enrichment of the few.

Now the mastery of technique in the Sanitary Service is the learning and the using of the technique of healing our wounded comrades who have fought for us and for whom we, in return, must fight. And the enemies we fight are death, disease, and deformity. Technique will conquer not all, but most of these enemies.

Technique is the term used, in general, to describe the mastery of materials and processes. It is the most improved, the most efficient way of doing things. It means that instead of being controlled by nature, we control her. So we may talk of the technique of sweeping a floor and the technique of the organization of a hospital; the technique of doing a dressing and of an operation, the technique of washing a patient, of lifting him and of making him comfortable. For each of these and a thousand other procedures, there is a right way and a wrong way. The correct way is called "good technique" and the wrong way "bad technique." We must learn the good technique.

Why must we learn the good technique? Because good technique in medicine and surgery means more quickly-cured patients, less pain, less discomfort, less death, less disease and less deformity. And all these things are our job. We have only one reason to offer, one excuse when our fighting comrades at the front ask us: "What are you doing in the anti-Japanese war?" Our answer is, "We are curing the wounds and healing the sick." They may say, "Are you doing it well?" And we say, "As well as we know how." But that last question we must ponder in our minds . . . "Are we doing it as well as we might?"

What is the duty of a doctor, of a nurse, of an orderly? There is only one duty. What is that duty? It is the duty to make our patients happy, to help them in their fight back to health and strength. You must consider each one as your own brother or father, for he is, in truth, more than either, he is your comrade. He must come first, in all things. If you do not consider him above yourself, there is no place for you in the Sanitary Service. In fact, there is no place for you in the 8th Route Army at all.

There is an old saying in the English hospitals . . . "A doctor must have the heart of a lion and the hand of a lady." That means he must be bold and courageous, strong, quick and decisive, yet gentle, kind and considerate. That applies to everyone who is engaged in treating the sick and wounded—doctors, nurses, orderlies. So be constantly thinking of your patients, constantly asking yourself—"Can I do more to help them?" Look for ways of improving your work and mastering your technique.

At first you will need instruction and you will need supervision. So you will need leaders. But you must not get into the habit of being supervised constantly. This is only temporary while you are learning. You must finally be able to supervise your own work. So you orderlies—go to your leaders, the Chief orderly, the doctors, and the nurses, and say to them, "What will I do next? Tell me what to do. Am I doing this correctly?" When you have finished the work you have given to do, go to him again and say, "Give me more work." After a while, he will get very tired of your insistence, and to get rid of you, he'll make you a nurse. And, when you're a nurse, go to the doctor of your team, to your leader, and say, "Show me how to do this. Am I doing this dressing correctly? Is there a better way to do it? What is the reason for this way? Give me more work to do." Then, he in his turn will get very tired of you and your insistence, indeed, and to get rid of you, he'll make you a doctor like himself. And, when you're a doctor, go on in the same way making a great nuisance of yourself, creating a big disturbance with your activities, go around eagerly looking for work. Do the work of two or three other doctors, be constantly studying how to improve your technique, be constantly thinking of the comfort and well-being of your patients. If other doctors go and see their patients once a day, or once every other day, you go two or three times a day to see them. Then, after a while, General Nieh will hear about you and he'll make you the Chief doctor of one of the military sub-districts. And there you behave as before, constantly discontented with yourself and your work, constantly thinking and planning to improve the conditions of your patients and constantly imparting instruction to others. Then Comrade Mao Tse-tung will hear about you and will want to make you the chief of the Sanitary System of the whole 8th Route Army. Then there will be a friendly fight between Comrade Nieh and Comrade Mao Tse-tung as to who will have you, for Comrade Nieh won't want to let you leave his division!

Now, comrades, we need technique and we need leaders to apply that technique. The ideal is the trained, conscientious technical leader. What are the qualities such a leader must possess (1) the ability to organize, (2) the ability to instruct, (3) the ability to supervise. Organization means planning—planning as a whole and planning in detail. Instruction means the communication of that plan to others, the teaching of correct technique; supervision means the constant inspection of the progress of the plan, the correction of faults, the modification of theory by practice. And above all—work, work, work.

The Army is hungry for leaders. Every department is looking for leaders. It needs leaders more than it needs rifles and food.

One of the tasks of this hospital is to develop leaders. And when I say leaders, you must not consider I am thinking only of generals, colonels, and chairmen of districts. No, I am thinking of the whole army and the whole district from the big leaders at the so-called top, to the little leaders at the so-called bottom. But there is, in truth, no top and no bottom. That is a false conception. Our organization is not like a house—settled, static and still. It is like a globe—round, fluid, moving and dynamic. It is held together like a drop of water, by the cohesion and co-operation of its individual parts. So, when I think of leadership, I think, principally, of the "little" leader of small units, and not so much of the big leaders of great units. This development of the "little" leaders is the absolute necessity for the revolutionary reorganization of human society into autonomously acting, socially conscious individuals. When that has been accomplished, leaders (like the State itself) will gradually disappear. So, even though you need leaders now, and will for a long time to come, you must begin to learn not to depend upon (I mean not to get into the habit of leaning heavily on) your leaders. Be a leader yourself, though you only lead yourself, for *every leader starts by first leading himself.*

Those of us who are your leaders now because of our experience, are trying hard to be displaced. We are eager for you to take over our jobs and our responsibilities. Then we will be able to sit back and admire you (yes, with friendly envy) for the way you have excelled us.

We need leaders and especially small leaders, to act as germinating centres to penetrate the whole masses of the people and arouse them to realities and show them the way out of poverty, ignorance and misery. It is the lack of small leaders who make dictators possible, and substitute instead so-called "great men," "great heroes," whom we are asked to admire and worship and to be led by them like sheep.

But to return to our particular work. Doctors —instruct and supervise your junior-doctors, nurses and orderlies. Lead them; show them an example of energy; of self-disregard; of consideration. Nurses—instruct your orderlies; lead and supervise them; be diligent and quick; don't talk so much and do more work; do not be so apt to give each other advice when you know no better yourselves. Learn to act independently without the help of a half-dozen others. Don't ask others to do things you can do yourself.

In regard to conferences, they are necessary and good, but only good if followed by action. Talk is no substitute for action. Words were invented by man to describe action. Use them for their original purpose.

Today we have accomplished what we set out to do—the fulfilment of our Five-Weeks' Plan of making this hospital the best in the 8th Route Army. I think it is the best in the 8th Army and I have seen most of the others. But we must not stop here. We must plan and work to make this hospital the best in the entire Chinese National Army of which we are a part. That is the goal we must set ourselves. It will take more than five weeks, I assure you. Can it be done? Yes, I am sure it can. How? By the hard work of every comrade. It must be done co-operatively, by energy, by enthusiasm. You have that energy and that enthusiasm—apply them to that great task. No work is small, no work is unimportant.

If one fails in his duty, all suffer in consequence—if one excels in his work, all gain as a result. Yet, one last word of warning, let us be on our guard, in spite of our success, against wishful thinking; against self-deception; against the confusion between our desires and our actual accomplishments. Let us be ruthless in our criticism, be cruel to personal vanities, be indifferent to age, rank or experience, if these stand in our way. Let all theories be subjected to the bright clear light of practice. Only in this way will our concepts mirror reality.

Let me conclude. I want to thank all who have made this splendid hospital, of which we are so proud. I thank the carpenters who have worked so hard making the buildings, the alterations, the ward furniture; the iron smith for the Thomas splints. I want to praise the doctors, nurses and orderlies for their splendid work. Especially is it just to praise the volunteer civilian nurses, many of them old in years, whose loving care for the wounded has been, and is, a daily lesson to all of us, in faithfulness and devotion to duty. The civilians of the village, both men and women have been co-operative and cheerful in accommodating such large numbers of wounded staff in their houses, often to the great inconvenience of themselves. I want to thank the Management Department and Superintendent's Branch. If I would mention names, I might mention a dozen worthy of praise, but I will mention only two. One is Comrade Liu, our political director, for his tireless activity; and Comrade Tung, my other self, assistant and interpreter, without whose patience, good humour and intelligence, I would be lost.

I cannot close without expressing my admiration for the courage and uncomplaining spirit of our wounded, both of the 8th Route Army and the Partisan Detachments. For these there is nothing we can do, less than to give them the utmost consideration, care and skill, in return for what they have endured and suffered for us. For they have fought, not only for the China of today, but that emerging, great, free, classless, democratic Chinese Republic of tomorrow, which they, and we, may never live to see. Whether they and we will ever live to see that peaceful and prosperous Republic of workers doesn't matter. The important thing is that both they and we, by our actions now, are making that new Republic possible, are assisting in its birth. But whether it will be born or not, depends on our actions today and tomorrow. It is not inevitable; it is not self-generating. It must be created by the blood and the work of all of us who believe in the future; who believe in man and his glorious man-made destiny. Only in this way is it inevitable. Let us raise our voices so that those who are lying in the wards and cannot move yet, hear us. Comrades, we salute you! We shall repay your suffering with our loving care. Before the graves of those who have fallen, whom we have been unable to save, let us say: we shall remember the sacrifices of the dead. Our goal is the free China for which they died. In their memory, in devotion to our great cause, let the living and the dying seal our comradeship. In struggle and sacrifice we shall have one purpose, one thought. Then we will be invincible. Then we will know that even if we do not live to see it, some day those who come after us will gather here, as we do today, to celebrate, not merely the building of a model hospital, but of a great and democratic republic for the liberated people of China.

Bethune worked in the Model Hospital for only a few days. In response to a Japanese autumn offensive, he was called away to West Hopei. Shortly after his departure Japanese troops moved into the valley to destroy the village of Sung-yen K'ou and the entire Model Hospital. General Nieh's worst fears had been realized.

The destruction of the Model Hospital finally convinced Bethune that stationary medical facilities were out of place in a guerrilla war. He turned his attention, therefore, to the development of a mobile medical team which, with adequate warning, could arrive in advance of planned military engagements. The first test of his unit was at the battle of Hei-ssu in late November. His report to General Nieh revealed his delight in the performance of his team. His experience at Hei-ssu convinced him that he must train similar units for every brigade in the Eighth Route Army.

Yang Chia Chuang, at Sub-District,
North Eastern Shansi,
Dec. 7, 1938.

General Nieh, Commanding Officer,
Chin-Ch'a-Chi Military District

Dear Comrade:

I have the honour to present the following report for the month of November of the Canadian-American Mobile Medical Unit.

Following our conference with you on October 29th, in which we received permission to go to the 1st Sub-District, we left Chang Yu on November 6th. Our unit consisted of Dr. Wang, Dr. Yu, Comrade Tung and myself. Drs. Wang and Yu were attached to our Unit for instruction in surgery. We travelled via Fu Ping to give Comrade Tung the opportunity to see his successors in the office of Magistrate of that Hsien [county]. We arrived at Chia Kuan on the 19th, being met by Dr. Ku, chief of the Sanitary Service of the 359th Brigade and Political Commissar Yuan of the same brigade. The Commander of the Brigade sent his regrets at not being there to meet us but was away on a tour of inspection of the front. The following day, we travelled to Ho Chien Tsun and Chu Hui Tze, two villages containing the wounded of the 359th Brigade to the number of 225. We operated on 7 cases here, then travelled to Hsia Shih Fan, the office of the Sanitary Service of the Brigade and examined 20 cases. Travelled to Chuan Lin Kiou and examined 27 more cases of wounded of the Brigade. On November 22nd, 35 wounded arrived from north of Lia Yuan, having been 3 days on the road without attention. We operated all night and the following day. As a result of my strongly expressed feelings of indignation that such lack of attention should have been shown the wounded by the Sanitary Service of the Brigade, the Commander, who stayed up all night and the following day while we were operating, agreed that a

Much of Bethune's deserved reputation in China derives from his concern for civilians. Traditionally the poor received no medical attention. Here he is examining a boy with a harelip.

radical change should be made and promised that on the next occasion of a planned action, that our Mobile Unit should be placed immediately behind the regiments in action, to render operative First Aid. He also agreed that Rest Stations should be placed on the road from the front to the rear. This was impressed on him by seeing two cases of gangrene of the arm occur as a result of tourniquets being left on for several days without attention.

On the 26th, we left for the Base Hospital at Yang Chia Chuang and inspected 60 cases. Decided to operate on 40, but owing to the receipt of a letter from the Commander on the evening of the 27th, that an action was planned for the morning of the 29th, north of Lin Chu, we left on the 28th and travelled 120 li northwest to Tsai Chia Yu. Here we were told to proceed to Hei Ssu, 55 li northwest. We arrived at 3 p.m. and found excellent arrangements had been made by the commander for our First Aid Station. We were 25 li behind the 8th Regiment attacking the Kuan Lin-Lin Chu motor road, and about 35 li from the 7th

Regiment and 45 li from the 9th Regiment, all in action on this road. A very fine organization of stretcher bearers had been formed. We received our first patient at 5:15 p.m.—seven hours and 15 minutes after he had been wounded. For the next 40 hours we worked without rest, and operated on 71 cases. We were joined on the 30th day by Dr. Lu of the Yenan Medical Unit and by another doctor of the Sanitary Service of the 359th Brigade, who relieved us for the evening of that day, permitting Drs. Yu and Wang and myself to take some rest. We finished operating at 10 a.m. on the first of December. By that time all the patients except two had been evacuated to the rear. These two were one perforation of the lung with hemorrhage that was unadvisable to transport for ten days and the other was a skull wound who refused to go to the rear. Only one patient died—a case of

multiple perforations of the intestines in whom a resection of the bowel had been done. He died from shock, in spite of a blood transfusion. Dr. Wang gave 500 ccs. of his own blood at 3 a.m. in the morning of the 30th and went on working for twelve hours. Very great praise should be given this doctor for this action. I desire to bring this to your official attention for commendation. I also wish to mention the work of Comrade Tung, who in spite of a severe tonsilitis and running a high fever, gave over 50 anaesthetics. The work of Drs. Yu and Chia was also very fine.

We left at 11:30 a.m. December 1st for the 8th Regiment accompanied by Brigade Commander Wang and his staff. Here we had a conference with the medical officers of the Regiment and critically reviewed the work of the past two days.

On December 3rd, we travelled to the Brigade

"I have operated all day and am tired. Ten cases, 5 of them very serious."

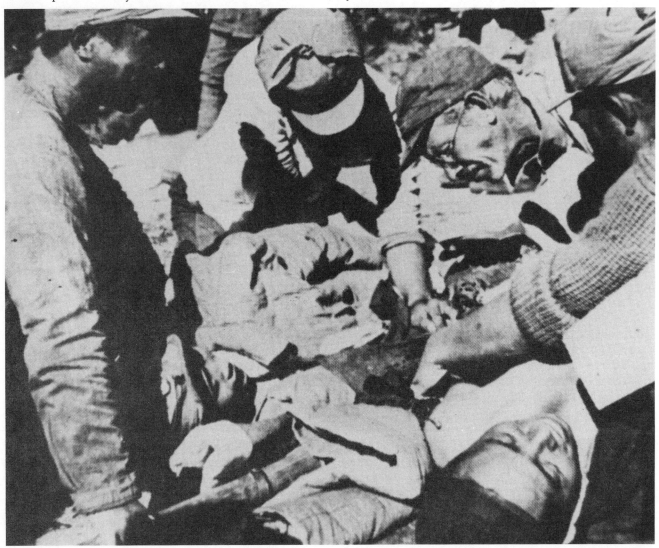

Hospital at Chu Hui Tsu to inspect the cases we had operated on at the front. The following is an analysis of the 71 cases seen on December 5th—4 days after operating by our Unit.

Number of cases traced	63
Number of cases untraced	4
Died	1
Left at front	2
No operation	1
	—
	71

We divided the traced cases into three classes:

Class A — clean wounds without infection	— 22 (34%)
Class B — wounds with very slight infection	— 21 (33.35%)
Class C — wounds with moderate infection (that is the usual infection seen in wounds arriving at hospital from the front)	— 20 (31.7%)
	63 cases

Incidence of fever.

Class A wounds — 6.2%	had fever.
Class B wounds — 44.4%	had fever.
Class C wounds — 50%	had fever.

Comments

It will be seen that one-third of all cases operated on escaped without infection. We regard this as a great advance. The incidence would have undoubtedly been high except for the unavoidable delay between the time the wound was received and the time on which it was operated. This, at the best, was 7 hours and 15 minutes and at the latest was 40 hours. The average was 24 hours for all wounded. I regard this as satisfactory as can be expected under the circumstances, as the country is very mountainous and transportation as a result slow.

Another important factor must not be forgotten, that these cases received no attention whatever between November 30th and December 3rd with their arrival at the Brigade Hospital—a distance of 110 li. There were two rest stations between but no arrangements made for dressings, at these stations. In spite of this, one-third arrived three days' later without infection! Now if these two factors of time between wound received and operation and the factor of intervening dressings between the Mobile Unit and the Base Hospital could be controlled, I feel that we could expect no more than 33% infections instead of 66% that occurred. The saving in time spent in hospital would be enormous, to mention only one result that would follow non-infected wounds.

No tourniquets were applied and no amputations done. All wounds were debrided. All fractures were operated on at once and splints applied. There were 4 fractures of the skull, with 3 herniation of the brain. None have died, to date.

Our equipment was found to be adequate. It consisted of a collapsible operating table, full set of surgical instruments, anaesthetics, antiseptics, 25 wooden leg and arm splints with ten iron Thomas leg and arm splints, sterile gauze, etc. All was placed on 3 mules. The three doctors and anaesthetist (Tung) were mounted. The remainder of the personnel of the Unit, namely operating room nurse, cook, 2 orderlies and 2 grooms were on foot. The unmounted personnel and mules with equipment were never more than 2 hours in arriving at a destination later than the mounted personnel. This was due to the very difficult country traversed which made walking practically as fast as riding.

Conclusion:

We have demonstrated to our own satisfaction and I hope to the satisfaction of the Army commanders the value of this type of treatment of wounds. It is expected that it will revolutionize our present concepts of the duties of the Sanitary Service. The time is past and gone in which doctors will wait for patients to come to them. Doctors must go to the wounded and the earlier the better. Every Brigade should have at its disposal a Mobile Operating Unit such as ours. It is the connecting link between the Regimental Aid posts and the Base Hospital. In this interval between the Regiment and the Rear, in the past, the wounded have been neglected. This neglect must cease.

I am perfectly aware of the difficulties of correct placement of such an Operating Unit in guerrilla warfare. But, if the communication by wireless of the separated military units be tightened up so that in the case of unanticipated action or spontaneous action, in which no time could be given to send word to the Operating Unit to get into position, the Operating Unit could immediately be dispatched to meet the wounded on their way back to the rear, a lot would be gained. The Operating Unit, in ordinary times should work at the base hospital and only go into action when the number of casualties are greater than the Regimental doctors can take care of efficiently.

That brings up a very important point of the improvement of the First Aid at the Regiments. I would suggest that these regimental doctors be given an intensive 2 week course of instruction at the Base Hospitals and that in addition they should have attached to them for their instruction a trained member of the Operating Unit, since the types of operations performed at the front and at the Base are entirely different.

We have now returned to the Base Hospital at Yang Chia Chuang where there are 147 sick and wounded. 130 are wounded, 40 are serious. All will require operation. We found Dr. Chang in charge. He has 16 nurses. The organization of the hospital is fair. The staff is inadequate. Owing to the inefficiency of the Sanitary Service of the 359th Brigade, it is imperative that all serious and moderately serious wounded be removed from the Brigade Hospital to our Base Hospital immediately and our Base Hospital reserved only for the serious wounded of the 359th Brigade and the 1st. Sub-District Regiments. To this end, I have discharged today 20 cases and have sent letters to the Chiefs of the 359th Brigade and 1st Sub-District Sanitary Services, that they should send us at once all their fractures, all head, chest and abdominal wounds. Frankly, I cannot trust these types of cases in the hands of the doctors and nurses of these Sanitary Services. Too frequently it is seen that owing to neglect, patients develop bed-sores that are more serious than their original wounds!

I would advise that this Base Hospital be strengthened by the permanent addition of both Dr. Wang and Dr. Yu, who I am now training in surgery and both of whom are making excellent progress. I have also attached, temporarily to our Unit, Dr. Lui of the Yenan Unit, for instruction. He will work in the 8th Regiment later. Owing to the poor quality of the medical work in this sub-District, I suggest that the Yenan Unit be broken up and its members dispersed among the hospitals here. This sub-District is a very active one from the Military point of view, has nearly 1000 wounded. The 359th Brigade is very energetic and as a result has a high proportion of casualties. These amount to at present in the neighborhood of 325 wounded (approximately 10% of strength)

With comradely greetings,
Norman Bethune

His was a lonely existence. Only his interpreter could speak English and Bethune learned little Chinese beyond a few standard words and phrases. His irritation was revealed to Dr. Ma.

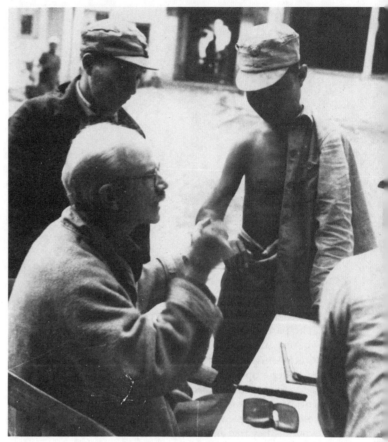

"The doctors who run this hospital range in age from 19 to 22, and not one of them has received any training in a modern hospital; the nurses are young people between 14 and 19. These are our greatest resource: they study diligently, strive to improve themselves, and are willing to listen to criticism. Sometimes I'm unhappy with them from the point of view of medical knowledge, but when I see their purity, their sincere efforts to study, their love of their comrades and their selfless diligence, I can always find a way to suppress my dissatisfactions."

Base Hospital,
Yang Chia Chuang 1st
    Sub-District
Commander Wang
359 Brigade
December 8th, 1938.

My dear Ma-

I'm getting used to not hearing from you! By God, I've got to! Another two months and no reply. The Yenan Medical Unit arrived on the 25th of November, but brought no letter from you. I had been looking

"The partisans are great people. Not regular soldiers, but workers in uniform. The average age of a soldier in the 8th Route Army is 22, while among the partisans many are 30 and over—up to 39 and 40. They are often big fellows—6 feet sometimes with strong, burnt-black faces; quiet, purposeful movements and an air of determination and courage. It's a pleasure to work on them. After I dress their wounds they rise and bow profoundly, with an inclination of the body from the waist. The father of the little boy knelt on the ground with his head at my feet to thank me."

forward to this Unit to bring me some books, magazines and papers and a letter from you telling me the news of the outsie world. But, they brought me instead an x-ray without a dynamo and without the upright (iron) so that the business won't work. They also brought me an opened tin of Canadian cigarettes, a bar of chocolate, a tin of cocoa, a tube of shaving soap. These were all very welcome, but I would have exchanged them all for a single newspaper or magazine or book. Incidentally, everything I have ever received from Yenan has been opened. This includes all my letters. Some parts of letters are missing. *Please*, double wrap all articles and letters in protective and seal. Chinese curiosity is very strong.

I have not seen an English language newspaper for over 6 months with the exception of the "Japan Advertiser" of April 18, left behind by the Japanese in a Shansi Village. I have no radio. My isolation is complete. If I did not have enough work to fill 18 hours a day, I certainly would feel discontented.

Will you do this for me? Just one thing! Send me 3

books a month, some newspapers and magazines, I won't ask you to write letters. I would like to know a few facts—"Is Roosevelt still president of the United States? Who is the prime minister of England? Is the Communist Party in power in France?" Some other facts would be welcome also—"What is the China Aid Council doing for China, for the 8th Route Army? How much money have they sent? Are they sending more doctors or technicians? Am I to have assistance? Am I to have the medical supplies I have been asking for for 5 months? I have exactly 27 tubes of catgut left and $1/2$ lb. of carbolic acid. I have one knife and 6 artery forceps—all the rest I have distributed. There remains $2^1/2$ lbs. of Chloroform. After that is finished we will operate without anaesthetics.

Now, for Marx' sake, get busy!

I am sending you a short story, "The Dud". It is based on an actual occurrence. Also an article called "Wounds". Duplicates are sent to Tim, in Toronto. I have been too busy to do more. Travelled 855 li last month, 113 operations. Set out first frontline Operating Unit on Nov. 29, 30 and operated on 71 cases in 40 hours. We were placed 25 li behind the 8th Regiment of the 359th Brigade in action. 33% of our operated cases escaped without infection, when seen 4 days later. Usual monthly report sent to Mao Tse-tung.

What is Ewen doing? What is Brown doing?

What does America say? What does Canada say?

All the above would seem that I was complaining bitterly of my lot. On the contrary. I'm having a swell time!

Best regards to Li Teh,

With comradely greetings,
Norman

Both his stories, "The Dud" and "Wounds," referred to in the previous letter were published in various American and Canadian left-wing publications in 1939.

The Dud

"Ai Yah," the old man murmured to himself and rested on his hoe, straightening his old bent back.

His face was burnt deep brown; wrinkles encircled his eyes, running down in deep grooves past the compressed corners of his mouth. The upper part of his body, from the waist, was bare. Below, he wore a many-patched pair of faded blue cotton trousers. His feet were bare. Around his head was wrapped a towel, from below the edges of which the white hair sprung, still strong and vigorous.

His body was bathed in sweat. It was very hot. Overhead, the sun was a great shimmering, brazen ball in a cobalt blue sky. Beneath, the brown, brittle earth threw back the sun's rays, like a reflector, into his bent face.

It was a morning in May, on the Hopei plain, outside the city of Pao Ting. Slender willow trees edged the little fields covered with the plushlike growth of the young green corn. The fields stretched away to the city's wall, rising in the near distance.

He could just make out with his old eyes the Japanese sentry standing, rifle in hand at the city's gate. Bluejays flashed their white striped wings in the sun, making, with their harsh cries, the heat even more intense.

"Ai Yah," the old man breathed. Life was very difficult. He had to eat much bitterness. First there was his cough. It never seemed to improve. Then his only son had left to fight and joined the Partisans, leaving no one at home to till the farm except him and his lame son-in-law.

Then the Japanese were hard people. They took half his crop and paid him nothing. They constantly bothered him with questions—where was his son, did he write, what did he say? They even threatened to shoot him. But the old man pretended to be stupid and would tell them nothing.

Then there were the weeds. Weeds everywhere. How could one keep up with their growth? Cut them down and they seemed to spring back to life again overnight. His life seemed to him to be just one great never-ending struggle with his enemy—weeds. There must be a weed devil in the earth, with a hundred thousand heads, a million lives; persistent, deathless, mocking.

For over seventy years the old man had fought his enemy and yet here they were as strong, as impudent, as unconquerable as ever. It was very discouraging.

Every trouble in the old man's life became for him a weed of some kind or another. His cough—that was a weed; his having to work in the fields again—that was a weed; the absence of his son—that was a weed; the Japanese—they were weeds, the biggest weeds of all.

And with the thought of weeds, there rose in the old man's mind the picture of a great green field. It was China. The whole of his country was for him just one vast farm—one big fertile acre of earth. And he saw this great field overrun with the weeds of the enemy, choking out the life of the young green corn; bold and arrogant. When he struck viciously at a particularly big, insolent weed with his hoe, he would murmur to himself, "Yeh Pen Kuei Tzu, Japanese devils, there, take that," as he dug it up, flung it aside and crushed out its life with the heel of his hoe.

The sun rose higher. The old man worked on. Coming to the end of a row, he stopped short in amazement. There, at the edge of the field, was a curious hole in the ground and sticking up in the centre of it, something that looked like a big black turnip with its top cut off.

For a moment he could not think what it could be. Then he remembered. Yes, there could be no doubt about it! It was a shell! He had seen hundreds of shells in the city, stacked up in rows like wood. The Japanese brought them from Pei Ping by train. Once he had been forced to unload a whole carload. He had seen the enemy put them into guns as long as his carrying pole and as big around as the black earthenware pot he had at home. These guns went off with a tremendous crash. They fired at men they couldn't even see, hundreds of li away.

He and his neighbors had often talked about these guns; what terrible weapons they were; how many the enemy had; and what a pity that our troops had none.

But to be sure, we did have one, just one. It had been captured in a raid the month before. He remembered his son, who had stolen home for a visit, telling him about this one gun of theirs; how proud the Partisans were of it; how much it must have cost; how few shells they had and how careful they had to be of them so that none were wasted.

Was it one of theirs or was it one of the enemies? It lay pointing towards the city. It must have been fired at the city and fallen short. Then there was no doubt of it. It belonged to the Partisans.

"Well, well," muttered the old man, "Isn't that just like those young fellows. Here they go simply throwing away one of their few precious shells. Why, it's scandalous! Young men are always wasteful."

He started at it with increasing indignation. A plan grew slowly in his old mind. Raising his head, he called, in a voice shaking with excitement and anger, to his son-in-law working in the next field. "Kuai Lai, Kuai Lai, come here quickly."

The young man hobbled over. "Look," said the old one, pointing at the shell, "just look at that. That's the way those young fellows of ours expect to win this war. Why, they have so many shells they can waste as

119

many as they please, it makes no difference," he exclaimed sarcastically. "That's the work of my son Chu. Undoubtedly, he is responsible. He was always extravagant. Don't you remember the time he spent a dollar, a whole dollar, for a book? Yes, it's that same careless one. If I had him here I would tell him what I think." His voice rose in indignation as he regarded the buried shell.

But the young man was paying him but little attention. With a cry of wonder and delight, he was down on his knees, scooping away the earth from the shell. In a moment he had it free. "Look, father, it's iron. This pointed end is brass. We will now be able to have a new ploughshare. Why, it's worth $10 at least. What a find. What luck."

He lifted it carefully, cradling it in his arms like a baby, regarding it with pleasure and pride, stroking its shining brass nose and smooth black sides with a living, rough brown hand, seeing already the new ploughshare and the brass lamp to be made from it. "Why, we're rich!" he exclaimed in excitement.

But the old man would have none of it. "No," he said firmly, "We must give it back to them. It mustn't be wasted. They must use it again." And in spite of the young man's protests, he made him fetch the donkey, made him place the shell in one of the wicker baskets, balancing the one on the other side with earth. Then with the shell covered with leaves to conceal it, he drove the donkey out of the field and turning its head away from the city, started down the long, dusty road in search of his son.

The great green chequered plain stretched ahead to the distant pale horizon. Bluebells and pink phlox flowers sprang up in the grass along the road. The brown water in the criss-cross irrigation ditches barely stirred. Poplar and willow trees stood tall and shining, each lifting its umbrella of green, motionless, into the still, blue sky.

The old donkey prodded on, the old man following in the cloud of dust stirred up by the feet of both. They were soon covered with a pale brown layer which clung to their skins and filled ears, nostrils and eyes, with its fine particles. Perspiration ran off the old man's face, making little rivulets down his cheeks. He wiped it off impatiently with his towel.

It was very hot. The whole air visibly vibrated. The dust particles danced in the waves of heat. The sun seemed like a heavy copper cap on his head. The distant line of the horizon moved up and down with a fine unsteady motion before his eyes. It was noon. Other farmers were stretched out beneath the trees for their noon day sleep, but still the old man plodded on, driven by determination and anger.

He collected burning words for his son like a man selecting jewels. Only the sharpest, the most bitter, would do. "I'll tell that young man what I think of him." He had a mission to perform, he had a work to do. He felt strong, proud and arrogant.

Li after li he urged the donkey on. Neither one of them had ever been so far away from home in their lives. "Why, I must have come fifty li," the old man muttered. They passed through village after village, which to him had been only names before, which he had never seen in all his seventy years. To all questions from whence he came, he replied, "I come from the east," and to those inquiries where he was going, the noncommital "I go to the west," was his answer.

Now, he didn't know exactly where he would find his son. Chu would never tell him where the Partisans were. "You see, father," he would say, "we Partisans never stay in the same place for long. One day we are here, the next, a hundred li away. We are like birds in the sky or like fish in a deep pool. Like a hawk, we swoop, and strike and fly as fast away. Like a fish we dart to the surface from beneath the shadow of a rock and as quickly swim away."

So the old man's task to find his son was likely to be a difficult one. And so it proved to be. To his questions where the Partisans were to be found, none knew, or if they did, would not tell. It was only by chance that late in the afternoon he happened to recognize a young neighbour of his standing in a village street. He knew that this neighbor and his son were in the same detachment, so his son could not be far away.

They greeted each other with the warmth of old friends. The young man expressed his surprise at the old man being so far away from home. "Why, Lao Pai, white-haired one, what are you doing here? Have you come to join the Partisans?" he asked jokingly. But the old man was serious. This was no time for jokes.

"Where's that son of mine?" he asked. "I've got something to tell that careless one. I've got something to give him, too," he added mysteriously. "He's not far away," said the neighbor. "Come, let us go and find him."

Close at hand they found the Partisans. They gathered around the old man and his donkey, in a great circle in the village street. Nearly a hundred of them. He knew most of them by sight and many by name, and they knew him. They were farmers like himself.

They greeted him with shouts of welcome. Yet for all that they were old neighbors of his, somehow they seemed strange to him. They seemed to have changed. Perhaps it was the faded green uniform of the Chin-Ch'a-Chi military district they wore, instead of the blue trousers and jacket of the farmer. Their faces seemed to have changed too. Burnt by a thousand suns, winds and rains to the color of the earth itself, they expressed determination and purpose. They carried themselves more erect. They seemed at the one and the same time to be more serious and yet more gay. They moved more quickly; spoke with more decision. It was very puzzling.

Perhaps it was the new Japanese rifles that each man carried; perhaps the yellow hand grenades on their belts, but the old man suddenly felt he knew them only as strangers. Even his own son seemed to have changed. Some of the anger and most of his assurance oozed out of his finger tips. He felt that superiority. They had become, instead of just old friends, that rather mysterious, separate, rather awe-inspiring Collective Thing—the Army. And he was just a lao pai hsing, a civilian, an individual.

So the old man suddenly forgot most of the bitter scornful words he had carefully been collecting all day long. He looked at their strong courageous faces and the arrogance melted out of him. When he spoke, the very sound of his voice surprised him, so gentle it was. Only his parental authority which they all would recognize as his right, supported him. He addressed his boy.

"My son, I have brought you something."

"Fine," they all shouted, "What is it? Cigarettes? We need those."

They crowded around the old man, and lifted up the leaves in the basket. "No, it's something that belongs to you." Bending over, he raised the shell in his arms.

"Here, that's yours, isn't it? Now, comrades," he spoke gently and almost apologetically, "I found this in my field, It didn't go off, so you must have fired it wrong. I've brought it back to you, so you can use it again."

For a moment there was silence in the crowd. The gales of laughter burst from their open mouths. The street rocked with their shouts. The old man looked at them in speechless amazement; waves of non-understanding passed across his face as clouds across the sky. He turned his head this way, then that. It was inexplicable. His brow wrinkled in perplexity. He shook his old white head. He could make nothing of it. It was beyond him. They were mad. He suddenly felt just a very tired old man.

Automatically, he placed the shell back in the donkey's basket. There was nothing to do but go home. His day had been wasted. He looked at the soldiers, at his own son, with sorrowful reproach. But none could speak; all were overcome with laughter. They thumped each other on the back, or collapsed into each other's arms, overcome by mirth. The old man picked up the donkey's reins and started to lead him out of the encircling laughing crowd.

His son was the first to recover and to understand. He laid his hand on the old man's sleeve. "No, father, you mustn't go."

"Comrades," he said, turning to the others, and indicating to them with his back to his father, that they must support him, "comrades, we are all greatly obliged to my father. He has done us a great service," scowling as he spoke, at one or two who threatened to burst into laughter again, at this remark.

"Yes, yes," they shouted, understanding at last the old man's mistake and eager that he should be deceived. "Yes, you have been a true soldier. We are grateful to you." Now they crowded about the old man and praised him. "We will use it again," they lied gracefully.

Gradually his old lined face broke into smiles. Gradually he began to feel important again. He felt he was one of them. He felt strong and authoritative. His assurance returned like a tide. They had made a mistake, but now they knew he was right. "My boy, you must never do that again."

"No, no," they all shouted earnestly. "We apologize. It was certainly wrong of us. In the future we will be more careful. We won't let that happen again, we tell you."

So the old man was happy again. He had rooted up a big weed that day. He had done something to clear the field of China.

Wounds

The kerosene lamp overhead makes a steady buzzing sound like an incandescent hive of bees. Mud walls. Mud floor. Mud bed. White paper windows. Smell of blood and chloroform. Cold. Three o'clock in the morning, Dec. 1, North China, near Lin Chu, with the 8th Route Army.

Men with wounds.

Wounds like little dried pools, caked with black-brown earth; wounds with torn edges frilled with black gangrene; neat wounds, concealing beneath the abcess in their depths, burrowing into and around the great firm muscles like a dammed-back river, running around and between the muscles like a hot stream; wounds, expanding outward, decaying orchids or crushed carnations, terrible flowers of flesh; wounds from which the dark blood is spewed out in clots, mixed with the ominous gas bubbles, floating on the fresh flood of the still-continuing secondary hemmorrhage.

Old filthy bandages stuck to the skin with blood-glue. Careful. Better moisten first. Through the thigh. Pick the leg up. Why it's like a bag, a long, loose, red stocking. What kind of stocking? A Christmas stocking. Where's that fine, strong rod of bone now? In a dozen pieces. Pick them out with your fingers; white as dog's teeth, sharp and jagged. Now feel. Any more left? Yes, here. All? Yes, No, here's another piece. Is this muscle dead? Pinch it. Yes, it's dead. Cut it out. How can that heal? How can those muscles, once so strong, now so torn, so devastated, so ruined, resume their proud tension? Pull, relax. Pull, relax. What fun it was! Now that is finished. Now that's done. Now we are destroyed. Now what will we do with ourselves?

Next. What an infant! Seventeen. Shot through the belly. Chloroform. Ready? Gas rushes out of the open peritoneal cavity. Odor of feces. Pink coils of distended intestine. Four perforations. Close them. Purse strong suture. Sponge out the pelvis. Tube. Three tubes. Hard to close. Keep him warm. How? Dip those bricks into hot water.

Gangrene is a cunning, creeping fellow. Is this one alive? Yes, he lives. Technically speaking, he is alive. Give him saline intravenously. Perhaps the innumerable tiny cells of his body will remember. They may remember the hot, salty sea, their ancestral home, their first food. With the memory of a million years, they may remember other tides, other oceans and life being born of the sea and sun. It may make them raise their tired little heads, drink deep and struggle back into life again. It may do that.

And this one. Will he run along the road beside his mule at another harvest, with cries of pleasure and happiness? No, that one will never run again. How can you run with one leg? What will he do? Why, he'll sit and watch other boys run. What will he think? He'll think what you and I would think. What's the good of pity? Don't pity him! Pity would diminish his sacrifice. He did this for the defense of China. Help him. Lift him off the table. Carry him in your arms. Why, he's as light as a child! Yes, your child, my child.

How beautiful the body is; how perfect its parts; with what precision it moves; how obedient; proud and strong. How terrible when torn. The little flame of life sinks lower and lower, and, with a flicker, goes out. It goes out like a candle goes out. Quietly and gently. It makes its protest and extinction, then submits. It has its say, then is silent.

Any more? Four Japanese prisoners. Bring them in. In this community of pain, there are no enemies. Cut away that blood-stained uniform. Stop that hemmorrhage. Lay them beside the others. Why, they're alike as brothers! Are these soldiers professional man-killers? No, these are amateurs-in-arms. Workman's hands. These are workers-in-uniform.

No more. Six o'clock in the morning. God, it's cold in this room. Open the door. Over the distant, dark-blue mountains, a pale, faint line of light appears in the East. In an hour the sun will be up. To bed and sleep.

But sleep will not come. What is the cause of this cruelty, this stupidity? A million workmen come from Japan to kill or mutilate a million Chinese workmen. Why should the Japanese worker attack his brother worker, who is forced merely to defend himself. Will the Japanese worker benefit by the death of the Chinese? No, how can he gain? Then, in God's name, who will gain? Who is responsible for sending these Japanese workmen on this murderous mission? Who will profit from it? How was it possible to persuade the Japanese workman to attack the Chinese workman—his brother in poverty; his companion in misery?

Is it possible that a few rich men, a small class of men, have persuaded a million poor men to attack, and attempt to destroy, another million men as poor as they? So that the rich may be richer still? Terrible thought! How did they persuade these poor men to come to China? By telling them the truth? No, they would never have come if they had known the truth. Did they dare to tell these workmen that the rich only wanted cheaper raw materials, more markets and more profit? No, they told them that this brutal war was "The Destiny of the Race," it was for the "Glory of the Emperor," it was for the "Honor of the State," it was for their "King and Country."

False. False as Hell!

The agents of a criminal war of aggression, such as this, must be looked for like the agents of other crimes, such as murder, among those who are likely to benefit from those crimes. Will the 80,000,000 workers of Japan, the poor farmers, the unemployed industrial workers—will they gain? In the entire history of Wars of Aggression, from the Conquest of Mexico by Spain, the capture of India by England, the rape of Ethiopia by Italy, have the workers of those "victorious" countries ever been known to benefit? No, these never benefit by such wars.

Does the Japanese workman benefit by the natural resources of even his own country, by the gold, the silver, the iron, the coal, the oil. Long ago he ceased to possess that natural wealth. It belongs to the rich, the ruling class. The millions who work those mines live in poverty. So how is he likely to benefit by the armed robbery of the gold, silver, iron, coal and oil of China? Will not the rich owners of the one retain, for their own profit, the wealth of the other. Have they not always done so?

It would seem inescapable that the militarists and the capitalists of Japan are the only class likely to gain by this mass murder, this authorized madness. That sanctified butcher, that ruling class, the true State stands accused.

Are wars of aggression, wars for the conquest of colonies, then just Big Business? Yes, it would seem so, however much the perpetrators of such national crimes seek to hide their true purpose under the banners of high-sounding abstractions and ideals. They make war to capture markets by murder; raw materials by rape. They find it cheaper to steal than to exchange; easier to butcher than to buy. This is the secret of this war. It is the secret of all wars. Profit. Business. Profit. Blood money.

Behind all stands that terrible, implacable God of Business and Blood, whose name is Profit. Money, like an insatiable Molloch, demands its interest, its return, and will stop at nothing, not even the murder of millions, to satisfy its greed. Behind the army stands the militarists. Behind the militarists stands finance capital and the capitalist. Brothers in blood; companions in crime.

What do these enemies of the human race look like? Do they wear on their foreheads a sign so that they may be told, shunned and condemned as criminals? No. On the contrary, they are the respectable ones. They are honored. They call themselves, and are

called, gentlemen. What a travesty on the name! Gentlemen! They are the pillars of the State, of the church, of society. They support private and public charity out of the excess of their wealth. They endow institutions. In their private lives they are kind and considerate. They obey the law, their law, the law of property. But there is one sign by which these gentle gunmen can be told. Threaten a reduction on the profit of their money and the beast in them awakes with a snarl. They become as ruthless as savages, brutal as madmen, remorseless as executioners. Such men as these must perish if the human race is to continue. There can be no permanent peace in the world while they live. Such an organization of human society as permits them to exist must be abolished.

These men make the wounds.

Isolation intensified Bethune's loneliness as this letter to a Canadian friend reveals.

Yang Chia Chuang, North-East Shansi,
Chin-Ch'a-Chi Military District, China
January 10, 1939

I received your last letter of July 17th on November 22, 1938 and was most certainly delighted to hear from you. As you know, I have no radio (Dodd forgot to give us the one he promised) and receive no newspapers, so am very ignorant of the affairs in the outside world. I have not seen an English newspaper for 8 months now. I receive mail about every 2 and half months apart. So you can well imagine my delight to receive your letters, especially as they give me important news of changes at home. In fact, if it were not for your letters, I should be in the dark as no one else writes me on these matters. I am sorry that the books you sent me have not arrived. I am very short of books as I have read and re-read all I have a dozen times.

My life is pretty rough and sometimes tough as well. It reminds me of my early days up in the Northern bush. The village is like all other Chinese Villages, made of mud and stone one-story houses, in groups (families) of compounds. Three or four houses are enclosed in a compound facing each other. In the compound are the pigs, dogs, donkeys, etc. Everything is filthy—the people, their houses, etc. I

After the destruction of the Model Hospital Bethune trained doctors and nurses wherever and whenever he was operating.

have one house to myself. It has a brick oven running along the single room. In this I have my cot and table. I have made myself a tin stove in which is burnt coal and wood. The windows (one) are papered with white paper. The floor is packed mud, so are the walls.

The country is mountainous and bare of trees except in the little valleys. Streams run in the valleys. They are now completely frozen over. There was an inch or so of snow in December, but that has gone in the January thaw. The weather is now mild—about 20 or 30 degrees above freezing in the day, but falling to 10 degrees above at night. The worst feature of the climate is the biting high winds that come down from the Gobi Desert to the northwest. They blow up great whirling clouds of dust and snow.

We are about 65 li (22 miles) south of Lin Chu, which is occupied by the Japs. The Japs are all around us—west on the Ta Tung-Tia Yuan railway, north on the Ta Tung-Kalgan line and the motor road which runs parallel to this, east and west about 50 miles south of it, to the east, the Japanese hold the big cities and towns between us and the Peiping-Hankow Line, while to the south, they hold the Tia Yuan-Shih Chua Chuan Line, also. Here they are putting in a wide gauge track to replace the old narrow gauge lines.

We are in close contact with the Manchurian troops in Suei Yuan province (inner Mongolia). These are our allies.

The Japanese plans are to drive west along the south and north. The south attack will be made along the

Lung Hai Line to Sian and then west to Lan Chow in Kan Su province. The northern drive will be west through Suei Yuan province and inner Mongolia, Also to Lan Chow or the Line from Lan Chow which goes northwest into Turkestan. This is very important as all our Russian aid comes down this line.

About the contradictions in the Chinese Government! I know nothing. There undoubtedly exists a set which are willing to make peace with Japan. This is, of course, exactly what the Japanese want to do now—a quick war and a quick peace. We want a long war and no peace until the Japanese are driven from China. I put this at a minimum of 4 years.

If we can prevent them cutting off our Russian supplies, we can go on for a long time. The country is independent for food. Its man power has just been touched and not exhausted. We believe the man power of Japan is nearly exhausted. Their troops are much older now. Conscription is digging deep into their available supply. There is no conscription as yet in China. At the beginning of the war it was said that in fighting efficiency 5 Chinese were equal to 1 Japanese. This has been reduced to 3 and 1. This year it will be lowered to 2 to 1. Then the tide will turn. Till

then guerrilla war and the avoidance of a stand face to face with the more technically efficient Japanese Army is the Military policy.

We are about 100 miles west of Peiping. Later on in the year, I will make an attempt to get into Peiping to buy medical supplies. I think it can be done. We have had foreign sympathizers come to us from the city and return.

Next week we leave this place and go east into Hopei (East Hopei). The following month we plan to cross the Pei-Han line into Mid-Hopei, which lies west of Tiensin. This large area is held by us.

Last month I sent to Canada one short story—"The Dud" and an article called "Wounds". This last is one of the best things I have written, I think. What happened to my articles on the "Cave University at Yennan," and the one about this District? Were they ever published? I wrote another called "Staff Conference." All of these were about 5000 words in length, each. I hope they have not been lost.

Well, I will leave you now. Let me confess that on the 1st of the New Year I had an attack of homesickness! Memories of New York, Montreal and Toronto! If I were not so busy I could find reasons enough for a holiday.

With the kindest remembrances of you all,

Norman Bethune,

Medical Advisor to the
Chin-Ch'a-Chi Military District.

There was very little time to ponder his loneliness. He was always involved, sometimes in matters which did not directly concern him. It is not known whether the suggestions made to General Nieh in the following letter were ever acted upon.

Nan Ping, 4th District
Oct. 22, 38.

General Nieh,
Commanding Officer,
Chin-Ch'a-Chi Military District.

Dear Comrade:

As a result of a visit to Headquarters of the 4th Sub-District, it has occurred to me that some methods

General Nieh made Bethune the present of a white horse captured from the Japanese. On occasion the Chinese delighted Bethune with coffee taken from the Japanese.

to encourage recruiting and to permit the soldiers to take a permissable pride in their army record and experiences and to deal (in part) with the problem of soldiers absent without leave or even deserters, would be useful at the present time. The following suggestions have been made to Commander Hsung. They were found extremely useful in the 1914-1918 war.

1. Service stripes. These are narrow strips of ribbon or braid about one inch long and a quarter of an inch wide, of red or any other color, worn on the uniform just above the lower end of the sleeve. Each strip represents any given time of service, say 6 months. A soldier with 2 years service would be entitled to wear 4 such stripes. They are sewn, horizontally, one above the other at a distance of ½ inch.

2. Wound stripes. The idea is the same as the service stripes, with a braid of a different color and worn on the opposite sleeve to the service stripes. They are sewn on the sleeve in a vertical manner, instead of horizontally. Every time a man is wounded on service he becomes entitled to wear one such stripe.

Unable to obtain supplies, Bethune frequently relied on his inventive capacity to fashion instruments, equipment and medicines. Here he is working with carpenters.

3. Army Enlistment Plaques. Of stone, on which the names of the men who have joined the army are cut. These plaques to be set up in each village in a prominent place, preferably at the village gate, for all to read and see. Sufficient space should be left on each to add additional names.

4. Soldiers' Families Stars. Made of paper, about one foot wide and printed in red, blue and white. To be distributed to the families who have sent men into the army. To be hung inside or outside the house. One star might be given for each man sent.

5. Medals for Mothers and Wives of soldiers killed or dying on service. Should be good quality, on enamel, with the soldier's name engraved on it.

6. Military funerals. Not sufficient attention or respect is paid to the dead in our hospitals. A cemetery should be set apart in each village. A meeting should be held in the dead soldier's village attended by political workers and representatives of the man's comrades from his regiment, to hold a short memorial service. His courage should be praised and the ideals for which he fought brought back to the attention of the villagers, and an appeal to replace him in the ranks made. Music-bands, bugles—are essential for the best effect of such a service.

7. To the relatives of every man killed in action or dying of wounds, letters should be written by the soldier's commander or by the doctor in the hospital, without delay. This letter should describe the manner of his death to his relatives. If the man dies in hospital, the doctor should notify the man's company commander. Then too, the Government should write or send to the relatives, an official letter of regret, printed or engraved in a suitable manner on good paper so that it may be hung or framed. This document should be countersigned by the Commanding Officer of the District.

8. All villages containing deserters or men absent without leave, should have sent to them representative soldiers of proved political worth and military experience to describe the truth to the villagers of life in the army and to counteract the injurious effects of deserters' stories—by means of which lies they defend their absence from the front. As frequently as circumstances will permit, men should be given leave to return to their own villages to describe the things they have seen of Japanese brutality and ruthlessness, to awaken the villagers to the situation.

With comradely greetings,
Norman Bethune, M.D.

A few days later he was suggesting more propaganda devices to the military command.

Chang Yu,
November 2, 1938.

Letter to Chin-Ch'a-Chi Military District.

We have, as you know, two wounded Japanese prisoners at Hua Mu Base Hospital. One is an officer of senior rank, on whom we have operated twice on his badly wounded leg. He is now able to walk with the aid of crutches. He is perfectly aware that it is entirely due to the good medical attention he has received that he did not either lose his leg or his life. The other has a moderately severe bayonet wound of the head which is nearly healed. Although neither of these prisoners can understand nor read Chinese, yet they manage to convey their gratitude to the staff of the hospital for their humane treatment.

When I was last at Hua Mu, on October 27th, I took photographs of these two prisoners in a group with Dr. Lin, dressed in his operating room gown marked with the red cross and wearing the arm band of the 8th Army. I myself was taken in a similar group.

Now I suggest we send these men a Japanese interpreter and have them write letters to their relatives in Japan and enclose the photos. In addition, we should have a statement of their letters printed with their photographs and use these as propaganda leaflets in enemy territory and abroad.

Greetings,
Norman Bethune, M.D.

The winter lull ended in January when Bethune led his mobile unit through Japanese lines to the Central Hopei plain. For the next four hectic months he moved from hospital to hospital inspecting, reorganizing, and training medical personnel. In the following report to the China Aid Council he summarized the unit's performance. K. H. refers to Kathleen Hall, a missionary from New Zealand. Before her death in the late 1960s she accepted an invitation from the People's Republic of China to revisit the areas in which she had worked.

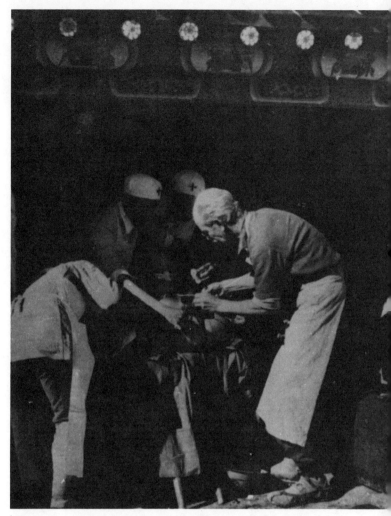

All of his surgery was performed in makeshift operating theatres as in this unused Buddhist temple in the spring of 1939. This photograph, one of the best known in China, was used in the design of a stamp commemorating Bethune issued in 1960.

Shin Pei, West Hopei, July 1/39

This report will be a survey of the work of the Canadian-American Mobile Medical Unit for the period from February 1, 1939 to July 1, 1939—a little over 4 months spent working in Central Hopei, south of Peiping and west of Tientsin, under very active conditions of guerrilla warfare. I have already submitted reports for February and March which included 3 memoranda on the sanitary service and suggestions for improvement.

Bethune was constantly writing: appeals to North America for funds; medical texts for training doctors and nurses; articles for publication in Canadian and American newspapers. Among his few personal possessions that the Chinese were able to save is this typewriter. It is in the Bethune Museum in Shichiachuang.

1. During the 4 months period, our Unit was in 4 battles—at Liu Han (at the crossing of the Hu To Ho) on March 14 to 19; at Ta Tuan Ting on April 15; at Chi Huei on April 26 to 28th; and at Sung Chia Chuang on May 18th. In none of these engagements was the Unit ever farther than 8 li from the firing line and times ever closer.

2. The total number of operations performed in the field were 315, not including 1st Aid dressings.

3. The total distances travelled in Mid Hopei were 1504 li (500 miles).

4. The number of operating rooms and dressing stations set up was 13.

5. The number of new Mobile Operating units organized was 2 (one for the troops of General Lui and the other for the troops of General Ho Lung).

6. Number of training courses given to doctors and nurses—2.

Comments:

1. The month of April was our busiest month at the battle of Chi Huei where out of a total of 400 Japanese engaged, 340 were either killed or wounded. Our casualties were 280. Our Unit was situated 7 li from the firing line and operated on 115 cases in 69 hours' continuous work.

2. The Unit was very nearly captured in the village of Szu Kung Tsun about 40 li north east of Ho Chien. With ten minutes warning at 5 a.m. we left one end of the village as 400 of the enemy entered. All the staff and equipment were saved owing to the smart work of our capable manager (W. Long) and to the fact that the entire staff were mounted and carried all equipment in saddle bags. If we had been carrying our equipment in the ordinary way it would have had to be abandoned with the mules. The patients were either hidden in straw or carried on the backs of the civilians. No patients were captured.

3. Two Japanese prisoners (wounded) were operated upon (one with an amputation of the thigh) and ten days later both returned to the enemy at Ho Chien.

4. Fifteen operations were performed without anaesthetic as we ran out of chloroform. We also ran short of antiseptics and gauze but a small quantity was obtained from Pao Ting.

5. At Chi Huei and at Sung Chia Chuang the temples in which our operating rooms were located were under artillery fire, but we had no casualties.

6. The transport of over 1000 wounded from Central Hopei to West Hopei was successfully accomplished without the loss of a single case. As this trip is a dangerous one, passing close to many enemy-held cities and takes over one week, it reflects the highest praise on the staff work of Headquarters and the intelligence department. All wounded were transported disguised as civilians.

7. There are now no hospitals in Mid-Hopei. All the former hospitals of the six sub-districts have been sent to the west, and the Sanitary work is being done by the regiments and brigades and partisan detachments Sanitary Services. It is hoped that the examples we were able to set up of Mobile Operating Units (really Divisional Field Hospitals but with only temporary bed accommodations) will be widely copied. This year it is hoped to set up 7 such Operating Units (one for each Division or each sub-district of partisan brigades).

8. The supply of drugs and medicines is pretty poor in most places in Central Hopei. Difficulty is being found in getting supplies from Tientsin. The missionaries are being closely watched. One lot of drugs were examined on the way by the Japanese and when told that they were going to a mission hospital, they made a note of all bottles and packages and later checked up on the Mission. The Mission reported that the drugs had been "stolen" by the partisans—to account for their non-arrival.

9. We were unable to construct a new form of transport for Field Hospital equipments to carry all necessary for an operating room, a dressing room and a drug room. All this equipment, sufficient for 100 operations, 500 dressings, and making up 500

prescriptions can be carried on two mules. A description of this transport will be found in the book which I am writing called "A manual of organization and technic for Divisional field hospitals in guerrilla war."

10. I enclose expense accounts up to date. (Note the original receipts will be sent to the Trustee Committee, Yenan.) Received $1,000 from General Nieh on February 2, 1939:

Feb. 20/39: Given to K.H. for drugs in Peiping $ 200

March 2/39: Sent K.H. a letter containing $500 from headquarters in Central Hopei to be spent for drugs in Peiping. This letter was given to the General but Miss H. never received it. It must have been stolen or lost in transit, as that particular time there was a big drive by the Japanese. An inquiry should be made for it from General Ho Lung. $ 500

April 2/39: For drugs purchased locally $ 14

May 15/39: For expenses to pay for transport and hospital care for a patient (Miss Shen, of the North West Service Group) sent to P.U.M.C., Peiping. $ 200

June 26/39: For drugs to be obtained by the Salvation Army Officer at Liu Tsoa $ 75

Balance: (current expenses) $ 11

———

$1000

11. Personal expenditures (food, etc.) as I cook my own meals:

April $30.30
May 21.60
June 18.62

These accounts are certified by the manager of the Unit (W. Long) and enclosed.

12. I believe that everyone was satisfied that operations can be successfully performed in the field by mobile operating units only one or two miles from the front. Not only can they be performed there, but it is essential that they should be. As an example of this,

He always lacked adequate equipment and supplies. The absence of rubber surgical gloves would lead to his death. He wrote the following in August 1938: "I have an infected finger—it's impossible to avoid them, operating without gloves in these dirty wounds. This is the third in 2 months."

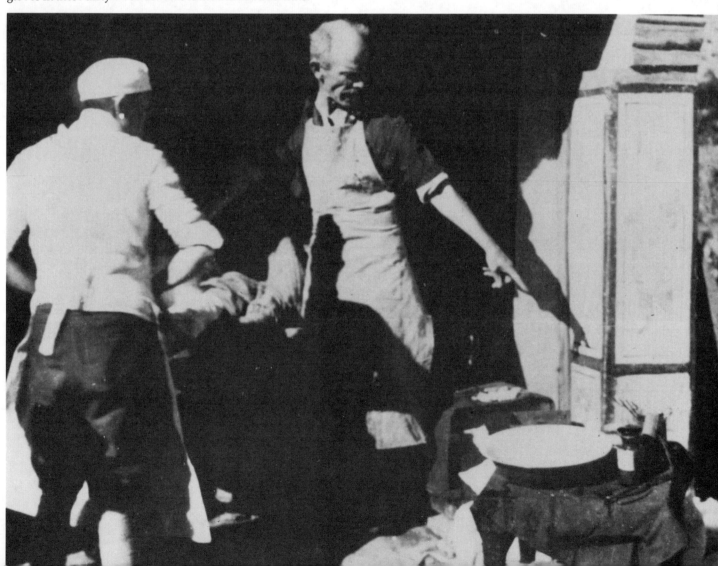

I will mention the two cases of perforation of the intestine by rifle bullets operated on. The first case was operated on 17 hours after wounded and the second 8 hours after being wounded. Both cases had almost identical wounds—the bullet entering the abdomen at the level of the umbilicus. Both had ten perforations and tears of the small and large intestine with escape of intestinal contents into the abdominal cavity (including round worms!). Also there was in both cases a big hemorrhage from tear of the mesenteric artery with the abdomen full of blood. Both were operated on at night in a dirty Buddhist temple by the light of candles and flashlights. The first case died the following day but the second made an uneventful recovery, in spite of being transported 60 li every night for the following week on a rough stretcher. The differences between life and death was the difference between 8 hours and 18 hours.

Two blood transfusions were given at the front in very difficult conditions. I would bring to your notice that Tung (my interpreter) saved another life by giving a second (in 4 months) blood donation; and to Dr. Chang who went on working for 12 hours after giving 300 c.c. of blood.

The successful application of Thomas Iron leg splints for fractured femurs was demonstrated. This should be routine practice especially for Mid-Hopei, where long transport from east to west must be done. Unfortunately, I have exhausted the supply of skin adherent I brought from America and we had no adhesive to use or elastic bandages.

Of course, the great obstacles to such treatment are two:

1. Untrained doctors.
2. No surgical instruments to give surgeons to do the work even if they were capable.

One of Bethune's most significant contributions was the development of the mobile medical team. During an inspection tour early in 1939, his unit of eighteen members included medical staff, interpreter, cook and his personal aide, Ho Tzu-shin.

I have come back with my mind thoroughly made up that the education of the doctors and nurses of this region is the main task of any foreign unit.

But, why, oh why, are we not receiving more help from both China and abroad? Think of it! 200,000 troops, 2,500 wounded always in hospital, over 1000 battles fought in the past year, and only 5 Chinese graduate doctors, 50 Chinese untrained "doctors" and one foreigner to do all this work.

13. In conclusion, the Unit left Mid-Hopei at the end of June as the rainy season was approaching and there was little expectation of fighting in the near future. I must thank all commanders (especially General Ho Lung and General Lui) and all ranks for the wonderful reception they gave us and the most splendid co-operation at all times.

Norman Bethune, M.D.

Medical Advisor to the Chin-Ch'a-Chi Military District.

Bethune's experiences with the mobile medical unit in Central Hopei had demonstrated its efficacy. If he were to form similar units for each of the various sub-divisions of the Border Region, he would need trained medical personnel. His only solution was to revive the scheme for a Model Hospital where he could train doctors and nurses. But where would he find the funds? The failure of the China Aid Council made him decide to return to North America to raise the money himself. In his monthly report, he explained his decision in detail.

Ho Chia Chuang, West Hopei.
August 1st/39

Since returning to West Hopei from Mid Hopei, I have been engaged in the past 4 weeks to organizational work. I have seen the director of the Medical School and his staff and talked over their problems with them. I have presented to them a memoranda on the organization of a Medical School with detailed curriculum and schedules of courses—both for doctors, surgeons, refresher courses for old doctors, nurses (specialist nurses) such as anaesthetists, masseurs, pharmacists, ward and operating room supervisors. I enclose a copy of this memoranda. I would like to put down some of my thoughts on this subject:

1. The importance of an efficient Medical School can not be exaggerated. This Region needs a Medical school badly. The present standard of both doctors and nurses is very low. It must be raised. But how?

2. There must be brought into the Sanitary Service a much higher grade of personnel than is entering it at present. The present policy of using young boys of 16 to 18 as nurses must cease. It is not only bad for the patients (such boys are young and careless) but their presence stops more intelligent and better educated men from entering, when they see young boys dressing wounds they are apt to think that such work is easily learnt and requires no special education or training. As a result, such superior men would rather go into other departments rather than the Sanitary Service. This is quite easily understood.

3. Not sufficient encouragement is given to women to enter the S.S. They are especially adapted to such work as pharmacists, anaesthetists, masseurs. There are a number of young women now entering other departments (such as the Political Department and Mass organizational work) which should be taken into the S.S.

4. A special appeal should be made to Kan Ta students to enter the S.S. after graduation. The same applies to the Party School.

5. Too few of the regimental, brigade and Divisional commanders realize their responsibility in supervision of the S.S. They may deplore, as often they do, the low state of this department, but I have found practically none who actually inspect and supervise their S.S. medical officers.

6. I feel too that the political workers among the S.S. are far too young in most cases.

7. Now that a number of graduate doctors have come from the Mid-Hopei S.S. to the West Hopei and have been taken to form the nucleus of the Medical school staff the standard of training should be raised considerably. But there is lacking still not only a number of trained staff doctors to act as instructors, but there are practically no books, no models for teaching anatomy, no histological or pathological sections, no bacteriological equipment. The school can only be set up by the expenditure of about $2000. It will then need a minimum of $3000 a month

to keep it going—counting 200 pupils and a staff of 100 at $10 a month each for maintenance. Another $1000 is not too much to spend on setting up a small Model Hospital of 100 beds to be run as an adjunct to the School for teaching purposes. I am aware of the pressing need for money in the Region and feel that an increased effort must be made to bring more money in, both from China and abroad. I am completely in the dark as to where the money from America (supposed to be over $1000 (gold) a month) is going to. I am not told where or how it is being used. I have written the Trustee committee in Yenan so often in the past 12 months without reply, that I am tired of writing them again. I have come to the conclusion that I must leave the Region temporarily and go to Yenan and return to America to raise the guaranteed sum of $1000 (gold) a month that the Medical School needs. How else can that money be raised except by wide-spread appeal of one such as myself who knows the needs of this region thoroughly after spending more than 15 months here?

8. I have come to some very definite conclusions as how best foreign comrades and friendly sympathizer technicians can help the Chinese in their great fight. One way (and not the best) is to come and work as independent Units and try to do as much work as themselves are capable of. This is the way missionaries work. It is not a good way. It is true that an energetic Unit can do a considerable amount of useful work in a year—as an example, any Red Cross Unit or even our own Canadian-American Unit which performed over 750 operations last year. But when such a Unit moves on, the essential conditions still remain. They have left no permanent record of their work outside of their cured patients. The Chinese themselves must be educated to carry on after such a foreign Unit moves away. That to my mind is the test of its real worth. How many Chinese technicians has such a Unit trained? Has the general standard of technical work been raised? Are the Chinese now capable of carrying on by themselves? The answer to such questions is the indication of the worth of foreign Units.

9. Such educational work is admittedly very difficult. First there is the great obstacle of the language, then the low standard of education of the workers to be trained, then the lessened amount of actual work that the Unit can do while training uneducated workers, its lessened efficiency during this period. The lack of standards of efficiency such as the western nations are trained in is very discouraging to western workers—the slackness, inability to master detail, carelessness in supervision by seniors and the whole general manner of haphazard working of the Chinese 8th Route Army Sanitary Service. Yet slow as this work is, it must be done. This is the heritage of the past and we have no other. We must work with the imperfect human material we have.

10. We must get more money, more and better men, more materials for work. I have been sending reports to the Chinese National Red Cross for over a year asking for help for this Region but have never had a reply in return. If the money from America and Canada is being sent to the Chinese Red cross and only a portion allotted to the 8th Route Army and from that only a still smaller part sent to this Region for my work, then I must return to America and Canada and tell the people about the needs of this Region to get money especially for the medical work here.

11. I have finished the book on the Organization and Technic for Divisional Mobile Operating Units. It will be about 150 pages with 50 illustrations. It is very detailed. It is based on my practical experiences for the past 6 months at the front. The translation is now under way by Comrade W. Long and should be finished in 3 weeks. I would like it printed here.

12. The medical supplies obtained in the past 3 months have chiefly been the result of the energy of Miss K. Hall of the Anglican Church Mission at Sung Chia Chuang. About $15,000 have been spent. This amount of supplies should see the S.S. thru the winter. As a result of her activities, her Mission has been burnt by the Japanese. I have always felt and expressed some months ago that too much should not have been asked of these sympathetic missionaries, but more organization of an underground transport service would have prevented this attack. Again, the local press were unwise enough to print an article praising Miss Hall for her assistance. This paper is undoubtedly read by the Japanese. Of course, there are other factors such as spies and the current manufactured so-called "Anti-British Sentiment" in China which does not exist except in the minds of the Japanese. There are still large amounts of supplies that have been bought in Peiping, Tientsin and Pao Ting that have not been brought out for the lack of a Chinese organized transport. This work must be organized at once. Miss Hall

can not be used again. Her life is already in danger owing to her help to the Region. The same applies to other missions such as the American Board Mission in Pao Ting. There have been many arrests of the Chinese there and the American Missionaries are nervous and dare do no more to help. In fact, when I asked one of them to send me 10 lbs. of Chloroform and 10 lbs. of Carbolic Acid when I was in Mid-Hopei in June, I received a reply that it would be done this time but I must not ask them to do it again.

So it comes down to this—either the Region organizes its own underground purchasing and transport service or else all materials must be brought from the south.

13. I am trying to persuade Miss Hall to join the Canadian-American Unit and give up her own missionary work. Around her I propose to gather a nucleus of trained graduate nurses from the P.U.M.C. (we have 2 now already) and with such a staff, set up a small model hospital to be used in connection with the teaching of the Medical school. She is considering the matter. It would mean her leaving (resigning) from her mission. She is also thinking of going to New Zealand to raise more money for this Region. Between the two of us, I feel that we can raise enough for the medical educational work of the Region, but it would mean that both of us would have to leave here temporarily for 6 months to 8 months.

14. One of the big problems that I am confronted with is what to do with the old former badly trained medical officers, many of whom have been in the Red Army. They have got into a lot of very bad habits and are tending to be very cliche and somewhat bureaucratic. They are technically inefficient but of course politically fine.

16. I would suggest the calling of a Conference of the Chiefs of the S.S. and discussing the points brought out in this letter.

> With warm comradely greetings,
> *Norman Bethune*, M.D.,
> Medical Advisor to the Chin-Ch'a-Chi Military District.

He planned to return to raise money but there is an obvious indication in his letter to John Barnwell that the trip would also serve as an antidote to his loneliness.

To be seriously wounded in a guerrilla war often meant to die or at best, to live without being able to fight or even work again. The knowledge that a qualified medical doctor was among them provided the troops of the Eighth Route Army with a great psychological lift.

On the border of north western Hopei, China, Chin-Ch'a-Chi Military District, August 13/39

Dear Comrade,

It seems such a long time since we last met and so much must have happened to you. It has certainly happened to me. These last (nearly two years) now, have been very full, so full that I hardly know where to start to describe them to you. So this account will be a disconnected one at best. But I am anxious that you should receive one letter at least of those I have written you, for I have written before, but I am supposing that you never received them as I have had no reply. That is what I have come to accept, more or less resignedly, as part of this life. The mails are very irregular. It takes at least 5 months for any letters to reach me after they have arrived in China. I calculate that I get only 1 in 25. Books and periodicals are even worse. I have received none in one and half years. My reading consists of years old San Franscisco papers used as wrappers for sugar, tea and cakes by merchants. I am thoroughly conversant with the doings of the "smart set" and the vagaries of

Hollywood, but of anything of importance, I know less than an Arctic explorer. He, at least, has a radio, I have none. It was three months before I knew that Madrid had fallen!

The work that I am trying to do is to take peasant boys and young workers and make doctors out of them. They can read and write and most have a knowledge of arithmetic. None of my doctors have ever been to college or university and none have ever been in a modern Hospital (most of them have never been in any hospital) much less a medical school. With this material, I must make doctors and nurses out of them, in 6 months for nurses and 1 year for doctors. We have 2300 wounded in hospital all the time. These hospitals are merely the dirty one-story mud and stone houses of out-of-the-way villages set in deep valleys overhung by mountains, some of which are 10,000 feet high. We have over 20 of these hospitals in our region which stretches from Peiping in the north to Tientsin in the east, south to Shi Chia Chuang, west to Tai Yuan. We are the most active Partisan area in China and engaged in very severe guerrilla warfare all the time.

The Japanese claim they "control" this region. The claim is absurd. What they control are the large towns and cities of the region which is an entirely different thing. There are 22 cities. They hold these. There are 100 large towns. They hold 75. There are 20,000 villages. They hold none. "Holding" a city means something like "holding" a tiger. You feel rather proud of "controlling" such a big fine beast but rather

afraid also of what he may do if you relax your vigilance.

The Puppet Governments set up by the Japs seem to work in a sort of fashion in the cities. In the countryside they are complete flops. Our own local governments are the only ones recognized by the people. To them they pay their taxes. Japanese taxes are pure and simple robbery and extortion, capricious, uncertain and based on the simple gunman principle—"How much have you got?" Our taxation is a fixed tax on the land such as the peasants are accustomed to paying for centuries. This year 1939, the taxes for 1940 have been paid as usual a year in advance. 90% of the customary amount ($1,200,000.00) has been already paid.

My own opinion is that the Japanese can never conquer China. I think it a physical impossibility. They haven't the troops to do it. The country is too big, the people too numerous, the feeling against the aggressor, among the masses too intense. Even at present, the Japanese army is nothing but a police force. They seem held up in their advance. And in the meantime, China is building an enormous army of 20,000,000 men. Next year this army will take the offensive.

The war will be a long one. We want it to be protracted. We are planning on a war lasting at least ten years.

The Anti-British sentiment in China is a purely Japanese manufactured article. The real Chinese feel very friendly to England and America.

We must help these splendid people more than we are doing. We must send them more money and men. Technicians of all kinds are badly needed, doctors, public health workers, engineers, mechanics —everybody that knows some technical specialty

well. Last year I travelled 3165 miles, of which 400 miles were marched on foot across Shansi, Shensi and Hopei Provinces. 762 operations were performed and 1200 wounded examined. The Sanitary Service of the army was re-organized, 3 textbooks written and translated into Chinese, a Medical Training School established.

It's a fast life. I miss tremendously a comrade to whom I can talk. you know how fond I am of talking! I don't mind the conventional hardships—heat and bitter cold, dirt, lice, unvaried unfamiliar food, walking in the mountains, no stoves, beds or baths. I find I can get along and operate as well in a dirty Buddhist temple with a 20-foot high statue of the impassive-faced god staring over my shoulder, as in a modern operating room with running water, nice green glazed walls, electric lamps and a thousand other accessories. To dress the wounded we have to climb up on the mud ovens—the k'angs. They have no mattresses, no sheets. They lie in their old stained uniforms, with their knapsacks as pillows and one padded cotton blanket over them. They are grand. They certainly can take it.

We have had tremendous floods this summer. It's been hellish hot and muggy. Rain for 2 months coming down like a steady shower-bath turned on full.

I am planning to return to Canada early next year. I must leave here sometime in November and go 500 miles on foot over to Yenan. From there by bus—I hope down thru French Indo-China. Then boat to Hong Kong, another boat (a freighter to Honolulu to avoid Japan) then another boat to San Francisco. I want to raise a guaranteed $1000 (gold) a month for my work here. I'm not getting it. They need me here. This is "MY" Region. I must come back.

I dream of coffee, of rare roast beef, of apple pie and ice cream. Mirages of heavenly food. Books—are books still being written? Is music still being played? Do you dance, drink beer, look at pictures? What do clean white sheets in a soft bed feel like? Do women still love to be loved?

How sad that, even to me once more, all these things may become accepted easily without wonder and amazement at my good fortune.

Goodbye for the present, dear friend and comrade.

Beth

In a brief letter to the Trustee Committee in Yenan he announced his intended visit to Canada.

G.H.Q. Chin-Ch'a-Chi Military Region
August 16, 1939.

Dear Comrades:

I am leaving this region to return to America about the first week of November if I can clean up my work before. My new book on "Organization and Technic for Division Field Hospitals in Guerrilla Warfare" has been written and is more than half translated. It will go to the press in about three weeks. Then I must make a fast inspection trip of all hospitals (20 now) before leaving. The medical school with 150 students is on its feet. We need 1000 medical books.

I plan to be away in America for 3 or 4 months returning next summer. I must have a guaranteed $1000 gold monthly for this region alone, I'm not getting it. I don't know where the money from America is going to. I can get no information from the Trustee Committee or America, so I'm going to find out for myself!

My teeth and eyes are bad. Completely deaf in one ear for three months, a little thing with the 8th Route Army chronic cough, otherwise OK.

Goodbye for the present. Inform Dr. Ma Hai Teh I received his letter written March 10, 1939 on June 2, 1939. I thank him for the information it contained.

With comradely greetings,
Norman Bethune
Medical Advisor to the Chin-Ch'a-Chi Military District.

There was much to do before he could leave. On a final inspection tour in late October he responded to a request for help from a brigade commander whose unit was under fire. He cut his finger during a hurried operation. His physical condition was far worse than he had admitted in his letters. When infection set in he was too weak to resist the blood poison that began to spread through his frail body.

Doctors were called to his bedside but it was too late. He wrote his last letter to Lang Lin, his interpreter.

On the north bank of Tang Ho near Hua Ta,
West Hopei,
November 11, 1939.

I came back from the front yesterday. There was no good in my being there. I couldn't get out of bed or operate. I left Shih Chia Chuang (I think) Hospital of Central Hopei troops on 7th. Pan and I went north. I then had infected finger . . . Reached Tu Ping Ti late at night . . . We go over west and joined at 3rd

Regiment sanitary service on 8th about 10 li east of Yin Fang. Had uncontrolled chills and fever all day. Temp. around 39.6 C., bad. Gave instructions I was to be informed of any abdominal cases of fractured femur or skull cases . . . Next day (9th), more vomiting all day, high fever. Next day (10th) regiment commander (3rd Regiment) instructed I be sent back, useless for work. Vomiting on stretcher all the day. High fever, over 40C. I think I have either septicaemia from the gangrenous fever or typhus fever. Can't get to sleep, mentally very bright. Phenacitin and aspirin, woven's powder, antipyrin, caffeine, all useless.

Dr. Ch'en arrived here today. If my stomach settles down will return to Hua Pai Hospital tomorrow. Very rough road over mountain pass.

I feel freely today. Pain over heart—water 120-130°. Will see you tomorrow, I expect.

Norman Bethune

Bethune died at twenty minutes past five on the morning of 12 November 1939, in a tiny peasant hut in the village of Huang-shih K'ou.

Unable to find any Canadian emblem, the Chinese draped Bethune's coffin with an American flag.

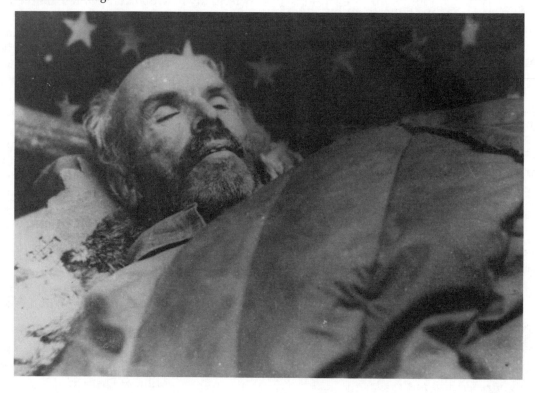

EPILOGUE

ethune spent less than two years in China, yet beyond the prominent members of the present Chinese leadership, no other name is so familiar to the nearly nine hundred million people of that country than Pai Ch'iu-en, (the transliteration of Bethune). The veneration of this foreigner, so unusual in a traditionally inward-looking nation, was assured by an essay written by Mao Tse-tung just five weeks after Bethune's death. He called it In Memory of Norman Bethune.

In Memory of Norman Bethune
Comrade Norman Bethune, a member of the Communist Party of Canada, was around fifty when he was sent by the Communist Parties of Canada and the United States to China; he made light of travelling thousands of miles to help us in our War of Resistance Against Japan. He arrived in Yenan in the spring of last year, went to work in the Wutai Mountains, and to our great sorrow died a martyr at his post. What kind of spirit is this that makes a foreigner selflessly adopt the cause of the Chinese people's liberation as his own? It is the spirit of internationalism, the spirit of communism, from which every Chinese Communist must learn. Leninism teaches that the world revolution can only succeed if the proletariat of the capitalist countries supports the struggle for liberation of the colonial and semicolonial peoples and if the proletariat of the colonies and semicolonies supports that of the proletariat of the capitalist countries. Comrade Bethune put this Leninist line into practice. We Chinese Communists

Upon Bethune's death, a temporary hospital in Chin-Ch'a-Chi was named after him. In 1952 the staff of this hospital, which included doctors and nurses trained by him, went to the city of Shichiachuang where the eight-hundred bed Norman Bethune International Peace Hospital was opened. At the end of the drive in front of the main entrance stands his statue.

On the hospital grounds a museum was built to outline the story of his life in photographs and line drawings. Within the museum is an exhibit containing the very few personal effects that they were able to retain.

Bethune was buried in Chu Ch'eng, a remote rural area in T'ang Hsien (county) southwest of Peking. The tomb and surrounding grounds were built by hundreds of Chinese, many of whom perilously evaded Japanese capture to bring needed materials to the site. It was dedicated on May Day, 1940.

must also follow this line in our practice. We must unite with the proletariat of all the capitalist countries, with the proletariat of Japan, Britain, the United States, Germany, Italy and all other capitalist countries, for this is the only way to overthrow imperialism, to liberate our nation and people and to liberate the other nations and peoples of the world. This is our internationalism, the internationalism with which we oppose both narrow nationalism and narrow patriotism.

Comrade Bethune's spirit, his utter devotion to others without any thought of self, was shown in his great sense of responsibility in his work and his great warm-

heartedness towards all comrades and the people. Every Communist must learn from him. There are not a few people who are irresponsible in their work, preferring the light and shirking the heavy, passing the burdensome tasks on to others and choosing the easy ones for themselves. At every turn they think of themselves before others. When they make some small contribution, they swell with pride and brag about it for fear that others will not know. They feel no warmth towards comrades and the people but are cold, indifferent and apathetic. In truth such people are not Communists, or at least cannot be counted as devoted Communists. No one who returned from the front failed to express admiration for Bethune whenever his name was mentioned, and none remained unmoved by his spirit. In the Shansi-Chahar-Hopei border area, no soldier or civilian was unmoved who had been treated by Dr. Bethune or had seen how he worked. Every Communist must learn this true communist spirit from Comrade Bethune.

Comrade Bethune was a doctor, the art of healing was his profession and he was constantly perfecting his skill, which stood very high in the Eighth Route Army's medical service. His example is an excellent lesson for those people who wish to change their work the moment they see something different and for those who despise technical work as of no consequence or as promising no future.

Comrade Bethune and I met only once. Afterwards he wrote me many letters. But I was busy, and I wrote him only one letter and do not even know if he ever received it. I am deeply grieved over his death. Now we are all commemorating him, which shows how profoundly his spirit inspires everyone. We must all learn the spirit of absolute selflessness from him. With this spirit everyone can be very useful to the people. A man's ability may be great or small, but if he has this spirit, he is already noble-minded and pure, a man of moral integrity and above vulgar interests, a man who is of value to the people.

Mao Tse-tung
Yenan, December 21, 1939

The Japanese desecrated the tomb but it was renovated by the Chinese. On April 1, 1975, to mark the thirty-seventh anniversary of Bethune's historic meeting with Mao, a total refurbishing of the site was completed.

Near the Bethune hospital in Shichiachuang is a huge memorial park, the site of the Martyrs' Tombs of the Military Region of North China. It pays tribute to twenty-five thousand Chinese who gave their lives in the struggle against the Japanese and the Kuomintang. Because it is a rail-junction city, less remote than Chu Ch'eng, Shichiachuang was chosen as the new site for Bethune's tomb. His remains were brought there in 1952.

142

The overwhelmingly dominant feature of the memorial park is the space given to Bethune. In August 1973, the Bethune Memorial Hall was opened. During his state visit to the People's Republic of China in October 1973, Prime Minister Trudeau presented to the museum officials models of two surgical instruments devised by Bethune in Canada. Along with photographs and statues, they are now on permanent display in the Memorial Hall.

Every year on the anniversary of Bethune's death (November 12) and on that of the writing of Mao's essay (December 21) special ceremonies are held at Bethune's tomb. The park is always open and thousands of Chinese and foreigners go there to pay their respects to the Canadian doctor.

143

Bethune spent two months (August and September 1938) in the village of Sung-yen K'ou. Deep in the Wu T'ai Mountains, it is 150 kilometres north of the city of Taiyuan, a distance that required more than four hours travel by car as late as 1975. During the Cultural Revolution, the inhabitants constructed their own Bethune Memorial Hall.

On the walls are photographs and line drawings that depict incidents during Bethune's brief stay in Sung-yen K'ou. One of these shows him greeting blood donors.

144

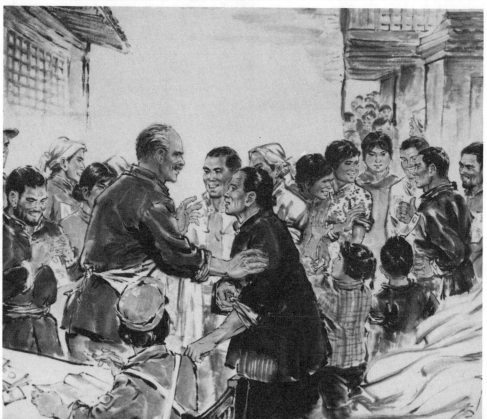

The survivors from the 1930s never forgot the Model Hospital, which they reconstructed in its entirety in the early 1970s. This is the stage from which Bethune spoke at the official opening on September 15, 1938.

At the opposite end is the operating room. On one side is the preparation room and on the other, the recovery room. In the rooms along the adjoining wings are many reconstructed instruments and pieces of equipment that he devised. The carpenter who worked with Bethune still lives in Sung-yen K'ou.

Two days before his death, Bethune was carried by stretcher to the village of Huang-shih K'ou. One of his attendants was Ti Tsuen-hsing, a youth of seventeen. The Ti family tried vainly to encourage Bethune to eat until the boy brought him some persimmon. Bethune liked the rich syrupy fruit and ate several. Guests who have come to pay their respects to Bethune are always served persimmon. Ti stands in the doorway of the little building in which Bethune died. He is the custodian of one of the most hallowed historic sites in modern China.

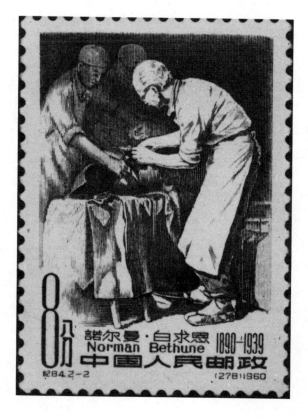

The speech bubble reads: "the password sounds like bethune."

There was considerable public controversy when Bethune was created an instant Canadian hero in 1972. A cynical and popular view of the real purpose of the Trudeau government's unprecedented recognition of a Communist was represented by Pilsworth's cartoon in the Toronto *Daily Star*. The man pushing the wheelbarrow was Canada's Minister of External Affairs in 1972.

It was not until the creation of the People's Republic of China in 1949 that many people outside of the former Border Region learned of Bethune. Study of his life became part of the school curriculum; statues were erected and posters were printed to commemorate him. Finally, in the Great Proletarian Cultural Revolution of the late 1960s, his reputation reached a new zenith. During this period of ideological controversy, Bethune was chosen as one of the symbolic vehicles that would forge the new revolutionary trend in Chinese society. Millions committed Mao's essay to memory and new books and pamphlets outlining his life and work appeared throughout China.

The reasons for the extraordinary degree of respect shown Bethune are within Mao's essay. His depiction of Bethune is that of a selfless, altruistic and totally dedicated individual who sacrificed his life for his beliefs. These are the characteristics of the model citizen of the new China.

Outside of his family and some left-wingers, few Canadians noted his passing. Until the 1970s, despite a biography, The Scalpel, The Sword *(1952) and a National Film Board documentary* Bethune *(1964), his name was virtually ignored.*

A sudden change occurred in 1972 after Canada and the People's Republic of China effected mutual diplomatic recognition. A decision by the Trudeau cabinet elevated Bethune to "a Canadian of national historic significance"

The official dedication of the Bethune Memorial House on 30 August 1976 brought a large delegation from Peking. Among the members of the delegation was Dr. Chang Yeh-shang, who had worked with Bethune in 1939. He later became vice-director of the Norman Bethune International Peace Hospital in Shichiachuang. He is seen here with the other members of the delegation and with Bethune's nurse in China, Jean Ewen.

and the house in which he was born in Gravenhurst was purchased in 1973. During the following three years, a restoration team renovated the building, restoring the ground floor and the nursery on the second floor to their condition at the time of Bethune's birth. The remainder of the second floor was given over to a series of exhibits outlining his career and achievements. On August 30, 1976 the Bethune Memorial Home was opened to the public as a national museum.

Henry Norman Bethune had come home.

The wooden sculpture borne by these beaming Chinese was donated by a visiting delegation from the People's Republic of China to the town of Gravenhurst several years ago. It is now on permanent display in the Bethune Memorial House.

Index